Photoshop
BRUSH
Directory

Photoshop
BRUSH
Directory

A Beginner's Guide to 4000 Selections and Settings

Susannah Hall

RotoVision

Copyright © 2011 Quarto plc

A QUARTO BOOK

Published and distributed by RotoVision SA
Route Suisse 9, CH-1295 Mies
Switzerland

RotoVision SA, Sales & Editorial Office
Sheridan House, 114 Western Road
Hove BN3 1DD, UK
Tel: +44 (0)1273 727268
Fax: +44 (0)1273 727269
Email: sales@rotovision.com
Web: www.rotovision.com

Conceived, designed, and produced by
Quarto Publishing plc
The Old Brewery
6 Blundell Street
London N7 9BH

Senior Editor: Katie Crous
Copy Editor: Liz Dalby
Art Director: Caroline Guest
Designer: Karin Skånberg
Picture Research: Sarah Bell
Proofreaders: Jan Seymour, Caroline West,
Sally MacEachern
Indexer: Diana Le Core
Creative Director: Moira Clinch
Publisher: Paul Carslake

ISBN 978-2-88893-165-2

10 9 8 7 6 5 4 3 2 1

Color separation by Modern Age
Printed in China by 1010 Printing International Ltd

Contents

Introduction

Welcome to the Best Digital Brushes for Photoshop directory. If you like painting in Photoshop, or even if you're a novice, you will find lots of ideas about how to play with your brush settings to create different painterly effects.

As well as being a browsing tool, where your eye might alight on a particular effect you like that you can then copy, you'll also find it gives you a thorough sense of how you can manipulate Photoshop's brush settings.

All the brushes that come with Photoshop's brush libraries have been included, and the Brush Directory shows between 14 and 28 effects for each brush. In addition, there is a comprehensive overview of how to use the brushes and how to adjust the settings, with an explanation of what each setting changes. You'll also find information about how to save your brush settings, how to load different libraries, and how to create your own brushes.

NEW USER OF PHOTOSHOP

If you are new to Photoshop, you will find instructions for using the brushes in Understanding Brushes (pages 22–55). These instructions assume you haven't used them before, so they start right at the beginning.

The Basics of Painting (pages 370–407) takes you through some other elements of Photoshop that you would need to know before you can start painting. Again, these assume no prior knowledge.

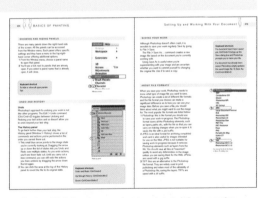

Basics of Painting shows you how to get started–from arranging your panels to which formats to save your files in.

EXPERIENCED USER OF PHOTOSHOP

If you've been using Photoshop for a while, you should still find some gems of information in the Understanding Brushes section (pages 22–55).

You'll also find an introduction to the Photoshop CS5 features, including the Mixer Brush (pages 40–42), the HUD Color Picker (page 43), and the Bristle Brushes (pages 346–369).

Using Previous Versions of Photoshop

This book has been written using Photoshop CS5. There have been a number of innovations that Adobe introduced to the brushes in this version. These are the main changes that were introduced compared to previous versions:

BRISTLE BRUSHES

The Bristle brushes are much more responsive to the use of a pen and tablet. See pages 346–369.

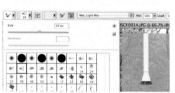

Photoshop CS5's new Bristle Brushes

MIXER BRUSH

You can use the Mixer Brush in combination with other brushes, and it offers an experience much more like painting with real wet paint that then mixes on the canvas. See pages 40–42.

Painting a photograph using the CS5 Mixer Brush

HUD COLOR PICKER

When using the new HUD Color Picker, the process of selecting a new color with which to paint is seamless. See page 43.

HUD Color Picker

NEW BRUSH LIBRARIES

There are two new brush libraries in CS5: the DP Brushes and M Brushes Libraries. They are both included in the Brush Directory—DP Brushes on pages 144–149 and M Brushes on pages 192–235.

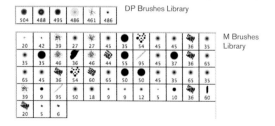

DP Brushes Library

M Brushes Library

OTHER DIFFERENCES: BRUSH SETTINGS

The Transfer settings are called Other Dynamics in previous versions of Photoshop.

The Size of a brush is referred to as the Diameter in earlier versions.

About This Book

There are three main sections in this book: Understanding Brushes, the Brush Directory, and The Basics of Painting. Understanding Brushes and The Basics of Painting explain how to use features within Photoshop, whereas the Brush Directory, the largest section of the book, shows examples of effects you can create with the brushes. Within each section there is a consistent style, which is outlined here so you can navigate your way around the pages with ease.

Photoshop CS5 and previous versions

Although Adobe have introduced some excellent new painting features in CS5, the brush libraries and settings have been left largely unchanged. Page 9 outlines the main differences you may encounter between CS5 and previous versions.

UNDERSTANDING BRUSHES AND BASICS OF PAINTING

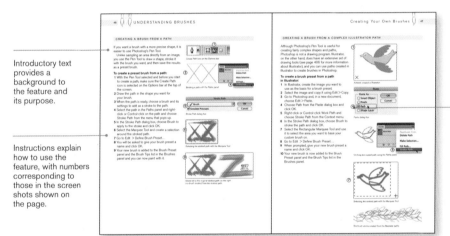

Introductory text provides a background to the feature and its purpose.

Instructions explain how to use the feature, with numbers corresponding to those in the screen shots shown on the page.

The number refers to the written instruction to the left, and you'll find a red highlight around the area you need to click or select in the screen shot.

Dual brushes

When a dual brush has been used, a screen shot of the brush tip is shown along with the tip name. Photoshop names many brush tips "Sampled Tip," which makes them difficult to identify by name. Use the screen shot, which shows the brush tips on either side of the tip selected as a dual brush, for additional reference.

BRUSH DIRECTORY

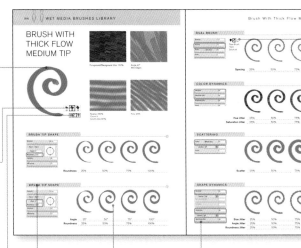

The main swatch shows how the brush, with its default settings, displays as a stroke.

The red highlight shows how the brush displays as a thumbnail in Photoshop, so you can find it easily.

Some brushes have a dual brush selected by default, which is indicated by this screen shot (see Dual brushes, opposite).

This heading tells you which area of settings to go to in the Brushes panel (see the screen shot). Tick the check box and the settings will appear to the right.

Each of these four spirals shows how the brush stroke changes as the settings rise or fall.

This screen shot is a reference to show what the settings options look like. The values change for each example, so the screen shot doesn't reflect the actual values used in the examples.

Where a dual brush has been added, you'll see the screen shot and details of the brush tip name.

Indicates the settings used and the values that have been applied. Only settings that change from the default have been displayed. So if the brush already has spattering applied by default, you can assume that the setting hasn't been changed unless it is indicated.

If a dual brush has been used, the icon is displayed here. The name of the brush tip is given in the settings below.

The details of the settings used are displayed in the order in which they appear in the Brushes panel: Brush Tip Shape, Shape Dynamics, Scattering, Texture, Dual Brush, Color Dynamics, Transfer, Noise, Wet Edges.

SOFT ROUND 18

These swatches show some examples of how the brush can look when painted in a block rather than as a single stroke.

Under each swatch are the details of the settings used to achieve the brush effect.

Digital Brush Art

Here are some digital paintings to inspire you, with details
of the brushes each artist has used to generate the effects
in their images.

The Brush Directory will give you some idea of the range of painting effects that Photoshop can offer with just the Photoshop brushes. There are many people developing their own custom brushes and making them available to download, and you can see how these can be used to good effect in the following images. For some useful Web sites to download brushes from, see Resources on page 408.

You'll notice that many of the images build up the effects with layers of brush strokes. Using a pen and tablet makes it much easier to vary each stroke because you can change the settings so they are responsive to how you adjust the angle and pressure of your pen.

You'll also find paintings that have only used a few brushes and are nonetheless striking in their simplicity.

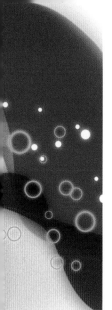

Circle brush

Floating Ribbons
GINA WALTON

These floating ribbons were created using brushes. You might recognize one of the circle brushes (pages 110–113) from the Photoshop Assorted Brushes Library, which has had Spacing and Scattering settings adjusted.

The World Outside Your Window
RICARDO MEDINA

Ricardo used a selection of brushes to create this image. He used the Chalk brush (page 72) and other dry media brushes with a variety of settings to paint over the edge of the window frame. He downloaded a number of brushes from the DeviantArt Web site: a flare brush created by Colorburned, Night Lights brushes from M-Ajinah, and Fractal brushes from ShadyMedusa. Ricardo built up the image with different layers of strokes, using a variety of blend modes (overlay, color dodge, and screen).

Fractal IV

Night Lights
Brush Set

Bristle brush
Size Jitter with Pen
Pressure; Minimum
Diameter 31%;
Minimum Roundness
1%; Opacity Jitter
20% with Pen
Pressure; Flow
Jitter 80%

Chalk brush
Size Jitter with Pen
Pressure; Minimum
Diameter 50%;
Angle Jitter with Initial
Direction; Opacity
Jitter and Flow Jitter
with Pen Pressure

Splatter brush
Size Jitter 10%
with Pen Pressure;
Minimum Diameter
60%; Angle Jitter
100%; Scatter (Both
Axes) 209%; Count 3;
Count Jitter, Opacity
Jitter, and Flow Jitter
with Pen Pressure

Phoenix
MIKE NASH

In general Mike uses brushes with plenty of texture (the
Chalk and Bristle brushes, for example) and builds up the
layers of paint using an opacity of 75%. He used a custom
cloud brush for the smoke and added the sparks and flecks
of ash using a Splatter brush. A custom bark brush and the
Charcoal brush (page 262) were also used to build up the
texture on the branches.

My Lovely
MICHAEL LAI

Cloud brush

Rose brush

Michael created a series of custom brushes from photos of clouds, roses, and trees for much of this image. He separated the objects of the photos from their background before turning them into brushes. As well as the custom brushes, Michael also used soft and hard basic brushes with a variety of settings.

19-pixel brush with 100% Hardness. A range of hard brushes were used.

300-pixel brush with 0% Hardness. Soft brushes were used at varying sizes.

Her
JONATHAN WONG

To produce this image, Jonathan used a combination of soft-edged and hard-edged brushes, along with scanned textures and splashes that he created himself. Even with straightforward hard and soft brushes, he found he could create a stunning effect with contrasting lines. He used the soft brushes to add a glow to the subject, enhancing the contrast by painting with white onto the colored background.

The Eve of Realisation
JONATHAN WONG

Many of the lines in this image have been created with a hard-edged brush, which has been combined with textures, a photo, and sketches to generate this delicate effect.

19-pixel brush with 100% Hardness. A range of hard brushes were used.

300-pixel brush with 0% Hardness. Soft brushes were used at varying sizes.

Brush 1: Hair
Spacing (on the
standard brush) 4%;
Size Jitter with Pen
Pressure.

**Brush 2: Face
and arms**
Simple Photoshop
hard brush: Spacing
10%; Size Jitter
with Pen Pressure;
Opacity and Flow
Jitter with Pen
Pressure; Airbrush
and Smoothing
selected.

**Brush 3: Skin and
clothing texture**
Spacing 6%; Size
Jitter with Pen
Pressure; Scattering
75% with Pen
Pressure.

Last Last Chance
ROB SHIELDS

For this painting, Rob created three
brushes in Photoshop using a Basic
brush (pages 58–63) with the Opacity
Jitter set to Pen Pressure: a brush for
the hair, one for the face and arms, and
another to add texture to the skin and
clothing. Using these brushes he
painted the image, varying the settings
as appropriate.

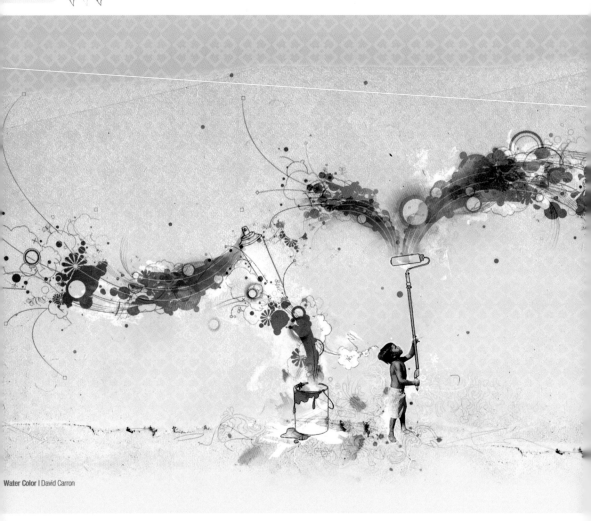

Water Color | David Carron

Chalk   Chalk

Soft Round   Watercolor

Hard Round   Watercolor

A selection of the
brushes used.

Water Color
DAVID CARRON

As could be expected from the title, David used a variety of
watercolor brushes to paint in texture and to erase areas
from some of the illustrations, lifting the image. He combined
the watercolor brushes with strokes from other brushes—
Chalk (page 72) and the Basic brush (pages 58–63) with
different settings of hardness—to build up the image.

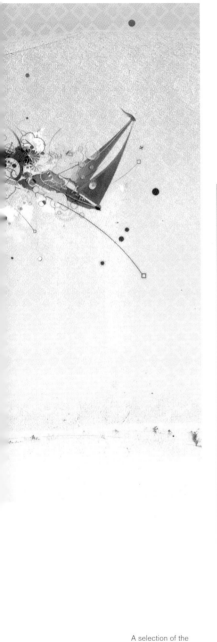

Lounge
DAVID CARRON

David made extensive use of soft-edged brushes in this image to create the dreamy atmospheric feel of the painting. Combining soft edges with hard-edged shapes gives depth to the painting by giving the impression of varying levels of focus.

A selection of the brushes used.

Soft Round   Hard Round

Airbrush Soft Round

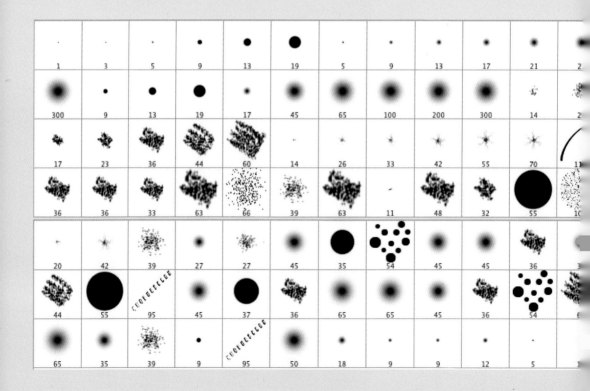

UNDERSTANDING BRUSHES

This section tells you everything you need to know about brushes, from selecting and changing your brushes right through to creating your own. There is also a handy overview of the brush libraries.

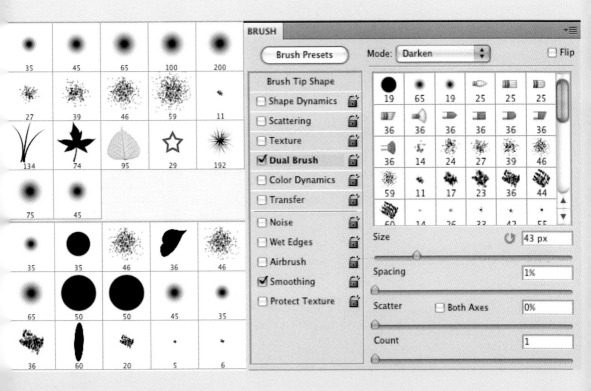

Brush Settings

Photoshop has many tools that use the Brush Settings: the Brush Tool, the Pencil Tool, the History Brush Tool, and the Healing Brush Tool to name just a few. Here you will learn how to use the Brush Settings to change your brush, and find a broad explanation of the effect of each of the ways you can change your brush.

Selecting a Brush (pages 25–26)

This section starts by explaining how to select a brush and change the color. It provides a starting point if you aren't familiar with using the Photoshop brush tools.

Changing Brush Settings (pages 27–35)

Once you have selected a brush, you can change a multitude of settings. This section explains how to change each of them and shows what effect the settings have on the brush. If necessary, you can use this as a reference section alongside the Brush Directory. It will remind you where to go to change the settings.

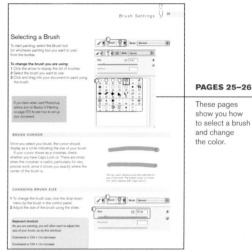

PAGES 25–26

These pages show you how to select a brush and change the color.

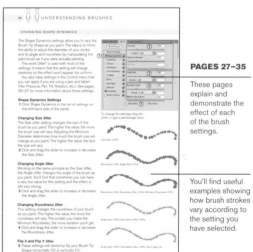

PAGES 27–35

These pages explain and demonstrate the effect of each of the brush settings.

You'll find useful examples showing how brush strokes vary according to the setting you have selected.

Selecting a Brush

To start painting, select the Brush tool
(or whichever painting tool you want to use)
from the toolbar.

To change the brush you are using:
1 Click the arrow to display the list of brushes.
2 Select the brush you want to use.
3 Click and drag into your document to paint using
   the brush.

If you have never used Photoshop
before, turn to Basics of Painting
on page 372 to see how to set up
your document.

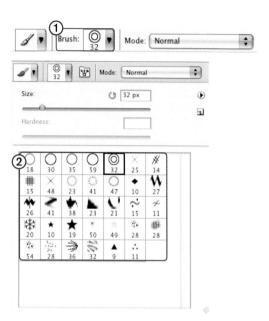

BRUSH CURSOR

Once you select your brush, the cursor should
display as a circle indicating the size of your brush.
   If your cursor shows as a crosshair, check
whether you have Caps Lock on. There are times
when the crosshair is useful, particularly for very
precise work, since it shows you exactly where the
center of the brush is.

The top cursor shows a circle that indicates the
size of the brush. The bottom cursor is a crosshair, which appears with Caps Lock on.

CHANGING BRUSH SIZE

1 To change the brush size, click the drop-down
   menu by the brush in the control panel.
2 Adjust the size of the brush using the slider.

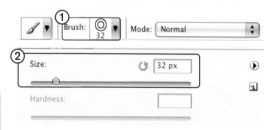

Keyboard shortcut

As you are painting, you will often want to adjust the
size of your brush, so try this shortcut:

Command or Ctrl + [to decrease

Command or Ctrl +] to increase

CHOOSING YOUR FOREGROUND COLOR

The color you will be painting with is determined by the color swatch selected for the Foreground Color at the bottom of the toolbar.

The swatch of color behind is known as the Background Color swatch. The Background Color won't affect your painting unless you have selected Foreground/Background Jitter as an effect (see page 34).

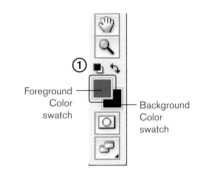

Foreground Color swatch

Background Color swatch

To change the Foreground Color:
1 Click and release the Foreground Color swatch and the Color Picker appears.
2 You can drag the slider up and down the vertical color wheel.
3 Click in the main square to choose your color.
4 When you click OK, the Foreground Color swatch will change to contain the color you selected.
5 When you paint, that is the color you will be using.
6 To add the color to the Swatches panel so it is always available for you to select, simply drag the swatch into the Swatches panel.

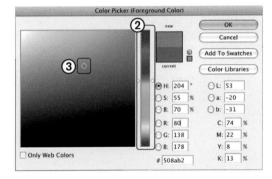

USING THE COLOR PANEL

To choose a color using the Color panel:
1 Display the Color panel by going to Window > Color.
2 Drag the sliders to create the color you want, or click in the color ramp at the bottom to select a color.

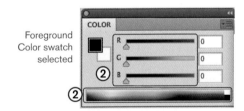

Foreground Color swatch selected

To change the Background Color:
1 Click on the Background Color swatch to highlight it (the highlight is very subtle!) and then choose the new color you want for the Background Color as you did above.

Background Color swatch selected

If you are working in an RGB document, RGB color sliders will be displayed. If your color mode is set up to be CMYK, the color will be defined in CMYK. For more information about the difference between RGB and CMYK, see page 376.

Changing Brush Settings

BLEND MODE, OPACITY, FLOW, AND AIRBRUSH

Changing the Blend Mode
1 When you change the Blend Mode (labeled "Mode"), you alter how the color you are painting with mixes with the colors underneath. You can create some great effects using the different modes; for a fuller explanation see page 390. To change the Blend Mode, click the drop-down menu and select a different mode.

Changing the Opacity
2 Changing the Opacity makes your brush strokes more or less translucent. If you paint with an Opacity of 0% you won't see your stroke—it will have become completely transparent. Painting with an Opacity of 50% will appear as though your stroke is mixing half and half with the colors underneath. To change the Opacity, type the percentage value you want.

Changing the Flow
3 The Flow determines how much paint appears to be on your brush. Having a low value makes it seem as though you have very little paint on your brush, and vice versa for a high value. To change the Flow, type a percentage for the level of Flow you want.

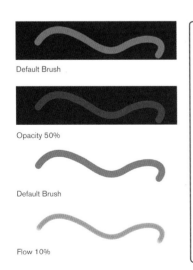

Default Brush

Opacity 50%

Default Brush

Flow 10%

Painting in Airbrush Mode
Clicking this button (1) turns on Airbrush Mode. It means that your "brush" seems to work more like an airbrush. So as you paint, if you hold the cursor in one place more paint is "sprayed" onto your canvas. Likewise, if you go over where you have already painted it appears to create layers of paint. Some brushes have Airbrush Mode turned on by default.

DISPLAYING THE BRUSH PANEL

The Brush panel contains all the settings that you can use to vary your brush tip. To display the Brush panel, go to Window > Brushes. This is the panel that appears.

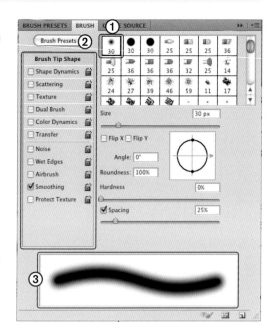

Using the Brush panel

1 The brush tip you have selected is highlighted with a black outline.
2 The settings are listed on the left-hand side of the panel. The settings above the line have options that display in the bottom right section of the panel when you click on the word to select them. The settings below the line are either on or off. Here the Brush Tip Shape is selected at the top (this setting can't be turned off for obvious reasons). You can see the settings in the bottom right section—Size, Angle, Roundness, Hardness, and Spacing. If you click on Shape Dynamics, you'll be able to change Size, Angle, and Roundness Jitter settings.
3 At the bottom of the panel there is a preview of how your brush stroke will look with the settings you selected. (The preview won't show changes you select in Color Dynamics settings because it only displays in black and white.)

USING NOISE AND WET EDGES

Using Noise
Turn Noise on by clicking the check box. Noise adds a grainy effect to your brush stroke, as you can see here.

Roundness 60%; Size Jitter 100%; Angle Jitter 100%; Noise

Using Wet Edges
Wet Edges is designed to mimic a watercolor effect where you have lots of water on your brush, so the paint is thin but concentrated more at the edge of your stroke.

You can turn the effect on by clicking the check box. You can see the effect here.

Roundness 60%; Size Jitter 100%; Angle Jitter 100%; Wet Edges

OTHER OPTIONS

Airbrush: When checked, your painting strokes will simulate the traditional airbrush.
Smoothing: Produces smoother curves when painting quickly, particularly when using a stylus.

Protect Texture: Applies the same pattern and scaling of the pattern to all brushes that have a texture applied.

CHANGING BRUSH TIP SHAPE SETTINGS

You can change the brush stroke drastically by changing the settings here, particularly Angle, Roundness, and Spacing.

Brush Tip Shape settings
1 Click Brush Tip Shape at the top of the list of settings on the left-hand side of the panel.

Brush Size or Diameter
As well as being able to change the size of your brush here, you can also use the Control Panel across the top of the screen, as explained on page 25.
2 Change the size of the brush by dragging the slider. The size is measured in pixels, which means it has a relationship to the size of your canvas—see page 372 for an explanation about how to set up your canvas in pixels.

Angle
Changing the Angle of your brush tip will make no difference if you have a circular brush. However, with a brush tip that isn't circular, this setting is like changing the angle you are painting with to a slightly flattened paint brush.
3 To change the Angle, type a new value or click and drag in the box.

Roundness
You can change the roundness of a brush, effectively squashing the tip.
4 To change the Roundness, type a percentage value or click and drag the black circles to push in or pull out the shape of the tip in the square to the right.

Hardness
5 You can only change the Hardness value on certain brushes. At 100% the brush is "hard" and has solid edges. As you decrease the value, the edges become softer.

Spacing
6 As you increase the Spacing, you create more space between each brush tip as you paint, making your stroke more "gappy."

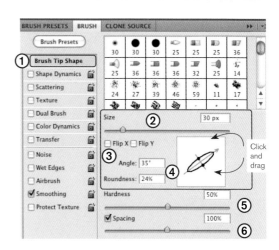

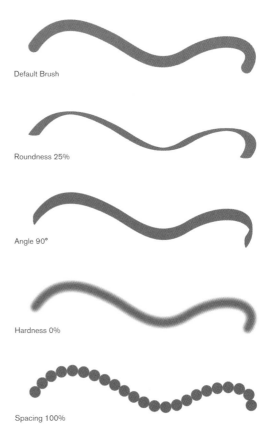

Default Brush

Roundness 25%

Angle 90°

Hardness 0%

Spacing 100%

CHANGING SHAPE DYNAMICS

The Shape Dynamics settings allow you to vary the Brush Tip Shape as you paint. The idea is to mimic the ability to adjust the diameter of your stroke and its angle and roundness by manipulating the paint brush as if you were actually painting.

The word "Jitter" is used with most of the settings; it means that the setting will change randomly so the effect won't appear too uniform.

You also have settings in the Control menu that you can apply if you are using a pen and tablet (Pen Pressure, Pen Tilt, Rotation, etc.). See pages 36–37 for more information about these settings.

Shape Dynamics Settings

1 Click Shape Dynamics in the list of settings on the left-hand side of the panel.

Changing Size Jitter

The Size Jitter setting changes the size of the brush as you paint. The higher the value, the more the brush size will vary. Adjusting the Minimum Diameter determines how much the brush size will change as you paint. The higher the value, the less the size will vary.

2 Click and drag the slider to increase or decrease the Size Jitter.

Changing Angle Jitter

Working on the same principle as the Size Jitter, the Angle Jitter changes the angle of the brush as you paint. You'll find that sometimes you can have a very low value for this setting and the effect is still very strong.

3 Click and drag the slider to increase or decrease the Angle Jitter.

Changing Roundness Jitter

This setting changes the roundness of your brush as you paint. The higher the value, the more the roundness will vary. The smaller you make the Minimum Roundness, the more variation you'll get.

4 Click and drag the slider to increase or decrease the Roundness Jitter.

Flip X and Flip Y Jitter

5 These settings will randomly flip your Brush Tip Shape horizontally (X) or vertically (Y).

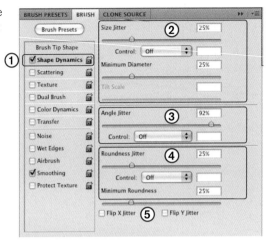

To change the settings, drag the slider or type a percentage value.

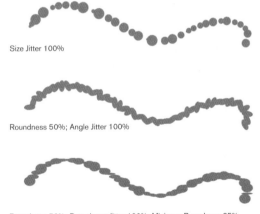

Size Jitter 100%

Roundness 50%; Angle Jitter 100%

Roundness 50%; Roundness Jitter 100%; Minimum Roundness 25%

Angle Jitter 100%; Roundness Jitter 100%

Angle Jitter 100%; Roundness Jitter 100%; Flip X Jitter On

CHANGING SCATTERING

Scattering literally scatters your brush tips as you paint. The higher the value, the more widely the tips are dispersed. Changing the Spacing (see page 29) spreads the tips out along the line you are painting. Scatter, on the other hand, spreads them out above and below the line.

You also have settings in the Control menu that you can apply if you are using a pen and tablet (Pen Pressure, Pen Tilt, etc.). See pages 36–37 for more information about these settings.

Scattering Settings
1 Click Scattering in the list of settings on the left-hand side of the panel.

Scatter
2 Change the value by dragging the slider or typing a percentage. You can check the Both Axes box to spread the tips in a circle instead of just above and below.

Count
3 The Count value changes the density of brush tips as you paint. The higher the value, the thicker and denser the effect.

Count Jitter
4 Count Jitter randomly varies the count value as you paint. The higher the value, the more variation in the density of the stroke.

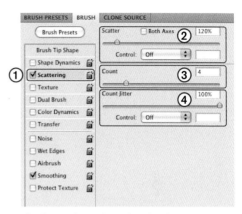

To change the settings, drag the slider or type a percentage value.

Scatter 120%

Scatter 120%; Count 4

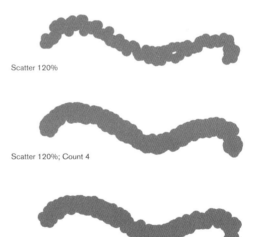

Scatter 120%; Count 4; Count Jitter 100%

TEXTURE

There are many textures that you can apply to your brush stroke. You'll find an example swatch of each texture on pages 334–345.

You also have settings in the Control menu (under Depth Jitter) that you can apply if you are using a pen and tablet (Pen Pressure, Pen Tilt, etc.)—see pages 36–37.

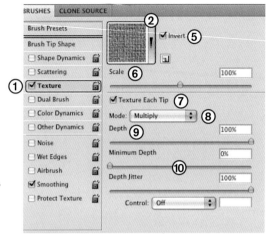

Texture settings

1 Click Texture in the settings list on the left-hand side of the panel.

2 Click the down arrow to see the menu.

3 Select your texture from the swatches displayed.

4 When you click the drop-down menu, another menu becomes available in the top-right corner, giving you the option to load other groups of textures: Artist Surfaces, Color Paper, etc. You can also adjust how your textures are displayed: as Small Thumbnail, Small List, etc.

Invert

5 The Invert check box has the effect of turning the texture inside out—all the raised elements become depressed and vice versa.

Scale

6 By adjusting the Scale you can determine the level of detail the texture has within the stroke.

Texture Each Tip

7 Texture Each Tip applies the texture to each "tip" of your stroke. (Select a wide spacing to see the individual tips that make up your brush stroke.)

Mode

8 Changing the Mode can result in the texture effect varying considerably.

Depth

9 Depth lets you control how "strong" your texture is. The higher the value, the greater the "impression" of the texture.

Minimum Depth and Depth Jitter

10 If you select Texture Each Tip, you can vary the depth as you paint by using Minimum Depth and Depth Jitter.

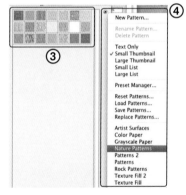

To change the settings (above), drag the slider or type a percentage value.

Dark Course Weave with Multiply Blend Mode

Dark Course Weave with Subtract Blend Mode

Dark Course Weave with Spacing 35%, Texture Every Tip, 0% Minimum Depth, and 100% Depth Jitter

DUAL BRUSH

You can create some great effects by using dual brushes. They offer an endless variety of possibilities.

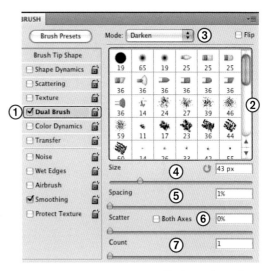

Dual Brush settings
1 Click on Dual Brush in the settings list on the left-hand side of the panel.

Choosing a Brush Tip
2 Start by clicking on a brush tip from the selection in the window.

Mode
3 You can change the mode at the top of the panel and experiment with different settings, since the mode can make a big difference to the way the dual brush blends with the original brush.

Size
4 You can change the Size of your dual brush. The brush you have selected as the dual brush will be "masked" by the actual brush you have selected. So if your actual brush is 50 pixels and you make your dual brush 75 pixels, you won't be able to see the edges of the brush you have selected as the dual brush.

Spacing
5 Spacing changes the amount of space between the dual brush tips horizontally along your stroke.

Scatter
6 Scatter spreads the brush tips vertically, or in a circular fashion if you select Both Axes.

Count
7 To increase the density of the effect of the dual brush, increase the Count value.

To change the settings, drag the slider or type a percentage value.

Basic Brush with Dual Brush of Grass using Multiply Blend Mode. Size 134 px; Spacing 25%; Scatter 139%; Count 3

As above but Size 30 px

Basic Brush with Dual Brush of Grass using Multiply Blend Mode. Size 30 px; Spacing 15%; Scatter 70%; Count 5

CHANGING COLOR DYNAMICS

There are many settings you can change within Color Dynamics. Although you can achieve dramatic effects by making the values high, lower settings can also give more subtle and therefore more realistic effects.

You also have settings in the Control menu (under Foreground/Background Jitter) that you can apply if you are using a pen and tablet (Pen Pressure, Pen Tilt, etc.)—see pages 36–37.

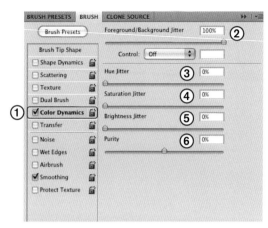

Color Dynamics settings

1 Click Color Dynamics in the settings list on the left-hand side of the panel.

Foreground/Background Jitter

2 As its name implies, this setting switches between the Foreground and Background Color Swatches while you are painting, so before you start make sure the two colors you want to use are selected as the Foreground and Background Colors (see page 26).

Hue Jitter

3 The Hue Jitter changes the colors as you are painting. A lower value gives a more subtle effect.

Saturation Jitter

4 As you increase the value of this setting, the more the saturation will vary.

Brightness Jitter

5 As with the previous settings, the higher the value the more your brush stroke will change from dark to light.

Purity

6 The value for Purity moves between −100% and +100%, with the default being 0%. At 0% it has no effect. Otherwise it determines levels of Saturation. At a value of −50% it would mean that the Saturation levels would never go above 50%, while at +50% it would mean the Saturation levels never went below 50%. At −100% the entire stroke has no Saturation and at +100% it has 100% Saturation.

To change the settings, drag the slider or type a percentage value.

Foreground/Background Jitter 100%

Hue Jitter 100%

Saturation Jitter 100%

Brightness Jitter 100%

Purity +100%

CHANGING TRANSFER SETTINGS

These settings all determine how the paint transfers onto the canvas—with more density or less, or with more transparency or less.
   You also have settings in the Control menu that you can apply if you are using a pen and tablet (Pen Pressure, Pen Tilt, etc.)—see pages 36–37.

Transfer settings
1 Click Transfer in the settings list on the left-hand side of the panel.

Opacity Jitter
2 This adjusts the opacity of your stroke as you are painting. The higher the value, the more the opacity changes. You can also set up controls that will respond to your pen strokes if you are using a pen and tablet.

Flow Jitter
3 Use this setting if you want to vary the flow as you paint. Lower percentages create more subtle variations and, as with many of the other settings, you can set up controls to use with your pen and tablet.

Wetness Jitter
4 This option is only available if you are using the CS5 new Mixer Brush (see page 40). It lets you vary randomly the amount of wetness applied to your brush.

Mix Jitter
5 As with Wetness Jitter, this option is only available when you have the new CS5 Mixer Brush selected (see page 40). This option varies the extent to which the colors are mixed as you paint with the Mixer Brush.

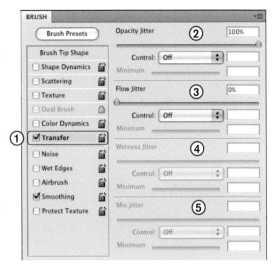

To change the settings, drag the slider or type a percentage value.

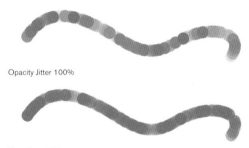

Opacity Jitter 100%

Flow Jitter 100%

Using a Pen and Tablet

Trying to paint using a mouse can be a frustrating experience because it's not at all like the traditional media that most of us were taught to draw or paint with. Graphics tablets and pens allow artists to use a more familiar method to create images on a computer.

A graphics tablet comes with a penlike device called a stylus that allows you to hand-draw images in a manner similar to using a pen.

As you draw with a stylus, the movements it makes on the tablet are translated to the computer's screen.

Graphics tablets also allow you to control the pressure or tilt of the stylus.

Changing Pen Settings in Photoshop

Photoshop's Brushes panel has Pen Settings, which gives you ways to control the stylus features.

FADE

Confusingly the first of the Pen Settings—Fade —is not actually controlled by a stylus. The Fade setting fades jitter settings—Opacity, Size, Angle, Roundness, and Flow—over a number of user-defined steps.

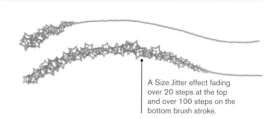

A Size Jitter effect fading over 20 steps at the top and over 100 steps on the bottom brush stroke.

PEN PRESSURE

The Pen Settings in the Brushes panel also allows you to control Opacity, Flow, Size, and Angle Jitters through the amount of pressure you apply to the stylus. The greater the pressure, the greater the jitter, and vice versa.

Using Size Jitter, the top stroke was made with a light pen pressure; the bottom stroke with a heavier pressure.

PEN TILT

The Pen Tilt controls respond to the angle that a stylus is being tilted during painting. Size Jitter controlled by Pen Tilt, for instance, would add greater jitter the more acute the stylus angle.

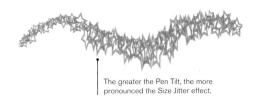

The greater the Pen Tilt, the more pronounced the Size Jitter effect.

STYLUS WHEEL

Some styluses have a wheel, which can be used to regulate the amount of jitter applied as you paint.

As the stylus wheel turns, the Size Jitter becomes more, or less, pronounced.

ROTATION

When you select Rotation, the brush stroke will respond and adjust as you rotate your pen.

INITIAL DIRECTION

Angle Jitter can be set so that the jitter angle of a painted stroke is based on the initial direction of the brush stroke (as in the example shown here).

The Angle Jitter ranges around the angle of the first brush tip.

DIRECTION

Angle Jitter can be set so that a painted stroke's jitter angle is based on the direction of the brush as it changes throughout the stroke.

The Angle Jitter responds to changes in angle as you paint.

Other Brush Tools

Apart from the paint brush, Photoshop has a huge range of other tools that use the brush tips and brush settings. Here is an overview of some of them.

PENCIL TOOL

The Pencil Tool merits only a brief mention here. It paints with hard-edged strokes, unlike the paint brush.

COLOR REPLACEMENT TOOL

The Color Replacement Tool replaces the color you are painting over with the Foreground Color. The tool has a cursor with a crosshair in the middle that you need to keep over the color you want to replace. The edges of the brush can stray into other colors but they won't be replaced.

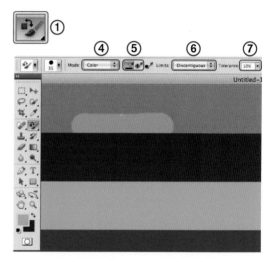

1 Select the Color Replacement Tool.

2 Select the Foreground Color you want as the new color.

3 Start painting, making sure the crosshair is over the color you want to replace. You should be painting in the new color.

4 By default, you will be using the Color blend mode when you paint. The Color mode replaces both the Hue and Saturation, and sometimes you might find that the Saturation values of the original are a little high. In this instance, you will achieve a better result by switching to just Hue. If the replacement color is lighter than the original, you might need to paint using the Luminosity mode first and then the Color mode.

5 If you only want to replace a single color, click Sample once, and the color under the crosshair when you first click will be the only one replaced.

6 Discontigous replaces the color regardless of where it appears under the pointer, while Contiguous will replace only adjacent pixels, and using Find Edges makes Photoshop find the edges of the color you are replacing.

7 The Tolerance setting determines the range of colors Photoshop will replace compared to the original pixel you selected. Use a lower tolerance to be more precise.

HISTORY BRUSH

The History Brush paints using a particular History state. What is particularly useful is that you can apply a filter to the whole image. In the History panel (see page 374), you can go back a step to undo the filter. You can then use the History Brush to paint the filter back in over particular areas of your image, using all the brush options—a fancy brush, changing the brush mode, settings, etc.

   Make changes to your picture so you have some steps in the History panel. In the example right, the History Brush has been used to paint in the Accented Edges step in the History panel over the bottom left half of the image with Multiple mode selected.

1 Select the History Brush Tool.
2 Select the History state you want to use to paint with by clicking the box to the left of the label.
3 Choose your brush tip, brush options, and settings.
4 Begin painting.

ART HISTORY BRUSH

The Art History Brush works in a similar way to the History Brush. You still choose a History state, but in addition, it has a number of "Art" effects you can apply that the History Brush doesn't have.

1 Select the Art History Brush.
2 Choose the History state you want to paint with from the History panel. Click in the box to the left of the History state.
3 Choose the Brush tip, Brush settings, and options for the History Brush.
4 Under Style, choose the Art effect you want.
5 Specifying the Area determines how many brush strokes there are as you drag the mouse. It appears to override the brush size, but in fact the brush size still determines the size of each brush dab, curl, etc.
6 The higher the Tolerance setting, the more minimal the effect.

Painting with the Mixer Brush

The Mixer Brush is new to Photoshop CS5. It provides a more realistic painting effect with its ability to "mix" colors as you paint, mimicking what happens in real life with wet paint as the colors on your canvas mix along your brush stroke.

CHOOSING COLORS FOR THE MIXER BRUSH

The Paint Brush Tool uses one color—the Foreground Color—and with it a solid stroke is painted onto the canvas. You still select a color with the Mixer Brush, as though you're loading paint onto an actual paint brush. With the Mixer Brush, the color you select is called the Reservoir. The Reservoir doesn't have to only contain a solid color. If you select the color from your Canvas, the brush will reflect the colors you picked up with the Eyedropper tool.

1 Here the Reservoir is filled with the solid Foreground Color.

2 With the Mixer Brush Tool selected, hold down "i" on the keyboard while you click the area of an image you want to sample. The brush will paint with the mixture of colors you have sampled.

Reservoir showing the solid Foreground Color selected

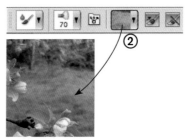

Reservoir showing the sampled pixels from this image

LOAD THE BRUSH AFTER EACH STROKE

You can choose whether or not to reload the brush after each stroke you paint. If you don't, depending on your settings your brush will continue painting without being refilled from the reservoir. In the example to the right, it means the brush starts with no color. To reload the brush after each stroke, press the button shown (1). Click it again to turn it off.

The Load After Each Stroke button

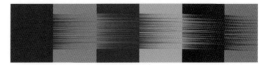

Painted stroke with Load After Each Stroke switched off, and with settings of Wet 100%, Load 100%, Mix 100%

CLEAN THE BRUSH AFTER EACH STROKE

You can choose whether to clean the brush after each stroke (1).

The example on the right shows a second stroke below the first that was not cleaned and, therefore, is still full of orange.

The Clean the Brush After Each Stroke button

Painted strokes with Clean Brush After Each Stroke switched off, and with settings of Wet 100%, Load 100%, Mix 100%

MIXER BRUSH PRESET SETTINGS

There are a number of combinations of settings that Photoshop supplies in a drop-down menu. They have different values for the settings that are described on the next page.

To the right are some examples of a brush stroke being used with different preset settings. They should give you an idea of the different effects possible.

Dry, heavy load

Moist, light mix

Wet

Very wet, heavy mix

MIXER BRUSH SETTINGS

Wet

The Wet setting determines how wet the paint on the canvas is. It doesn't define how wet the paint on the brush is. So the wetter the paint on the canvas, the more it will spread and mix.

Wet 100%, Load 1%, Mix 0%

Load

The higher the load value, the more paint loads on the brush, which means the stroke will be sustained for longer.

Wet 0%, Load 100%, Mix 0%

Mix

This determines how much color is loaded on the brush and how much is taken from the canvas as you paint. The higher the value, the more paint is taken from the canvas, and, conversely, the lower the value, the more paint comes from the color reservoir.

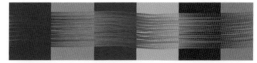

Wet 1%, Load 1%, Mix 100%

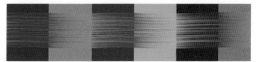

Wet 100%, Load 100%, Mix 0%

Wet 1%, Load 100%, Mix 100%

Wet 100%, Load 100%, Mix 100%

PAINTING A PHOTOGRAPH

You can use the Mixer Brush to create a painting from a photograph.

1 Create a new Layer to paint on so you don't affect the original photograph.

2 Make sure that Sample All Layers is checked in the Options bar so that the paint will mix with the original photograph.

3 Remember that you can sample pixels from the photograph to paint with.

Using the HUD Color Picker

The HUD Color Picker is a new feature in Photoshop CS5. (HUD stands for Heads Up Display, in case you were wondering!) It is designed to make it a lot easier to select a new color on the fly while you are painting. Having said that, it uses a complicated combination of keyboard shortcuts that take some practice to master.

With one of the Brush tools selected, hold down Ctrl+Alt+Cmd on a Mac or Shift+Alt+right-click on a PC. The HUD Color Picker appears. Keep your mouse held down and you can scroll around the window showing the Saturation and Brightness. The Saturation is displayed from left to right and the Brightness from top to bottom.

To move to the Hue slider (which can be displayed as a wheel around the outside or a strip), keep the mouse held down (as soon as you release the mouse, you have to start again!), and hold down Spacebar while you move the cursor over to the circle on the Hue slider. Release the Spacebar (NOT the mouse) when you reach the circle and you'll be able to drag around to the Hue you want.

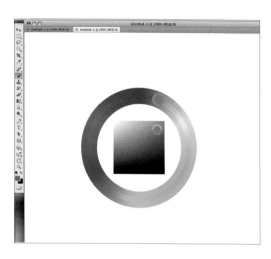

CHANGING PREFERENCES

The HUD Color Picker Preferences determine how the HUD Color Picker displays. You have a choice between a Strip and a Wheel for the Hue display, and you can also choose how large the display will be.

1 Go to Preferences: on a PC, select Edit > Preferences and General; on a Mac, select Photoshop > Preferences > General.
2 Toward the top of the General section, there is a drop-down menu where you can select the option you want for the HUD Color Picker.

> **Keyboard shortcut**
> To display General Preferences:
> Ctrl/Cmd+K

Creating Your Own Brushes

It is very simple to create your own brush in Photoshop. You just select an area on the canvas and then tell Photoshop that you want to use the sampled (i.e. selected) area as a brush.

When you paint with the brush you've created, Photoshop repeats the area you sampled along the length of your painted stroke.

Photoshop ignores any color information in the area you've sampled and simply looks at the brightness of the pixels. It uses these brightness values to determine how opaque areas of the new brush should be.

Areas in the original sample that are darker will be more opaque, and areas that were lighter will be more transparent.

Once you've created a custom brush, you can paint with it as you would a normal brush; all the Brushes panel settings such as Shape Dynamics, Color Dynamics, and so on are available so you can adjust your brush. The one setting that can't be changed is the Hardness value.

The black smudge above has been used as the basis of a custom brush, which was then used to create the blue paint stroke below it.

CREATING CUSTOM BRUSHES

To create a custom brush from a sample:
1 Select the area you want to sample with the Rectangular Marquee Tool.
2 Go to Edit > Define Brush Preset…
3 Give your custom brush a name and it will be added to the Brush Presets panel and the Brush Tip thumbnails.

Edit	Image	Layer	Select	Filter
Undo Rectangular Marquee				⌘Z
Step Forward				⇧⌘Z
Step Backward				⌥⌘Z
Fade…				⇧⌘F
Cut				⌘X
Copy				⌘C
Copy Merged				⇧⌘C
Paste				⌘V
Paste Into				⇧⌘V
Clear				
Check Spelling…				
Find and Replace Text…				
Fill…				⇧F5
Stroke…				
Free Transform				⌘T
Transform				▶
Auto-Align Layers…				
Auto-Blend Layers				
Define Brush Preset…				
Define Pattern…				
Define Custom Shape…				

ADAPTING AND SAVING PHOTOSHOP'S BRUSHES

Photoshop's preset brushes provide a useful starting point for the creation of your own unique brushes.

1 Start by selecting a preset brush that you want to customize.

2 Make adjustments to the preset brushes by altering settings such as Roundness, Scattering, and so on in the Brushes panel.

3 When you've found settings that you're happy with, choose New Brush Preset from the Brushes panel menu, or click the New Brush Preset icon at the bottom of the Brushes panel. Photoshop will remember all these settings as a new brush preset.

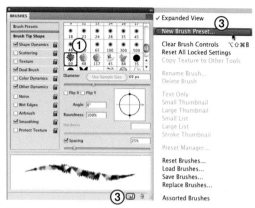

Saving a new brush preset

SAVING BRUSH SETTINGS WITH THE TOOL PRESETS PANEL

Although the Brush Presets panel will remember most of the settings you can use with a brush, some things, notably the Opacity setting and the color you were painting with are not remembered in the Brushes panel.

If you want to have Photoshop retain all the settings that can be associated with a brush, use the Tool Presets panel.

To create a tool preset that you can access from the Tool Presets panel:

1 First select the brush you want to save as a tool preset.

2 Choose the color you want to save with the brush as the Foreground Color and set Opacity and Flow if required.

3 Open the Tool Presets panel (Windows > Tool Presets).

4 Click the New Tool Preset icon or select New Tool Preset from the panel menu and name your new tool preset.

Saving a new tool preset

CREATING A BRUSH FROM A PATH

If you want a brush with a more precise shape, it is easier to use Photoshop's Pen Tool.

Unlike sampling an area directly from an image, you use the Pen Tool to draw a shape, stroke it with the brush you want, and then save the results as a preset brush.

Create Path icon on the Options bar

To create a preset brush from a path:

1 With the Pen Tool selected and before you start to create a path, make sure the Create Path icon is selected on the Options bar at the top of the screen.

2 Draw the path in the shape you want for your brush.

3 When the path is ready, choose a brush and its settings to add as a stroke to the path.

4 Select the path in the Paths panel and right-click or Control-click on the path and choose Stroke Path from the menu that pops up.

5 In the Stroke Path dialog box, choose Brush to apply to the stroke and click OK.

6 Select the Marquee Tool and create a selection around the stroked path.

7 Go to Edit > Define Brush Preset...

8 You will be asked to give your brush preset a name and click OK.

9 Your new brush is added to the Brush Preset panel and the Brush Tips list in the Brushes panel and you can now paint with it.

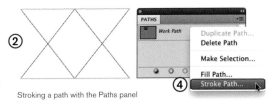

Stroking a path with the Paths panel

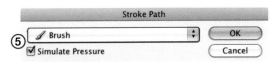

Stroke Path dialog box

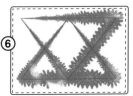

Selecting the stroked path with the Marquee Tool

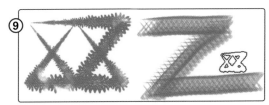

Above left is the original stroked path; on the right is a brush created from the stroked path.

CREATING A BRUSH FROM A COMPLEX ILLUSTRATOR PATH

Although Photoshop's Pen Tool is useful for creating fairly complex shapes and paths, Photoshop is not a drawing program. Illustrator, on the other hand, does have an extensive set of drawing tools (see page 406 for more information about Illustrator), and you can use paths created in Illustrator to create brushes in Photoshop.

Artwork created in Illustrator

To create a brush preset from a path in Illustrator:

1 In Illustrator, create the image you want to use as the basis for a brush preset.
2 Select the image and copy it using Edit > Copy.
3 Go to Photoshop and, in a new document, choose Edit > Paste.
4 Choose Path from the Paste dialog box and click OK.
5 Right-click or Control-click Work Path and choose Stroke Path from the Context menu.
6 In the Stroke Path dialog box, choose Brush to stroke the path and click OK.
7 Select the Rectangular Marquee Tool and use it to select the area you want to base your custom brush on.
8 Go to Edit > Define Brush Preset…
9 When prompted, give your new brush preset a name and click OK.
10 Your new brush is now added to the Brush Preset panel and the Brush Tips list in the Brushes panel.

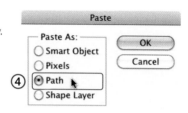

Paste dialog box

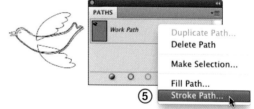

Stroking the copied path using the Paths panel

Selecting the stroked path with the Marquee Tool

The brush stroke created from the Illustrator paths

Keyboard Shortcuts

They might take a while to grow accustomed to, but once you do, keyboard shortcuts will save you lots of time and effort. It is worth trying to remember the ones that you will use most often from the list below.

PAINTING

To select the Brush Tool:

Press **b** and you switch to that tool.

To cycle through the tools with the Brush Tool:

Hold down **Shift+b** repeatedly and you select each tool in turn (the Pencil, Color Replacement, and Color).

To change the way the brush cursor displays (from a circle that reflects the size of the brush):

Press **Caps Lock** and the cursor changes to a crosshair. For further options to change the way the cursor displays: go to Preferences, press **Ctrl/Cmd+K** and then **Ctrl/Cmd+5** to select the Cursors panel (below).

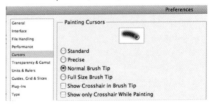

To increase/decrease the brush size in 10-pixel increments:

Press **[** to decrease and **]** to increase.

To increase/decrease the hardness of your brush in 25% increments:

Press **Shift+[** to decrease and **Shift+]** to increase.

To cycle through the brush presets:

Press **,** (comma) to go to the previous preset brush and **.** (period) to go to the next preset brush. Add **Shift** to jump to the first or last preset in the library.

To cycle through the brush blend modes (Normal, Dissolve, etc.):

Press **Shift+** or **Shift−**

To fade your previous brush stroke, go to Edit > Fade:

Press **Ctrl/Cmd+Shift+F**

CHANGING COLORS

To select a new Foreground Color from the Canvas:

Hold down **Alt** and click on the pixels with the color you want.

To switch the Foreground and Background Colors:

Press **x**

To display the Color panel:

Press **F5**

To fill an area with a color:

Press **Shift+Backspace** and the Fill dialog box appears.

To fill an area with the Foreground Color:

Press **Alt+Backspace**

CREATING YOUR OWN KEYBOARD SHORTCUTS

To set up your own keyboard shortcuts, go to Edit > Keyboard Shortcuts.

1 Select the area of Photoshop where you want to adjust or create new keyboard shortcuts.

2 Click the triangle to see the individual commands or panel items.

3 When you select a command, a box is selected in which you can type the keyboard shortcut you want to use.

4 Click Add Shortcut.

5 To delete a shortcut, click Delete Shortcut.

6 If the keyboard shortcut conflicts with one that is already set, a warning appears and you can choose either to go ahead with the shortcut or Undo Changes.

7 Once you have finished changing your keyboard shortcuts, either click OK or click the disc icon with a tiny arrow to save a new keyboard shortcut set.

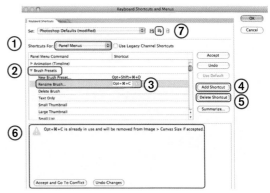

Keyboard Shortcuts dialog box

USEFUL KEYBOARD SHORTCUTS

1 Go to the Panel Menus under Shortcuts For.

2 Under Brush Presets, you can set shortcuts to Load Brushes and to load each of the Photoshop libraries.

3 A useful keyboard shortcut to create under Brushes is Clear Brush Controls (removes all the changes you have made to the Brush settings).

Saving Your Brush Settings

Once you have your brush just the way you want it, after having fiddled with the settings, you can, thankfully, save the brush with its settings as a "Brush Preset." This means that if you want to use the brush again, you can simply select the Brush Preset and you'll be ready to paint.

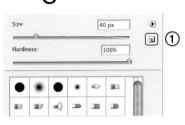

Creating a Brush Preset:

1 Go to the Brush drop-down menu in the Options bar and click the very small button on the top right of the area that drops down. It is indicated on the right. (You can also click the menu and select New Brush Preset.)

2 This dialog box appears asking you to give the Brush Preset a name.

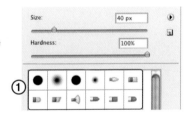

3 When you click OK, you'll see that the Brush Preset has been added to the list of brushes and you can select it.

RETURNING TO THE BRUSH DEFAULT SETTINGS

There is a quick and easy way to return to the default brush settings, which is very useful if you have been playing around and can't remember the settings the brush originally had.

1 Click the brush again, here in the Brush Preset picker, and the settings return to the default.

The only settings that don't return to their default are the settings in the Application Bar across the top: the Blend Mode, Opacity, and Flow. So if you are painting and wondering why your stroke appears faint, check the Opacity or Flow values.

Changing Libraries

There are many brush libraries that come with Photoshop. They are described on the following pages, and, in the Brush Directory, you'll see the brushes in all the libraries shown with a variety of different settings.

To load a new library:
1 Click the Brush Preset picker in the Options bar and...
2 ...from the menu on the right-hand side, select the library (you'll see them listed at the bottom of the menu).
3 A dialog box appears asking whether you want to append or replace the existing library. Click either Append or OK.

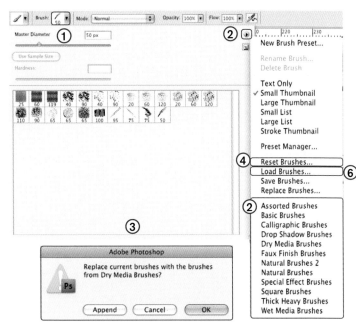

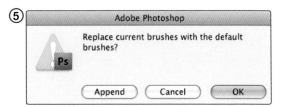

RESETTING YOUR BRUSH LIBRARY TO DEFAULT BRUSHES

4 If you want to return to the default brushes library, go to the Brush Preset picker as above, select the menu on the right, and select Reset Brushes.
5 A dialog box appears. Click either Append or OK. (Append will add the library of brushes to those already loaded.)

⑤ **Adobe Photoshop**

Replace current brushes with the default brushes?

Ps

[Append]   [Cancel]   [OK]

LOADING OTHER LIBRARIES

You can also load libraries of brushes from other sources.
6 When you select Load Brushes from the menu, a dialog box appears asking you to select a library. Brush libraries have the extension ".abr."
7 Navigate to the library you want to load and click Load.

Overview of the Brush Libraries

Before launching into the Brush Directory, here is an overview of the brush libraries, briefly describing the kinds of brushes that each one contains.

The libraries generally fall into two categories. There are libraries that mimic the effects of using natural tools to paint and draw. These are:

Dry Media Brushes page 150
Faux Finish Brushes page 176
Natural Brushes 2 page 236
Natural Brushes page 258
Thick Heavy Brushes page 280
Wet Media Brushes page 290

There are also libraries that contain shapes that can produce wild and interesting effects. They are:

DP Brushes (CS5 only) page 144
M Brushes (CS5 only) page 192
Special Effects Brushes page 266
The Default Brushes contain a mixture of both natural and shape types of brushes.

There are additional brush libraries containing brushes with similar shapes but different sizes:

Basic Brushes and **Calligraphic Brushes** (in the Default Brushes Library, page 58)
Drop Shadow Brushes A series of soft-edged square brushes
Square Brushes A series of square brushes at different sizes

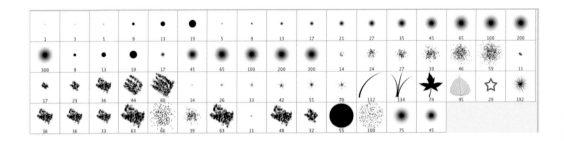

Default Brushes Library, page 58

This is the library of brushes you'll find pre-loaded when you start Photoshop from the box. It contains a varied selection of brushes—from the Dune Grass brush to Oil Heavy Flow Dry Edges. There is a brush to mimic almost any form of drawing or painting. There are dry media brushes: Chalk, Charcoal Large Smear, Hard Pastel on Canvas, and Oil Pastel Large.

The painting brushes include: Dry Brush Tip Light Flow, Dry Brush, Watercolor Loaded Wet Flat Tip, Watercolor Small Round Tip, Oil Heavy Flow Dry Edges, Oil Medium Wet Flow, Wet Sponge, and Rough Round Bristle.

Interesting effects can be created by combining brushes as dual brushes (see page 33). Try using some of the painterly brushes with the shape brushes as the dual brush.

Assorted Brushes Library, page 110

The Assorted Brushes Library contains a huge selection of shape brushes. They vary widely—ornaments, textures, crosshatches, and circles. As well as creating some great effects on their own, they can be used as dual brushes with brushes from other libraries. Try loading two libraries at the same time (see page 51) and combining brushes as dual brushes.

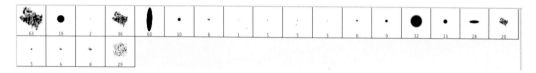

DP Brushes Library, page 144

A new library for Photoshop CS5, this contains some striking, big-effect brushes. The shapes are interesting and again could be combined with brushes from other libraries as dual brushes.

Dry Media Brushes Library, page 150

There are brushes in this library to mimic many of the drawing media. The library includes pencils, crayons, charcoal, graphite, pastels, and even permanent markers.

Faux Finish Brushes Library, page 176

The Faux Finish Brushes Library contains a selection of brushes designed to mimic painting with tools, to give textures rather than shapes. There are brushes to create washes with cotton or terry rags and sponges, along with texture combs and veining brushes.

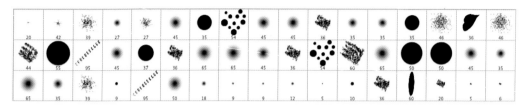

M Brushes Library, page 192

The M Brushes are new to CS5. The library contains a large range
of mainly shape brushes, with lots of interesting effects applied to
them by default. Many of them already use dual brushes and you can
achieve variations by adjusting their Dual Brush settings.

Natural Brushes 2 Library, page 236

This library contains some very useful painterly brushes offering
"dark" and "light" versions of a number of brushes and a selection of
watercolor brushes.

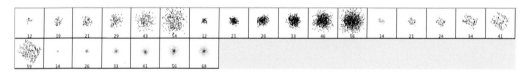

Natural Brushes Library, page 258

There are only a few actual brushes in this library since it
offers each of the brushes at different sizes. This is useful since it
means you can more easily avoid the pixelated effect you can get
when you increase the size of some brushes.

Special Effects Brushes Library, page 266
These brushes are not all they seem. For instance, a brush that looks like a soft round basic brush in fact sprays daisies everywhere. The brushes have plenty of effects applied to them by default. You'll find some interesting shapes to combine with brushes in other libraries.

Thick Heavy Brushes Library, page 280
These are what they say they are—thick and heavy. You'll get some great effects.

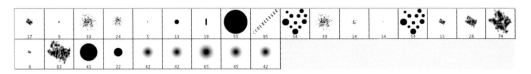

Wet Media Brushes Library
These offer a good selection of painterly brushes. Many of the brushes have interesting textures applied by default and there are variations on different brushes, including six varieties of watercolor brush.

BRUSH DIRECTORY

This extensive resource features examples of over 4,000 digital brush effects, organized by library, and provides all the settings information you need to access the brushes easily and quickly on your own system.

BASIC BRUSH

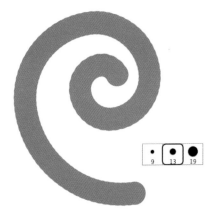

Scatter 100%
Count 1
Count Jitter 50%
Opacity Jitter 100%

Scatter 100%
Count 2
Count Jitter 100%
Foreground/Background Jitter 100%
Flow Jitter 100%

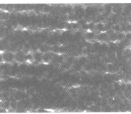

Flow 50%
Size Jitter 100%
Angle Jitter 100%
Roundness Jitter 50%
Minimum Roundness 1%

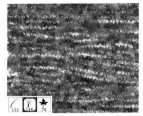

Dual Brush: Grass
Size 20px
Spacing 10%
Foreground/Background Jitter 100%

BRUSH TIP SHAPE

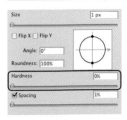

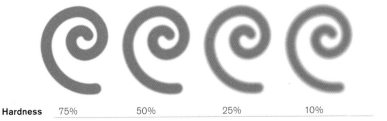

| Hardness | 75% | 50% | 25% | 10% |

BRUSH TIP SHAPE

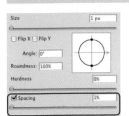

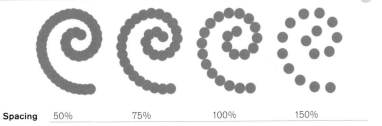

| Spacing | 50% | 75% | 100% | 150% |

FLOW

| Flow | 75% | 50% | 25% | 10% |

SHAPE DYNAMICS

| Size Jitter | 25% | 50% | 75% | 100% |

SHAPE DYNAMICS

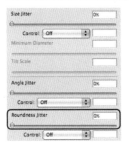

| Rndnss Jitter | 25% | 50% | 75% | 100% |

SHAPE DYNAMICS

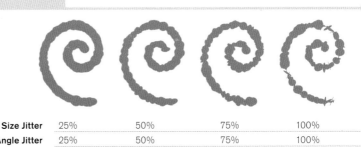

Size Jitter	25%	50%	75%	100%
Angle Jitter	25%	50%	75%	100%
Rndnss Jitter	25%	50%	75%	100%

SCATTERING

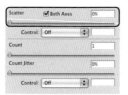
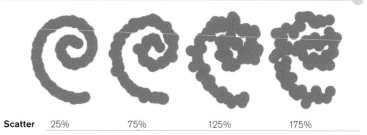

Scatter   25%   75%   125%   175%

COLOR DYNAMICS

Foreground/Background Jitter   25%   50%   75%   100%

COLOR DYNAMICS

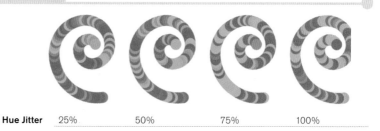

Hue Jitter   25%   50%   75%   100%

COLOR DYNAMICS

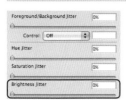

Brightness Jitter   25%   50%   75%   100%

COLOR DYNAMICS

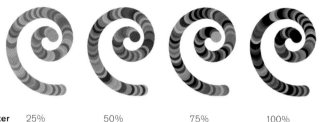

Brightness Jitter	25%	50%	75%	100%

COLOR DYNAMICS

Foreground/Background Jitter	100%	100%	100%	100%
Purity	-100%	-50%	+50%	+100%

COLOR DYNAMICS

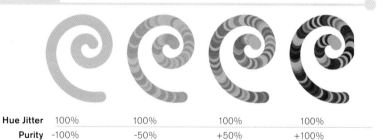

Hue Jitter	100%	100%	100%	100%
Purity	-100%	-50%	+50%	+100%

TRANSFER

Opacity Jitter	25%	50%	75%	100%

TRANSFER

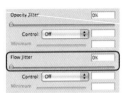

Flow Jitter	25%	50%	75%	100%

SHAPE DYNAMICS • COLOR DYNAMICS

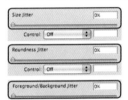

Size Jitter	25%	50%	75%	100%
Roundness Jitter	100%	100%	100%	100%
Foreground/Background Jitter	25%	50%	75%	100%

BRUSH TIP SHAPE • SHAPE DYNAMICS • COLOR DYNAMICS

Hardness	25%	25%	25%	25%
Angle and Roundness Jitters	100%	100%	100%	100%
Saturation Jitter	25%	50%	75%	100%

BRUSH TIP SHAPE • COLOR DYNAMICS

Spacing	75%	75%	75%	75%
Hue Jitter	25%	50%	75%	100%
Saturation Jitter	25%	50%	75%	100%

BRUSH TIP SHAPE · COLOR DYNAMICS

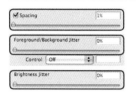

Spacing	1%	1%	1%	1%
Foreground/Background Jitter	25%	50%	75%	100%
Brightness Jitter	25%	50%	75%	100%

SCATTERING · COLOR DYNAMICS · TRANSFER

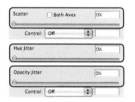

Scattering	25%	50%	75%	100%
Hue Jitter	25%	50%	75%	100%
Opacity Jitter	25%	50%	75%	100%

DUAL BRUSH

Dual Brush: Dune Grass

Size	112 px	50 px	25 px	10 px

DUAL BRUSH

Dual Brush: Dune Grass

Count	4	8	12	16

CALLIGRAPHIC BRUSH

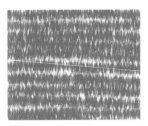

Angle 90°; Roundness 0%
Spacing 1%; Size Jitter 100%
Minimum Diameter 12%
Angle Jitter 5%

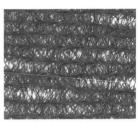

Angle 45°; Roundness 0%
Spacing 1%; Size Jitter 100%
Minimum Diameter 50%
Angle Jitter 50%
Foreground/Background Jitter 50%

Angle 45°
Roundness 0%
Spacing 1%

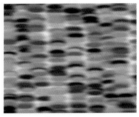

Angle 0°; Roundness 28%
Hardness 25%; Spacing 50%
Scatter 20%; Hue Jitter 25%
Saturation Jitter 100%

Angle 45°; Roundness 45%
Hardness 100%; Spacing 25%
Foreground/Background Jitter 100%
Hue Jitter 100%; Brightness
Jitter 50%; Purity +100%; Opacity
Jitter 100%; Flow Jitter 100%

BRUSH TIP SHAPE

Calligraphic settings

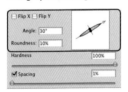

Angle	30°	30°	30°	30°
Roundness	10%	25%	50%	75%

BRUSH TIP SHAPE

Calligraphic settings

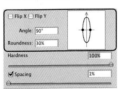

Angle	90°	60°	30°	10°
Roundness	30%	30%	30%	30%

BRUSH TIP SHAPE

Calligraphic settings

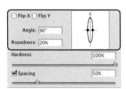

Roundness	20%	15%	10%	5%
Spacing	50%	75%	100%	150%

BRUSH TIP SHAPE

Calligraphic settings

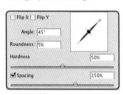

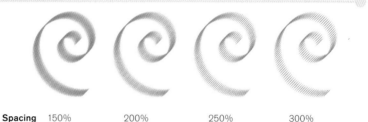

Spacing	150%	200%	250%	300%

BRUSH TIP SHAPE

Calligraphic settings

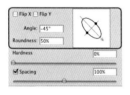

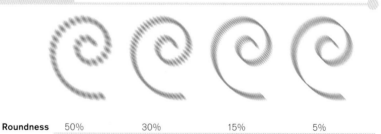

Roundness	50%	30%	15%	5%

BRUSH TIP SHAPE

Calligraphic settings

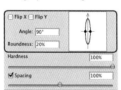

Angle	90°	60°	45°	30°
Roundness	20%	15%	10%	5%

BRUSH TIP SHAPE • SHAPE DYNAMICS

Calligraphic settings

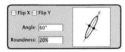
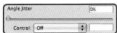
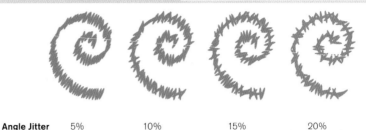

Angle Jitter	5%	10%	15%	20%

BRUSH TIP SHAPE • SHAPE DYNAMICS

Calligraphic settings

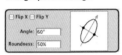

Angle Jitter	100%	100%	100%	100%
Roundness	50%	25%	5%	0%

BRUSH TIP SHAPE • SHAPE DYNAMICS

Calligraphic settings

Roundness Jitter	25%	50%	75%	100%

BRUSH TIP SHAPE • SHAPE DYNAMICS

Calligraphic settings

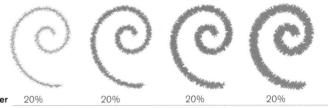

Angle Jitter	20%	20%	20%	20%
Rndnss Jitter	2%	25%	50%	75%

BRUSH TIP SHAPE • SHAPE DYNAMICS

Calligraphic settings

Size Jitter	100%	100%	100%	100%
Angle Jitter	0%	5%	10%	15%
Rndnss Jitter	0%	10%	20%	30%

BRUSH TIP SHAPE • SCATTERING

Calligraphic settings

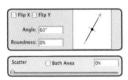

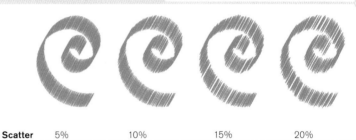

Scatter	5%	10%	15%	20%

BRUSH TIP SHAPE • SCATTERING

Calligraphic settings

Scatter	50%	50%	50%	50%
Count	1	2	3	4
Count Jitter	100%	100%	100%	100%

BRUSH TIP SHAPE • SCATTERING

Calligraphic settings

Scatter	50%	75%	100%	125%

BRUSH TIP SHAPE • SHAPE DYNAMICS • SCATTERING

Calligraphic settings

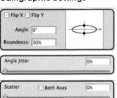

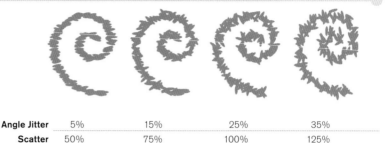

Angle Jitter	5%	15%	25%	35%
Scatter	50%	75%	100%	125%

BRUSH TIP SHAPE • SHAPE DYNAMICS • SCATTERING

Calligraphic settings

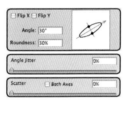

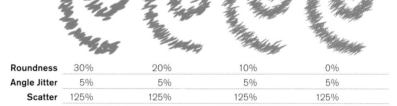

Roundness	30%	20%	10%	0%
Angle Jitter	5%	5%	5%	5%
Scatter	125%	125%	125%	125%

BRUSH TIP SHAPE • SHAPE DYNAMICS • SCATTERING

Calligraphic settings

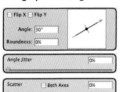

Angle Jitter	5%	5%	5%	5%
Roundness Jitter	5%	15%	25%	35%
Scatter	125%	125%	125%	125%

BRUSH TIP SHAPE • SCATTERING

Calligraphic settings

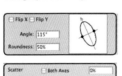

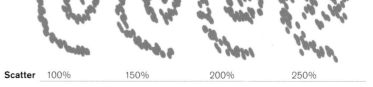

Scatter	100%	150%	200%	250%

BRUSH TIP SHAPE • SHAPE DYNAMICS • SCATTERING

Calligraphic settings

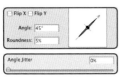

Angle Jitter	5%	5%	5%	5%
Scatter	0%	20%	40%	60%

BRUSH TIP SHAPE • SHAPE DYNAMICS

Calligraphic settings

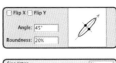

Angle	45°	90°	130°	180°
Size Jitter	50%	50%	50%	50%

BRUSH TIP SHAPE • SHAPE DYNAMICS

Calligraphic settings

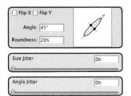

Size Jitter	25%	50%	75%	100%
Angle Jitter	25%	50%	75%	100%

BRUSH TIP SHAPE • SHAPE DYNAMICS

Calligraphic settings

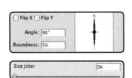

Spacing	60%	80%	100%	120%
Size Jitter	25%	50%	75%	100%

SPATTER

Roundness 50%

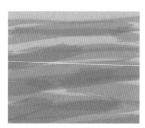

Roundness 50%
Opacity 50%

Size Jitter 100%
Opacity 50%

Dual Brush: Scattered Leaves
Wet Edges

BRUSH TIP SHAPE

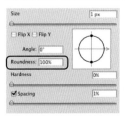

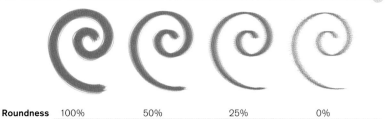

| Roundness | 100% | 50% | 25% | 0% |

SHAPE DYNAMICS

| Size Jitter | 0% | 25% | 50% | 100% |

SCATTERING

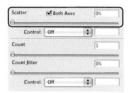
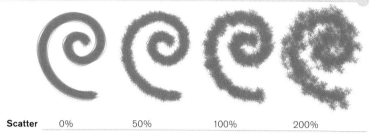

Scatter	0%	50%	100%	200%

SCATTERING • TRANSFER

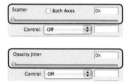

Scatter	50%	50%	50%	50%
Opacity Jitter	0%	50%	75%	100%

BRUSH TIP SHAPE

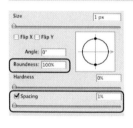
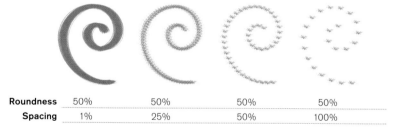

Roundness	50%	50%	50%	50%
Spacing	1%	25%	50%	100%

DUAL BRUSH

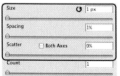

Dual Brush: Scattered Leaves

Size	50 px	35 px	35 px	35 px
Spacing	50%	1%	1%	1%
Scatter	0%	50%	400%	1000%

CHALK

Spacing 30%
Scatter 120%
Count 3
Count Jitter 100%

Scatter 500%
Foreground/Background Jitter 100%
Hue Jitter 100%

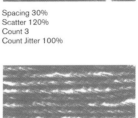

Spacing 35%
Size Jitter 100%

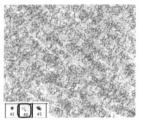

Dual Brush: Sampled Tip
Dual Brush Diameter 50 px
Saturation Jitter 100%
Purity +100%
Opacity Jitter 100%

SCATTERING

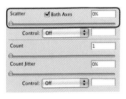

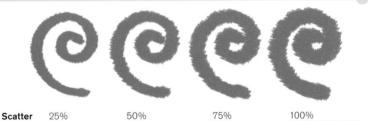

Scatter	25%	50%	75%	100%

SHAPE DYNAMICS

Size Jitter	50%	50%	100%	100%
Angle Jitter	0%	25%	50%	100%
Roundness Jitter	50%	50%	100%	100%

BRUSH TIP SHAPE • COLOR DYNAMICS

Spacing	10%	15%	20%	25%
Hue Jitter	25%	50%	75%	100%
Saturation Jitter	100%	75%	50%	25%

SCATTERING • TRANSFER

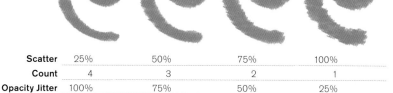

Scatter	25%	50%	75%	100%
Count	4	3	2	1
Opacity Jitter	100%	75%	50%	25%

DUAL BRUSH • COLOR DYNAMICS

Dual Brush:
Sampled
Tip

Spacing	10%	20%	30%	40%
Scatter	100%	200%	300%	400%
Foreground/Background Jitter	25%	50%	75%	100%

BRUSH TIP SHAPE

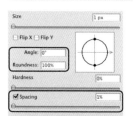

Angle	45°	60°	75°	90°
Roundness	0%	25%	35%	45%
Spacing	25%	20%	15%	10%

STAR

Default Brush

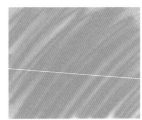

Flow 50%

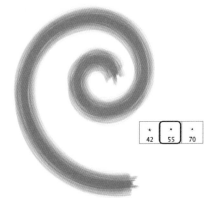

Hue Jitter 100%
Purity +100%

Dual Brush: Flowing Stars

BRUSH TIP SHAPE · SHAPE DYNAMICS

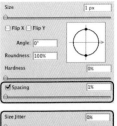

Spacing	0%	0%	0%	20%
Size Jitter	0%	50%	100%	100%

SCATTERING

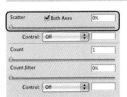

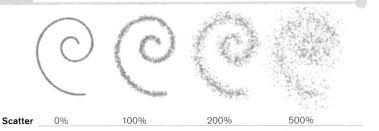

Scatter	0%	100%	200%	500%

COLOR DYNAMICS

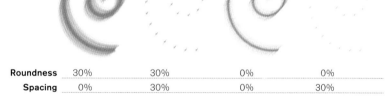

Foreground/Background Jitter	50%	100%	100%	100%
Hue Jitter	0%	0%	50%	100%

BRUSH TIP SHAPE

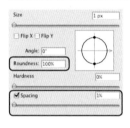

Roundness	30%	30%	0%	0%
Spacing	0%	30%	0%	30%

DUAL BRUSH

Dual Brush:
Flowing
Stars

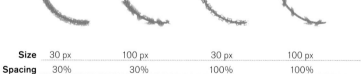

Size	30 px	100 px	30 px	100 px
Spacing	30%	30%	100%	100%

COLOR DYNAMICS • DUAL BRUSH

Dual Brush:
Grass

Foreground/Background Jitter	0%	100%	100%	100%
Hue Jitter	0%	0%	50%	100%

DUNE GRASS

Default Brush

Spacing 100%

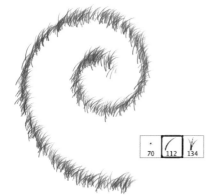

70   112   134

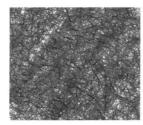

Angle Jitter 100%

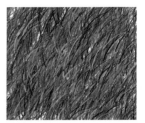

Hue Jitter 100%

COLOR DYNAMICS

Foreground/Background Jitter	0%	100%	100%	100%
Hue Jitter	0%	0%	50%	100%

SCATTERING

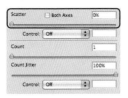

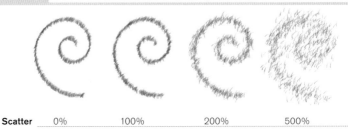

Scatter	0%	100%	200%	500%

SHAPE DYNAMICS

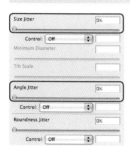

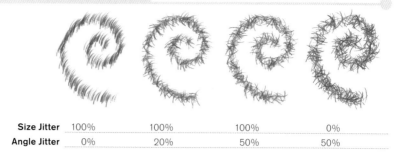

Size Jitter	100%	100%	100%	0%
Angle Jitter	0%	20%	50%	50%

BRUSH TIP SHAPE

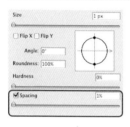

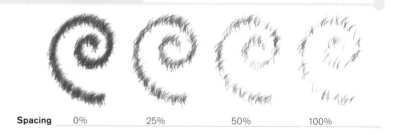

Spacing	0%	25%	50%	100%

DUAL BRUSH

Dual Brush:
Hard Pastel
on Canvas

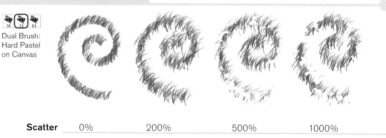

Scatter	0%	200%	500%	1000%

SCATTERING

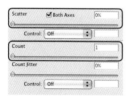

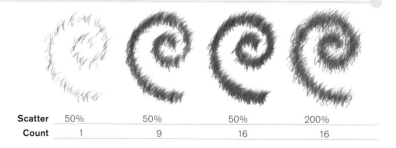

Scatter	50%	50%	50%	200%
Count	1	9	16	16

GRASS

Default Brush

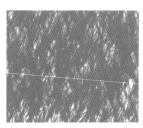

Foreground/Background Jitter 0%
Hue Jitter 0%

Size Jitter 100%
Foreground/Background Jitter 0%
Hue Jitter 0%

Roundness 30%
Foreground/Background Jitter 0%
Hue Jitter 0%

SCATTERING

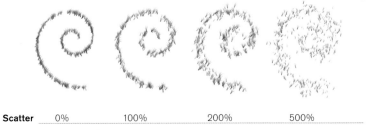

Scatter	0%	100%	200%	500%

COLOR DYNAMICS • SCATTERING

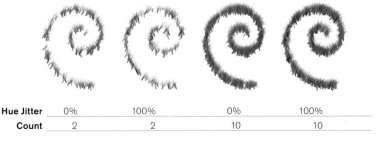

Hue Jitter	0%	100%	0%	100%
Count	2	2	10	10

BRUSH TIP SHAPE • SHAPE DYNAMICS

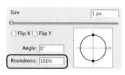

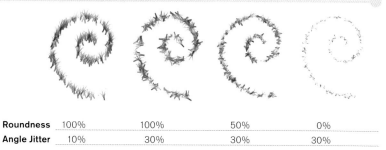

Roundness	100%	100%	50%	0%
Angle Jitter	10%	30%	30%	30%

BRUSH TIP SHAPE

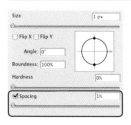

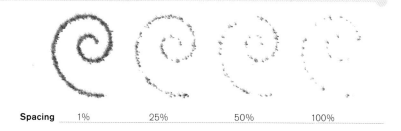

Spacing	1%	25%	50%	100%

FLOW • SHAPE DYNAMICS

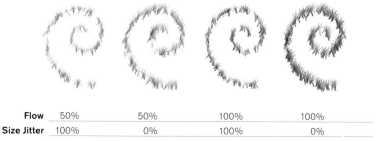

Flow	50%	50%	100%	100%
Size Jitter	100%	0%	100%	0%

BRUSH TIP SHAPE • SHAPE DYNAMICS • DUAL BRUSH

Dual Brush: Chalk

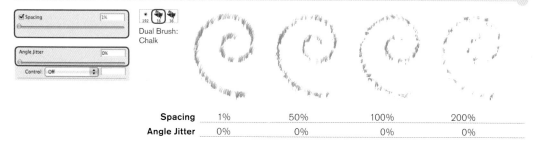

Spacing	1%	50%	100%	200%
Angle Jitter	0%	0%	0%	0%

SCATTERED MAPLE LEAVES

Default Brush

Scatter 0%

Hue Jitter 100%

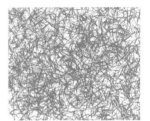

Roundness 4%

SCATTERING

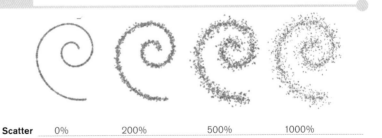

Scatter	0%	200%	500%	1000%

BRUSH TIP SHAPE • COLOR DYNAMICS

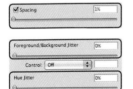

Spacing	25%	25%	25%	400%
Foreground/Background Jitter	100%	100%	100%	0%
Hue Jitter	0%	50%	100%	0%

DUAL BRUSH

Dual Brush:
Scattered
Leaves

Size	7 px	50 px	100 px	150 px
Spacing	1%	1%	1%	8%
Scatter	0%	0%	1000%	500%

COLOR DYNAMICS • TRANSFER

 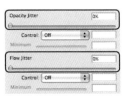

Hue Jitter	20%	20%	20%	0%
Opacity Jitter	0%	100%	100%	100%
Flow Jitter	100%	100%	0%	100%

SCATTERING

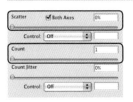

Scatter	400%	400%	400%	100%
Count	1	8	16	16

SCATTERING • TRANSFER

  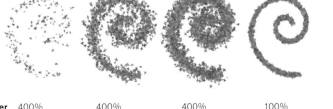

Scatter	100%	100%	100%	400%
Count	16	16	16	16
Opacity Jitter	0%	50%	100%	100%

SCATTERED LEAVES

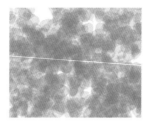

Default Brush

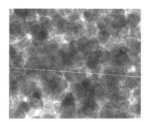

Foreground/Background Jitter 100%

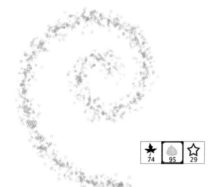

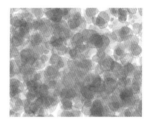

Hue Jitter 100%

Size Jitter 100%

BRUSH TIP SHAPE

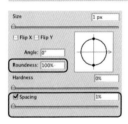

Roundness	100%	100%	30%	1%
Spacing	1%	50%	50%	1%

SCATTERING

Scatter	0%	200%	500%	300%
Count	1	1	1	16

COLOR DYNAMICS

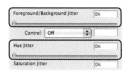

Foreground/Background Jitter	100%	0%	0%	100%
Hue Jitter	0%	50%	100%	100%

DUAL BRUSH

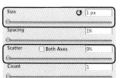

Dual
Brush:
Dry Brush
Tip Light
Flow

Size	50 px	150 px	50 px	50 px
Scatter	400%	400%	0%	1000%

BRUSH TIP SHAPE • SCATTERING

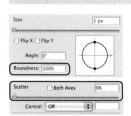

Roundness	0%	45%	45%	45%
Scatter	400%	400%	100%	5%

TRANSFER

Opacity Jitter	0%	0%	50%	100%
Flow Jitter	0%	50%	100%	100%

FLOWING
STARS

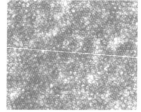

Default Brush

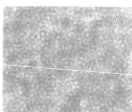

Opacity 50%

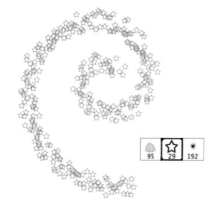

Scatter 100%

Scatter 0%

SCATTERING

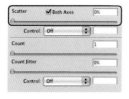

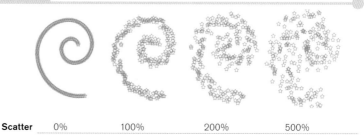

Scatter	0%	100%	200%	500%

SCATTERING

Scatter	250%	250%	250%	250%
Count	1	5	10	16

COLOR DYNAMICS

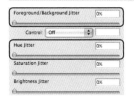

Foreground/Background Jitter	100%	0%	0%	100%
Hue Jitter	0%	50%	100%	100%

TRANSFER

Opacity Jitter	0%	0%	50%	100%
Flow Jitter	0%	50%	100%	100%

BRUSH TIP SHAPE

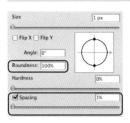

Roundness	100%	45%	45%	45%
Spacing	20%	20%	20%	40%

DUAL BRUSH

Dual Brush:
Oil Pastel
Large

Size	60 px	120 px	240 px	480 px
Count	6	6	6	16

FUZZBALL

Default Brush

Scatter 300%

Foreground/Background Jitter 100%

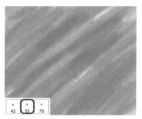

Dual Brush: Star

COLOR DYNAMICS

Foreground/Background Jitter	100%	0%	0%	100%
Hue Jitter	0%	50%	100%	100%

SCATTERING

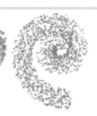

Scatter	0%	100%	200%	500%

BRUSH TIP SHAPE

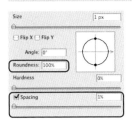
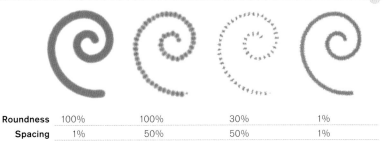

Roundness	100%	100%	30%	1%
Spacing	1%	50%	50%	1%

DUAL BRUSH

Dual Brush: Dune Grass

Size	13 px	40 px	40 px	80 px
Spacing	90%	90%	200%	200%

SCATTERING • DUAL BRUSH

Dual Brush: Sampled Tip

Count	6	4	2	1
Size	100 px	100 px	100 px	100 px

BRUSH TIP SHAPE

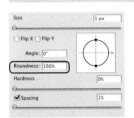
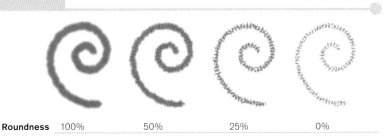

Roundness	100%	50%	25%	0%

CHARCOAL LARGE SMEAR

Opacity 50%

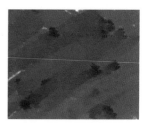

Size Jitter 100%

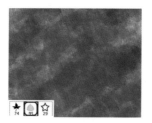

Dual Brush: Scattered Leaves

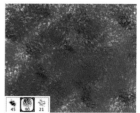

Dual Brush: Sampled Tip

BRUSH TIP SHAPE

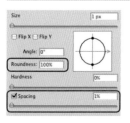

Size: 1 px
Flip X Flip Y
Angle: 0°
Roundness: 100%
Hardness: 0%
Spacing: 1%

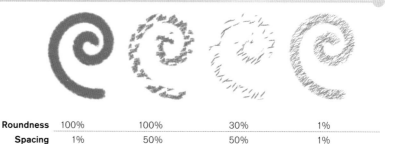

Roundness	100%	100%	30%	1%
Spacing	1%	50%	50%	1%

COLOR DYNAMICS

Foreground/Background Jitter: 0%
Control: Off
Hue Jitter: 0%
Saturation Jitter: 0%
Brightness Jitter: 0%

Foreground/Background Jitter	100%	0%	0%	100%
Hue Jitter	0%	50%	100%	100%

DUAL BRUSH

Dual Brush:
Chalk

Size	24 px	24 px	50 px	50 px
Spacing	5%	30%	30%	80%

DUAL BRUSH • COLOR DYNAMICS

Dual Brush:
Chalk

Spacing	80%	80%	80%	0%
Foreground/Background Jitter	0%	100%	100%	100%
Hue Jitter	0%	0%	50%	100%

SHAPE DYNAMICS • TRANSFER

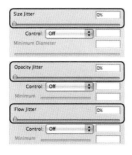

Size Jitter	100%	100%	100%	100%
Opacity Jitter	100%	100%	50%	0%
Flow Jitter	100%	0%	0%	0%

BRUSH TIP SHAPE

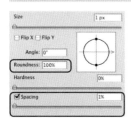

Roundness	12%	12%	12%	12%
Spacing	100%	70%	50%	5%

HARD PASTEL ON CANVAS

Default Brush

Foreground/Background Jitter 100%

Spacing 100%

Opacity Jitter 100%

COLOR DYNAMICS

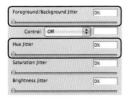

Foreground/Background Jitter	100%	0%	0%	100%
Hue Jitter	0%	50%	100%	100%

BRUSH TIP SHAPE

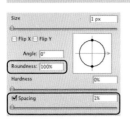

Roundness	100%	100%	30%	1%
Spacing	1%	50%	50%	1%

SCATTERING

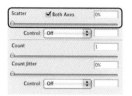

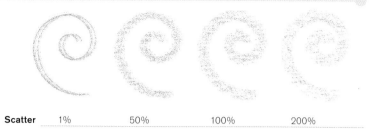

| **Scatter** | 1% | 50% | 100% | 200% |

BRUSH TIP SHAPE • SCATTERING

Scatter	350%	350%	350%	350%
Count	16	16	16	16
Spacing	1%	20%	50%	100%

BRUSH TIP SHAPE • COLOR DYNAMICS

| **Spacing** | 1% | 20% | 50% | 100% |
| **Hue Jitter** | 100% | 100% | 100% | 100% |

SHAPE DYNAMICS

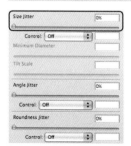

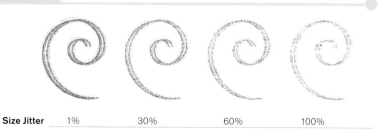

| **Size Jitter** | 1% | 30% | 60% | 100% |

OIL PASTEL LARGE

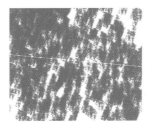

Scatter 500%

Opacity Jitter 100%

Spacing 100%

Foreground/Background Jitter 100%
Hue Jitter 100%

SCATTERING

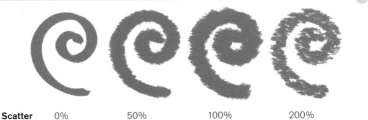

Scatter   0%   50%   100%   200%

SHAPE DYNAMICS

Size Jitter   0%   25%   50%   100%

TRANSFER

Opacity Jitter	0%	25%	50%	100%

BRUSH TIP SHAPE

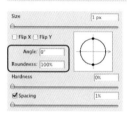

Angle	45°	45°	45°	45°
Roundness	100%	50%	25%	0%

BRUSH TIP SHAPE

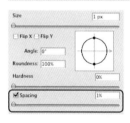
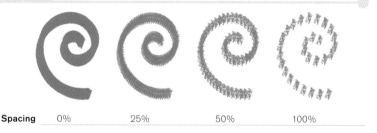

Spacing	0%	25%	50%	100%

BRUSH TIP SHAPE • COLOR DYNAMICS

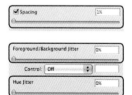

Spacing	10%	10%	10%	10%
Foreground/Background Jitter	0%	100%	50%	100%
Hue Jitter	0%	0%	50%	100%

DRY BRUSH TIP LIGHT FLOW

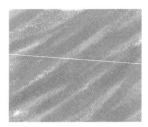

Default Brush

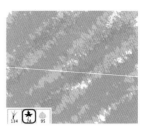

Dual Brush: Scattered Maple Leaves

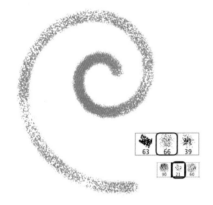

Dual Brush: Grass
Hue Jitter 100%

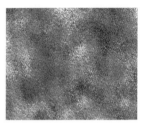

Hue Jitter 100%

SCATTERING

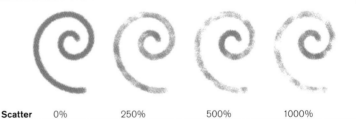

| Scatter | 0% | 250% | 500% | 1000% |

BRUSH TIP SHAPE

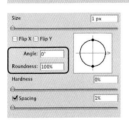

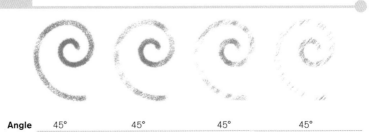

| Angle | 45° | 45° | 45° | 45° |
| Roundness | 100% | 50% | 25% | 0% |

BRUSH TIP SHAPE

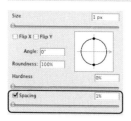

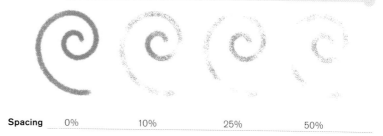

Spacing	0%	10%	25%	50%

DUAL BRUSH

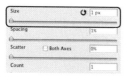

Dual Brush:
Sampled Tip

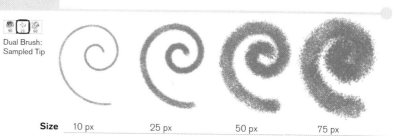

Size	10 px	25 px	50 px	75 px

BRUSH TIP SHAPE • SCATTERING • DUAL BRUSH

Dual Brush:
Sampled Tip

Spacing	0%	20%	60%	100%
Scatter	0%	200%	400%	600%

COLOR DYNAMICS

Dual Brush:
Grass

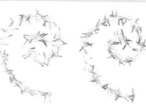

Dual Brush	on	on	on	off
Hue Jitter	0%	25%	100%	100%

DRY BRUSH

Default Brush

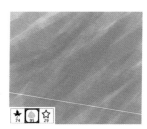

Dual Brush: Scattered Leaves

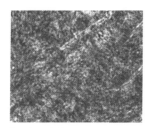

Roundness 20%

Hue Jitter 50%

BRUSH TIP SHAPE

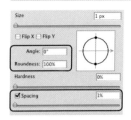

Angle	45°	45°	45°	45°
Roundness	25%	25%	25%	100%
Spacing	0%	10%	20%	30%

DUAL BRUSH

Dual Brush:
Sampled Tip

Size	20 px	60 px	100 px	100 px
Count	0	0	0	6

DUAL BRUSH

Dual Brush:
Sampled
Tip

Spacing	0%	25%	50%	100%
Scatter	200%	200%	200%	200%

SCATTERING • DUAL BRUSH

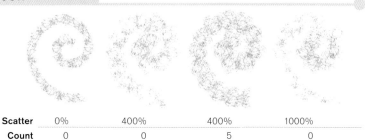

Scatter	0%	400%	400%	1000%
Count	0	0	5	0

FLOW

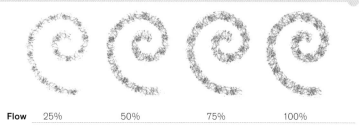

Flow	25%	50%	75%	100%

DUAL BRUSH • COLOR DYNAMICS

Dual Brush:
Scattered
Leaves

Dual Brush	on	on	on	off
Hue Jitter	0%	50%	100%	100%

WATERCOLOR LOADED WET FLAT TIP

Default Brush

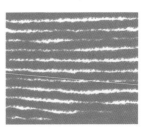

Size Jitter 100%

Opacity Jitter 100%

Dual Brush: Star
Diameter 117 px
Wet Edges

BRUSH TIP SHAPE

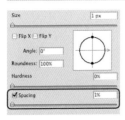

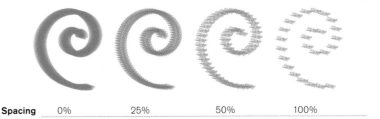

| Spacing | 0% | 25% | 50% | 100% |

SHAPE DYNAMICS • TRANSFER

| Size Jitter | 0% | 50% | 75% | 100% |
| Opacity Jitter | 0% | 50% | 100% | 100% |

BRUSH TIP SHAPE

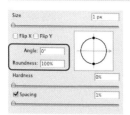

Angle	45°	45°	45°	45°
Roundness	100%	50%	25%	0%

SCATTERING

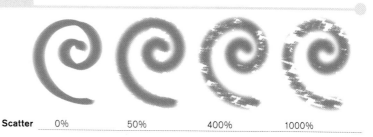

Scatter	0%	50%	400%	1000%

DUAL BRUSH

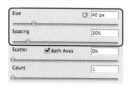

Dual Brush: Soft Round

Size	10 px	50 px	100 px	100 px
Spacing	0%	0%	50%	100%

COLOR DYNAMICS

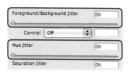

Foreground/Background Jitter	50%	100%	0%	0%
Hue Jitter	0%	0%	50%	100%

WATERCOLOR SMALL ROUND TIP

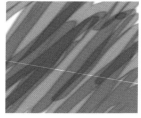

Default Brush

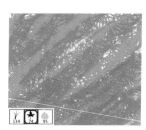

Dual Brush: Scattered Maple Leaves

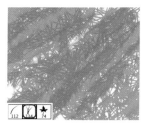

Dual Brush: Grass

Spacing 140%

BRUSH TIP SHAPE • SHAPE DYNAMICS

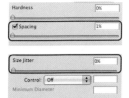

Spacing	0%	100%	200%	400%
Size Jitter	100%	100%	100%	100%

SCATTERING

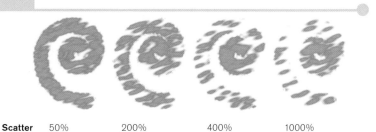

Scatter	50%	200%	400%	1000%

COLOR DYNAMICS

Fgnd/Bgnd Jitter	50%	100%	100%	100%
Hue Jitter	0%	50%	100%	100%
Purity	0%	-100%	-100%	-100%

DUAL BRUSH • WET EDGES

Dual Brush: Sampled Tip

Size	90px	90px	22px	12px
Spacing	75%	75%	75%	75%
Wet Edges	on	off	off	on

DUAL BRUSH

Dual Brush: Dune Grass

Size	50 px	150 px	100 px	100 px
Spacing	25%	25%	200%	400%

BRUSH TIP SHAPE • TRANSFER

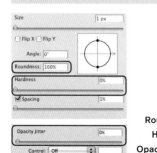   

Roundness	30%	30%	100%	100%
Hardness	10%	100%	10%	100%
Opacity Jitter	100%	100%	100%	100%

OIL HEAVY FLOW DRY EDGES

Flow 50%

Hue Jitter 100%

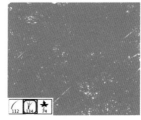

Dual Brush: Grass

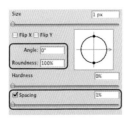

Dual Brush: Flowing Stars

BRUSH TIP SHAPE

Angle	4°	4°	90°	70°
Roundness	72%	8%	0%	0%
Spacing	130%	0%	0%	50%

SHAPE DYNAMICS

Size Jitter	30%	100%	100%	100%
Minimum Diameter	0%	0%	0%	100%
Angle Jitter	0%	0%	50%	50%

BRUSH TIP SHAPE · SCATTERING

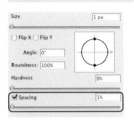
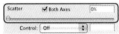

Spacing	0%	0%	0%	40%
Scatter	100%	400%	800%	400%

DUAL BRUSH

Dual Brush: Default

Size	40 px	100 px	100 px	20 px
Spacing	30%	30%	100%	100%

DUAL BRUSH

Dual Brush: Grass

Dual Brush: Scattered Leaves

Dual Brush	Grass	Scattered Leaves	Scattered Leaves	Grass
Spacing	30%	30%	100%	100%

COLOR DYNAMICS

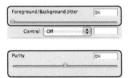

Foreground/Background Jitter	100%	100%	100%	50%
Purity	-100%	0%	+100%	+100%

OIL MEDIUM WET FLOW

Opacity 50%

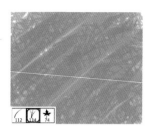

Dual Brush: Grass

Scatter 500%

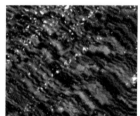

Hue Jitter 50%

BRUSH TIP SHAPE

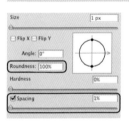

Roundness	32%	32%	10%	0%
Spacing	0%	30%	30%	60%

SHAPE DYNAMICS

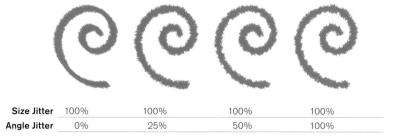

Size Jitter	100%	100%	100%	100%
Angle Jitter	0%	25%	50%	100%

SCATTERING

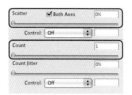

Scatter	125%	250%	800%	800%
Count	1	1	1	4

DUAL BRUSH

Dual Brush: Flowing Stars

Size	30 px	80 px	80 px	400 px
Scatter	100%	100%	300%	0%

SCATTERING • DUAL BRUSH • COLOR DYNAMICS

Dual Brush: Scattered Maple Leaves

Scatter	100%	100%	100%	100%
Foreground/Background Jitter	100%	100%	100%	100%
Hue Jitter	0%	50%	100%	100%

BRUSH TIP SHAPE • TRANSFER

Spacing	0%	0%	0%	35%
Opacity Jitter	0%	100%	100%	100%
Flow Jitter	0%	0%	100%	100%

WET SPONGE

Default Brush

Size Jitter 100%

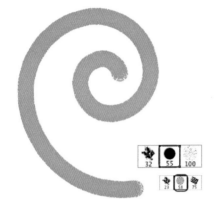

Foreground/Background Jitter 100%

Dual Brush: Scattered Maple Leaves

BRUSH TIP SHAPE

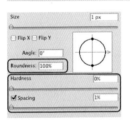

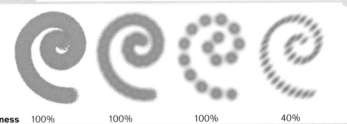

Roundness	100%	100%	100%	40%
Hardness	0%	0%	0%	0%
Spacing	0%	30%	100%	100%

SHAPE DYNAMICS

Size Jitter	50%	100%	100%	100%
Roundness Jitter	0%	0%	50%	100%
Minimum Roundness	50%	50%	50%	1%

BRUSH TIP SHAPE • TRANSFER

Spacing	30%	30%	80%	200%
Opacity Jitter	50%	100%	100%	100%

DUAL BRUSH

Dual Brush: Star

Size	30 px	70 px	100 px	200 px

DUAL BRUSH

Dual Brush: Star

 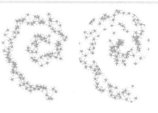

Spacing	10%	30%	10%	10%
Scatter	0%	0%	50%	100%

DUAL BRUSH • COLOR DYNAMICS

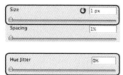

Dual Brush: Scattered Maple Leaves

Dual Brush	off	off	on	on
Size	60 px	60 px	60 px	120 px
Hue Jitter	0%	100%	100%	100%

ROUGH ROUND BRISTLE

Flow 60%

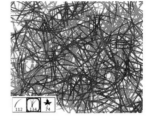

Dual Brush: Grass

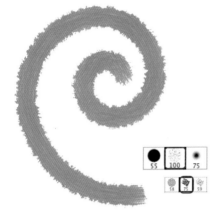

Hue Jitter 23%

Roundness 16%

BRUSH TIP SHAPE

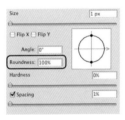

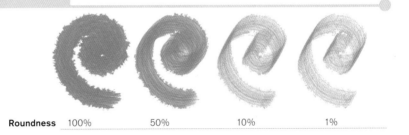

| **Roundness** | 100% | 50% | 10% | 1% |

SCATTERING

| **Scatter** | 100% | 200% | 400% | 1000% |

BRUSH TIP SHAPE • COLOR DYNAMICS

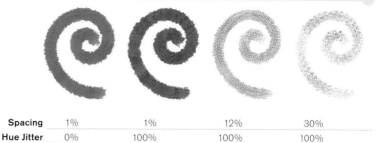

Spacing	1%	1%	12%	30%
Hue Jitter	0%	100%	100%	100%

DUAL BRUSH

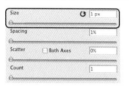

Dual Brush:
Scattered
Leaves

Size	30 px	70 px	200 px	500 px

DUAL BRUSH

Dual Brush:
Star

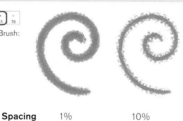
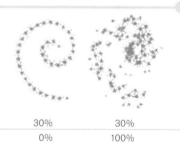

Spacing	1%	10%	30%	30%
Scatter	0%	0%	0%	100%

DUAL BRUSH

Dual Brush:
Grass

Size	50 px	50 px	100 px	50 px
Spacing	12%	12%	30%	1%
Scatter	500%	500%	500%	500%

CIRCLE 1

Spacing 66%
Foreground/Background Jitter 50%
Hue Jitter 30%
Flow Jitter 75%

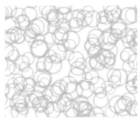

Size Jitter 50%
Scatter 200%

Scatter 500%
Foreground/Background Jitter 100%

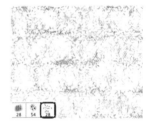

Size Jitter 70%
Dual Brush: Size 100 px
Brightness Jitter 100%

SETTINGS

Scatter 100%

Size Jitter 50%
Scatter 200%
Count Jitter 50%

Scatter 100%
Count 7

Scatter 350%
Count 2
Foreground/Background
Jitter 50%
Purity +100%
Opacity Jitter 60%
Flow Jitter 75%

Scatter 225%
Count 2
Foreground/Background
Jitter 50%
Hue Jitter 100%
Opacity Jitter 60%

Foreground/Background
Jitter 100%

Scatter 230%
Count 8
Foreground/Background
Jitter 100%

Scatter 300%
Count 1
Foreground/Background
Jitter 100%
Hue Jitter 100%
Opacity Jitter 50%

Scatter 100%
Count 16
Foreground/Background
Jitter 100%
Hue Jitter 100%
Opacity Jitter 50%

Scatter 500%
Count 4
Foreground/Background
Jitter 50%
Hue Jitter 50%
Opacity Jitter 50%

CIRCLE 2

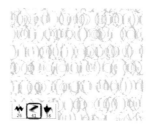

Roundness 3%
Size Jitter 80%
Dual Brush: Ornament

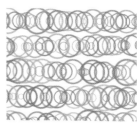

Size Jitter 80%
Foreground/Background Jitter 50%

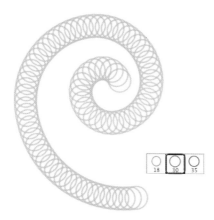

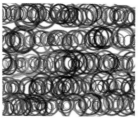

Size Jitter 80%
Scatter 30%
Count 2
Foreground/Background Jitter 100%

Size Jitter 80%
Scatter 530%
Count 2
Foreground/Background Jitter 50%
Hue Jitter 50%
Purity +100%

SETTINGS

Size Jitter 50%

Size Jitter 50%
Roundness
Jitter 100%
Scatter 105%
Count 4

Size Jitter 50%
Scatter 105%
Count 4
Foreground/Background
Jitter 50%
Saturation Jitter 100%

Size Jitter 50%
Scatter 105%
Count 5
Foreground/Background
Jitter 25%
Saturation Jitter 100%
Purity +100%

Size Jitter 100%
Scatter 300%
Count 5
Foreground/Background
Jitter 100%
Hue Jitter 50%
Brightness Jitter 100%

Size Jitter 100%
Scatter 150%
Count 2; Count Jitter 50%
Foreground/Background
Jitter 100%
Hue Jitter 50%
Brightness Jitter 50%

Scatter 30%
Count 6
Foreground/Background
Jitter 100%

Scatter 100%
Count 3
Foreground/Background
Jitter 100%
Hue Jitter 75%
Brightness Jitter 100%
Purity +100%

Scatter 100%
Count 3
Foreground/Background
Jitter 10%
Saturation Jitter 100%
Brightness Jitter 100%
Purity +100%

Scatter 25%
Count 16
Brightness Jitter 100%
Flow Jitter 60%

CIRCLE 3

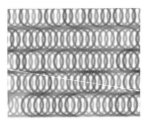

Foreground/Background Jitter 100%

Scatter 100%
Foreground/Background Jitter 100%

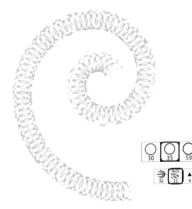

Scatter 100%
Foreground/Background Jitter 100%
Hue Jitter 50%
Brightness Jitter 50%

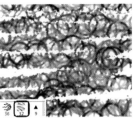

Scatter 100%
Dual Brush: Texture 6
Hue Jitter 100%
Brightness Jitter 50%

SETTINGS

Size Jitter 50%
Scatter 100%

Size Jitter 50%
Scatter 100%
Count 3
Count Jitter 100%

Size Jitter 50%
Scatter 200%
Count 6

Size Jitter 50%
Scatter 100%
Count 6
Foreground/Background
Jitter 100%
Hue Jitter 55%

Size Jitter 50%
Roundness Jitter 100%
Scatter 100%
Foreground/Background
Jitter 50%
Hue Jitter 55%

Size Jitter 50%
Roundness Jitter 100%
Scatter 300%
Count 2
Foreground/Background
Jitter 50%
Hue Jitter 100%

Size Jitter 100%
Scatter 100%
Count 16
Hue Jitter 100%

Size Jitter 100%
Scatter 100%
Count 5
Hue Jitter 10%

Scatter 30%
Count 4
Count Jitter 100%
Foreground/Background
Jitter 15%
Hue Jitter 10%
Brightness Jitter 50%

Scatter 30%
Count 4
Count Jitter 100%
Foreground/Background
Jitter 15%
Hue Jitter 75%
Purity +100%

CIRCLE 4

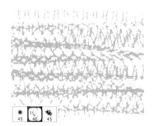

Dual Brush: Texture 4

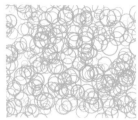

Size Jitter 50%
Scatter 300%
Count 3

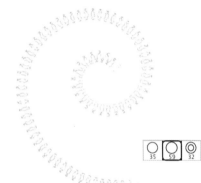

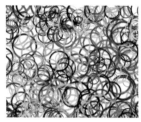

Size Jitter 100%
Scatter 200%
Count 5
Foreground/Background Jitter 100%
Brightness Jitter 50%

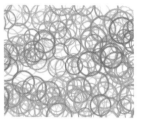

Size Jitter 50%
Scatter 100%
Count 2
Foreground/Background Jitter 50%
Purity +100%
Opacity Jitter 75%

SETTINGS

Size Jitter 100%

Size Jitter 100%
Scatter 120%
Count 2
Foreground/Background
Jitter 85%

Size Jitter 100%
Scatter 120%
Count 2
Foreground/Background
Jitter 100%
Hue Jitter 50%

Size Jitter 100%
Scatter 120%
Count 2
Foreground/Background
Jitter 100%
Hue Jitter 100%

Size Jitter 100%
Scatter 120%
Count 2
Hue Jitter 100%
Saturation Jitter 100%
Opacity Jitter 50%

Size Jitter 100%
Scatter 200%
Count 2
Hue Jitter 50%
Saturation Jitter 100%
Opacity Jitter 50%

Size Jitter 100%
Scatter 200%
Count 2; Foreground/
Background Jitter 100%
Hue Jitter 100%
Saturation Jitter 100%
Opacity Jitter 50%

Scatter 220%
Count 3
Foreground/Background
Jitter 100%
Hue Jitter 100%
Purity +100%

Count 4
Foreground/Background
Jitter 100%
Hue Jitter 100%

Scatter 130%
Count 16; Foreground/
Background Jitter 125%
Hue Jitter 100%
Brightness Jitter 100%
Opacity Jitter 100%
Flow Jitter 50%

CONCENTRIC CIRCLES

Scatter 100%

Scatter 245%
Foreground/Background Jitter 50%
Hue Jitter 50%

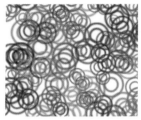

Size Jitter 50%
Scatter 120%
Foreground/Background Jitter 100%
Hue Jitter 50%

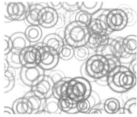

Size Jitter 50%
Scatter 120%
Foreground/Background Jitter 50%
Purity +100%
Flow Jitter 85%

SETTINGS

Size Jitter 100%
Roundness Jitter 50%

Size Jitter 100%
Scatter 115%
Foreground/Background
Jitter 20%

Size Jitter 50%
Scatter 100%
Count 2
Foreground/Background
Jitter 20%
Brightness Jitter 100%

Size Jitter 50%
Scatter 150%
Count 3
Foreground/Background
Jitter 100%
Purity +70%
Opacity Jitter 100%

Scatter 100%
Foreground/Background
Jitter 50%
Hue Jitter 10%
Purity +100%

Scatter 70%
Count 2
Foreground/Background
Jitter 100%
Hue Jitter 50%
Opacity Jitter 50%

Size Jitter 100%
Foreground/Background
Jitter 100%
Saturation Jitter 60%

Count 2
Opacity Jitter 100%

Size Jitter 100%
Scatter 110%
Flow Jitter 50%

Size Jitter 100%
Scatter 150%
Count 2; Count Jitter 100%
Foreground/Background
Jitter 100%; Hue Jitter 10%
Saturation Jitter 60%
Flow Jitter 50%

CROSSHATCH 1

Spacing 100%
Size Jitter 60%
Hue Jitter 100%

Spacing 50%
Size Jitter 100%
Count 3
Foreground/Background Jitter 100%
Hue Jitter 25%

Spacing 15%
Scatter 80%
Foreground/Background Jitter 25%
Hue Jitter 10%
Purity +100%
Opacity Jitter 50%

Roundness 40%
Spacing 10; Size Jitter 50%
Angle Jitter 10%
Scatter 80%
Foreground/Background Jitter 50%
Purity +50%

SETTINGS

Scatter 30%
Count 2
Wet Edges

Scatter 70%
Count 3
Count Jitter 50%
Hue Jitter 50%

Spacing 50%
Angle Jitter 25%
Scatter 70%
Count 3
Hue Jitter 100%
Purity +100%

Roundness 50%
Spacing 50%
Angle Jitter 50%
Scatter 20%
Count Jitter 50%
Hue Jitter 100%
Purity +100%

Spacing 50%
Size Jitter 100%
Angle Jitter 45%
Scatter 20%
Count 7
Count Jitter 50%
Hue Jitter 100%
Wet Edges

Spacing 30%
Size Jitter 100%
Angle Jitter 45%
Roundness Jitter 20%
Scatter 50%; Count 2
Foreground/Background
Jitter 100%

Spacing 30%
Size Jitter 100%
Angle Jitter 45%
Scatter 100%
Count 3
Foreground/Background
Jitter 100%

Spacing 50%
Size Jitter 100%
Angle Jitter 5%
Count 16; Foreground/
Background Jitter 50%
Hue Jitter 100%
Purity +100%

Spacing 50%
Size Jitter 100%
Angle Jitter 50%
Count 9; Foreground/
Background Jitter 50%
Hue Jitter 60%
Purity +100%

Spacing 50%
Size Jitter 50%
Angle Jitter 5%
Roundness Jitter 25%
Count 16; Foreground/
Background Jitter 50%
Purity +100%; Wet Edges

CROSSHATCH 2

Spacing 55%
Size Jitter 50%
Angle Jitter 15%

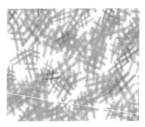

Spacing 35%
Size Jitter 50%
Angle Jitter 15%
Scatter 200%
Count 2; Hue Jitter 50%

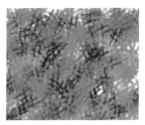

Spacing 20%
Size Jitter 20%
Angle Jitter 15%
Scatter 120%
Count 2
Hue Jitter 50%

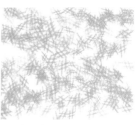

Roundness 50%
Spacing 30%
Size Jitter 50%
Angle Jitter 45%
Scatter 120%
Count 2; Flow Jitter 95%

| 14 | 15 | 48 |

SETTINGS

Roundness 50%
Spacing 30%

Spacing 30%
Size Jitter 75%
Roundness Jitter 100%

Spacing 30%
Size Jitter 75%
Roundness Jitter 50%
Foreground/Background
Jitter 100%

Spacing 30%
Size Jitter 50%
Roundness Jitter 50%
Foreground/Background
Jitter 100%
Hue Jitter 20%
Purity +100%

Spacing 100%
Size Jitter 75%
Angle Jitter 15%
Count 3
Foreground/Background
Jitter 100%
Hue Jitter 20%

Spacing 1%
Size Jitter 75%
Angle Jitter 15%
Foreground/Background
Jitter 100%
Hue Jitter 20%

Spacing 20%
Size Jitter 80%
Angle Jitter 15%
Foreground/Background
Jitter 100%
Hue Jitter 50%

Spacing 20%
Size Jitter 75%
Angle Jitter 5%
Foreground/Background
Jitter 100%
Hue Jitter 50%
Purity +100%

Spacing 20%
Size Jitter 75%
Angle Jitter 5%
Hue Jitter 100%
Purity +100%

Spacing 20%
Size Jitter 75%
Angle Jitter 5%
Scatter 100%
Hue Jitter 100%
Opacity Jitter 50%

CROSSHATCH 3

Foreground/Background Jitter 100%
Purity +100%

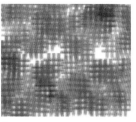

Scatter 110%
Foreground/Background Jitter 75%
Hue Jitter 45%

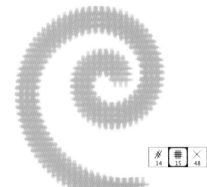

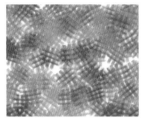

Size Jitter 20%
Angle Jitter 15%
Roundness Jitter 20%
Scatter 20%
Hue Jitter 100%

Size Jitter 40%
Angle Jitter 25%
Scatter 200%
Hue Jitter 100%
Wet Edges

SETTINGS

Angle 45°
Roundness 45%

Spacing 50%
Size Jitter 75%
Angle Jitter 10%

Size Jitter 75%
Angle Jitter 10%
Scatter 75%
Count 2
Wet Edges

Spacing 1%
Size Jitter 75%
Angle Jitter 10%
Scatter 75
Count 2
Foreground/Background
Jitter 100%
Wet Edges

Spacing 50%
Scatter105%
Count 2
Foreground/Background
Jitter 50%
Purity +100%

Spacing 50%
Scatter 105%
Count 2
Foreground/Background
Jitter 50%
Hue Jitter 50%
Purity +100%

Spacing 50%
Scatter 50%
Count 2; Foreground/
Background Jitter 50%
Hue Jitter 50%
Purity +50%
Opacity Jitter 75%

Spacing 30%; Size Jitter 100%
Roundness Jitter 100%
Scatter 150%
Count 2; Foreground/
Background Jitter 50%
Hue Jitter 50%; Purity +50%
Wet Edges

Angle 45°
Roundness 45%
Foreground/Background
Jitter 75%
Purity +55%
Opacity Jitter 75%
Wet Edges

Angle 45°; Roundness 100%
Scatter 50%
Foreground/Background
Jitter 75%; Hue Jitter 50%
Purity +55%
Opacity Jitter 75%
Wet Edges

CROSSHATCH 4

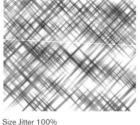

Size Jitter 100%
Scatter 30%
Count 3
Foreground/Background Jitter 100%

Size Jitter 100%
Scatter 239%
Count 4
Foreground/Background Jitter 100%
Purity +50%

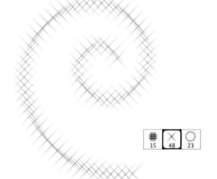

Angle 45°
Size Jitter 100%
Scatter 240%; Count 4
Foreground/Background Jitter 50%
Hue Jitter 20%
Purity +50%

Spacing 10%
Size Jitter 100%
Roundness Jitter 50%
Scatter 110%; Count 3
Foreground/Background Jitter 50%
Brightness Jitter 100%

SETTINGS

Angle 45°
Spacing 10%

Spacing 40%
Size Jitter 50%
Angle Jitter 15%
Scatter 30%
Count 3
Foreground/Background
Jitter 100%

Spacing 40%
Size Jitter 50%
Angle Jitter 15%
Scatter 50%
Count 4; Foreground/
Background Jitter 100%
Hue Jitter 50%

Spacing 40%
Size Jitter 50%
Roundness Jitter 50%
Scatter 50%
Count 4; Foreground/
Background Jitter 100%
Hue Jitter 100%

Spacing 40%
Size Jitter 100%
Scatter 50%
Count 4
Foreground/Background
Jitter 100%
Hue Jitter 50%

Spacing 40%
Size Jitter 50%
Scatter 50%; Count 4
Foreground/Background
Jitter 100%
Hue Jitter 100%
Purity +100%

Spacing 20%
Size Jitter 100%
Angle Jitter 7%
Scatter 50%
Count 4
Hue Jitter 100%
Purity +100%

Spacing 20%
Size Jitter 100%
Angle Jitter 7%
Scatter 50%
Count 4
Hue Jitter 100%
Purity +50%

Spacing 1%
Angle Jitter 20%
Scatter 50%
Purity +100%
Wet Edges

Spacing 1%
Angle Jitter 20%
Scatter 50%
Foreground/Background
Jitter 50%
Hue Jitter 20%
Purity +100%

DASHED CIRCLES 1

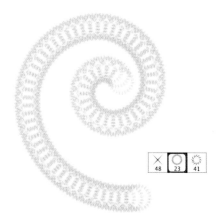

Size Jitter 50%
Hue Jitter 50%
Purity +100%
Wet Edges

Size Jitter 50%
Scatter 250%
Hue Jitter 50%
Purity +100%

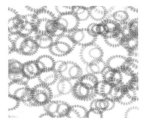

Size Jitter 50%
Roundness Jitter 50%
Scatter 250%
Hue Jitter 50%
Purity +100%

Size Jitter 50%
Roundness Jitter 50%
Scatter 150%
Foreground/Background Jitter 50%
Hue Jitter 50%

SETTINGS

Scatter 30%

Scatter 75%
Count 2

Spacing 50%
Size Jitter 50%
Scatter 75%
Count 2

Spacing 50%
Size Jitter 50%
Count 3
Foreground/Background
Jitter 100%

Spacing 100%
Size Jitter 50%
Count 3
Foreground/Background
Jitter 100%
Hue Jitter 20%

Spacing 100%
Size Jitter 50%
Count 3
Foreground/Background
Jitter 100%
Hue Jitter 50%
Purity +100%

Spacing 20%
Size Jitter 50%
Count 3
Foreground/Background
Jitter 100%
Hue Jitter 50%
Purity +100%

Spacing 40%
Size Jitter 50%
Scatter 100%
Count 3; Foreground/
Background Jitter 100%
Hue Jitter 50%
Purity +100%

Spacing 40%
Scatter 145%
Count 5
Hue Jitter 100%

Spacing 40%
Scatter 100%
Count 6
Foreground/Background
Jitter 100%
Hue Jitter 100%
Brightness Jitter 50%

DASHED
CIRCLES 2

Size Jitter 50%
Roundness Jitter 100%
Foreground/Background Jitter 100%

Spacing 15%
Size Jitter 100%
Roundness Jitter 100%
Foreground/Background Jitter 50%
Hue Jitter 50%

Roundness Jitter 100%
Foreground/Background Jitter 100%
Hue Jitter 50%
Opacity Jitter 50%

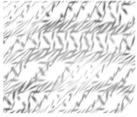

Angle 45°
Roundness 33%
Roundness Jitter 100%
Hue Jitter 50%
Purity +100%
Wet Edges

SETTINGS

Size Jitter 50%
Scatter 100%
Foreground/Background
Jitter 100%

Spacing 10%
Size Jitter 50%
Scatter 100%
Foreground/Background
Jitter 50%
Purity +100%

Spacing 10%
Size Jitter 50%
Scatter 50%
Count 2
Foreground/Background
Jitter 50%
Saturation Jitter 50%
Purity +100%

Spacing 50%
Size Jitter 50%
Scatter 50%
Count 2
Foreground/Background
Jitter 50%
Hue Jitter 75%
Saturation Jitter 100%

Spacing 15%
Roundness 50%
Size Jitter 50%
Foreground/Background
Jitter 50%
Hue Jitter 75%
Size Jitter 100%

Spacing 15%
Roundness 50%
Size Jitter 50%
Foreground/Background
Jitter 50%
Hue Jitter 75%
Purity +100%

Spacing 100%
Size Jitter 50%
Foreground/Background
Jitter 50%
Hue Jitter 75%
Purity +100%
Wet Edges

Spacing 10%
Size Jitter 100%
Scatter 50%
Count 2
Foreground/Background
Jitter 100%
Purity +50%

Spacing 10%
Size Jitter 100%
Roundness Jitter 100%
Scatter 50%; Count 2
Foreground/Background
Jitter 100%; Hue Jitter 33%
Purity +50%; Wet Edges

Spacing 10%
Size Jitter 100%
Roundness Jitter 100%
Scatter 50%
Count 2; Hue Jitter 50%
Purity +100%
Wet Edges

DASHED CIRCLES 3

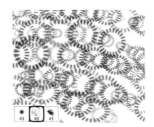

Spacing 30%
Size Jitter 75%
Roundness Jitter 50%
Foreground/Background Jitter 50%
Hue Jitter 100%; Purity +100%

Spacing 30%
Size Jitter 75%
Roundness Jitter 50%
Foreground/Background Jitter 50%
Hue Jitter 100%

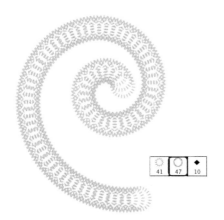

Spacing 15%
Size Jitter 75%
Hue Jitter 10%
Purity +50%

Spacing 15%
Size Jitter 75%
Hue Jitter 100%
Purity +100%
Wet Edges

SETTINGS

Size Jitter 50%
Purity +50%

Roundness 50%
Size Jitter 50%
Purity +100%

Roundness 50%
Size Jitter 50%
Roundness Jitter 100%
Foreground/Background
Jitter 30%
Purity +100%

Size Jitter 50%
Roundness Jitter 100%
Count 2
Foreground/Background
Jitter 100%
Purity +100%

Size Jitter 50%
Angle Jitter 10%
Roundness Jitter 100%
Scatter 0%
Count 2
Hue Jitter 20%
Purity +50%

Spacing 50%
Angle Jitter 50%
Roundness Jitter 100%
Scatter 0%
Count 3
Hue Jitter 20%
Purity +50%

Spacing 30%
Angle Jitter 50%
Roundness Jitter 100%
Scatter 100%
Count 4
Hue Jitter 50%
Purity +50%

Spacing 1%
Angle Jitter 50%
Roundness Jitter 100%
Scatter 100%
Count 4
Hue Jitter 100%
Wet Edges

Spacing 100%
Angle Jitter 50%
Scatter 190%
Count 8
Hue Jitter 100%

Spacing 75%
Size Jitter 33%
Angle Jitter 50%
Scatter 100%
Count 4
Hue Jitter 100%
Purity +100%

DIAMOND

Dual Brush: Star Large
Spacing 50%
Hue Jitter 50%

Size Jitter 100%
Roundness Jitter 100%
Brightness Jitter 50%

Angle 45°
Roundness 50%
Roundness Jitter 50%
Brightness Jitter 50%
Purity +50

Angle 45°
Roundness 50%
Roundness Jitter 50%
Brightness Jitter 50%
Hue Jitter 10%
Purity +100%
Wet Edges

SETTINGS

Angle 45°
Roundness 50%

Angle 45°
Roundness 50%
Size Jitter 50%
Angle Jitter 10%

Spacing 75%
Size Jitter 50%
Scatter 150%
Count 2
Hue Jitter 50%
Brightness Jitter 100%
Opacity Jitter 50%

Spacing 75%
Size Jitter 50%
Scatter 150%
Count 3
Hue Jitter 50%
Brightness Jitter 100%

Spacing 100%
Size Jitter 50%
Scatter 150%; Count 2
Hue Jitter 50%
Brightness Jitter 100%
Opacity Jitter 50%
Wet Edges

Spacing 50%
Size Jitter 100%
Angle Jitter 10%
Scatter 150%
Count 2
Hue Jitter 100%

Spacing 50%
Size Jitter 100%
Angle Jitter 10%
Scatter 150%
Count 6
Hue Jitter 100%

Spacing 100%
Size Jitter 100%
Purity +50%

Spacing 60%
Size Jitter 50%
Brightness Jitter 50%
Purity +50%

Spacing 60%
Size Jitter 50%
Hue Jitter 25%
Brightness Jitter 50%
Purity +100%
Wet Edges

ORNAMENT 1

Angle 45°
Roundness 50%
Size Jitter 50%

Spacing 100%
Scatter 30%

Spacing 100%
Angle Jitter 50%
Scatter 30%
Count 2
Brightness Jitter 100%

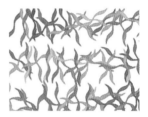

Spacing 100%
Angle Jitter 45%
Scatter 30%
Count 2
Hue Jitter 50%
Brightness Jitter 100%
Wet Edges

SETTINGS

Scatter 100%

Size Jitter 100%
Angle Jitter 15%
Scatter 100%
Count 1

Size Jitter 100%
Angle Jitter 15%
Scatter 100%
Count 2
Hue Jitter 25%

Size Jitter 100%
Angle Jitter 15%
Scatter 100%
Count 2
Hue Jitter 100%

Size Jitter 100%
Angle Jitter 15%
Scatter 100%
Count 2
Hue Jitter 100%

Spacing 100%
Size Jitter 50%
Angle Jitter 50%
Scatter 100%; Count 2
Saturation Jitter 50%
Brightness Jitter 100%
Purity +100%

Angle 45°
Size Jitter 50%
Angle Jitter 75%
Scatter 100%
Count 4
Brightness Jitter 100%
Purity +100%

Angle 45°
Scatter 100%
Count 2
Brightness Jitter 100%
Purity +100%

Spacing 100%
Size Jitter 100%
Angle Jitter 75%
Scatter 200%
Count 1
Hue Jitter 50%
Brightness Jitter 50%

Spacing 1%
Size Jitter 100%
Angle Jitter 75%
Scatter 200%
Count 1
Hue Jitter 50%
Brightness Jitter 50%

ORNAMENT 2

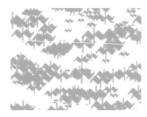

Size Jitter 100%
Scatter 290%
Count 1

Spacing 10%
Size Jitter 100%
Scatter 290%
Count 1
Brightness Jitter 100%

Spacing 20%
Hue Jitter 100%
Purity +100%

Spacing 50%
Angle Jitter 50%
Scatter 33%
Count 1
Foreground/Background Jitter 100%
Hue Jitter 50%
Brightness Jitter 50%

SETTINGS

Spacing 25%
Size Jitter 100%
Brightness Jitter 100%

Spacing 25%
Size Jitter 100%
Brightness Jitter 100%
Purity +100%

Spacing 1%
Size Jitter 100%
Scatter 75%
Count 2
Brightness Jitter 100%
Purity +100%

Spacing 20%
Size Jitter 100%
Angle Jitter 35%
Scatter 100%
Count 2
Brightness Jitter 100%
Purity +100%
Opacity Jitter 100%

Spacing 20%
Size Jitter 100%
Angle Jitter 35%
Scatter 100%
Count 2
Hue Jitter 30%
Purity +50%

Spacing 30%
Size Jitter 100%
Angle Jitter 35%
Hue Jitter 100%
Purity +50%

Spacing 30%
Size Jitter 100%
Angle Jitter 35%
Scatter 200%
Count 2
Hue Jitter 100%
Brightness Jitter 25%

Spacing 30%
Size Jitter 100%
Angle Jitter 35%
Scatter 200%; Count 2
Hue Jitter 50%
Brightness Jitter 25%
Wet Edges

Spacing 30%
Size Jitter 100%
Angle Jitter 35%
Scatter 300%
Count 2
Hue Jitter 50%
Brightness Jitter 25%

Spacing 40%
Size Jitter 25%
Angle Jitter 35%
Scatter 250%
Count 2
Hue Jitter 50%
Purity +100%

ORNAMENT 3

Angle 45°
Spacing 100%

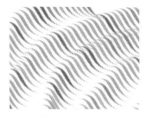

Angle 45°
Spacing 100%
Hue Jitter 50%

Angle 45°
Spacing 100%
Angle Jitter 7%
Scatter 50%
Count 1
Brightness Jitter 100%

Spacing 25%
Size Jitter 25%
Roundness Jitter 25%
Scatter 50%
Count 1
Hue Jitter 5%
Brightness Jitter 50%

SETTINGS

Size Jitter 100%

Size Jitter 100%
Angle Jitter 20%
Purity +50%
Wet Edges

Size Jitter 100%
Angle Jitter 20%
Scatter 100%
Count 1
Purity +50%

Spacing 10%
Size Jitter 100%
Angle Jitter 50%
Scatter 200%
Count 2
Brightness Jitter 100%
Purity +100%

Spacing 10%
Size Jitter 100%
Angle Jitter 50%
Scatter 200%
Count 4
Hue Jitter 20%
Brightness Jitter 100%
Purity +100%

Size Jitter 100%
Angle Jitter 100%
Scatter 150%
Count 5
Hue Jitter 50%
Brightness Jitter 100%

Spacing 50%
Angle Jitter 50%
Count 5
Hue Jitter 50%
Brightness Jitter 100%

Spacing 150%
Angle Jitter 50%
Count 5
Hue Jitter 50%
Brightness Jitter 100%
Purity +100%
Wet Edges

Spacing 150%
Angle Jitter 50%
Scatter 300%
Count 2
Hue Jitter 100%
Brightness Jitter 100%
Purity +100%

Angle Jitter 50%
Scatter 100%
Count 8
Hue Jitter 100%
Brightness Jitter 50%
Purity +100%

ORNAMENT 4

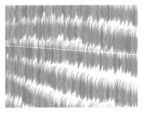

Angle 90°
Size Jitter 100%
Brightness Jitter 25%

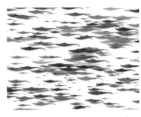

Size Jitter 100%
Scatter 445%
Count 1
Brightness Jitter 100%

Size Jitter 100%
Angle Jitter 10%
Scatter 100%
Count 1
Hue Jitter 25%
Wet Edges

Size Jitter 100%
Angle Jitter 25%
Scatter 200%
Count 2
Hue Jitter 50%
Purity +100%

SETTINGS

Scatter 30%
Brightness Jitter 50%

Scatter 100%
Count 1
Brightness Jitter 50%
Wet Edges

Spacing 90%
Angle Jitter 100%
Scatter 100%
Brightness Jitter 50%

Spacing 90%
Angle Jitter 100%
Count 1
Hue Jitter 100%
Brightness Jitter 100%

Spacing 60%
Angle Jitter 10%
Scatter 135%
Count 2
Count Jitter 100%
Hue Jitter 100%
Brightness Jitter 100%

Spacing 60%
Angle Jitter 20%
Scatter 300%
Count 2
Hue Jitter 100%
Brightness Jitter 100%
Purity +100%

Spacing 25%
Count 2
Hue Jitter 100%
Saturation Jitter 50%
Purity +100%

Scatter 25%
Count 2
Hue Jitter 50%
Purity +25%
Opacity Jitter 25%

Spacing 100%
Angle 45°
Scatter 120%
Count 2
Brightness Jitter 75%
Purity +100%

Angle 45°
Spacing 100%
Angle Jitter 5%
Scatter 120%
Count 2
Hue Jitter 100%
Purity +100%

ORNAMENT 5

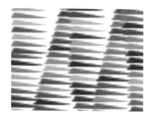

Spacing 100%
Brightness Jitter 50%

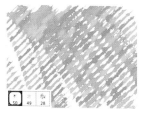

Dual Brush: Starburst Small
Spacing 75%
Brightness Jitter 50%
Wet Edges

Spacing 100%
Angle Jitter 25%
Saturation Jitter 50%
Brightness Jitter 10%

Spacing 50%
Hue Jitter 33%
Brightness Jitter 10%

SETTINGS

Angle 45°
Brightness Jitter 50%

Angle 45°
Angle Jitter 5%
Brightness Jitter 50%
Purity +50%

Angle 45°
Angle Jitter 5%
Scatter 100%
Count 1
Brightness Jitter 50%
Purity +50%

Angle Jitter 10%
Scatter 100%
Count 1
Saturation Jitter 100%

Angle Jitter 10%
Scatter 100%
Count 1
Brightness Jitter 100%

Angle Jitter 50%
Scatter 220%
Count 1
Brightness Jitter 100%
Purity +100%

Angle 90°
Scatter 200%
Count 2
Hue Jitter 100%
Purity +50%

Spacing 10%
Size Jitter 100%
Scatter 220%
Count 1
Hue Jitter 50%
Purity +100%
Wet Edges

Angle 10°
Size Jitter 100%
Scatter 100%
Count 4
Brightness Jitter 100%
Hue Jitter 50%
Purity +100%

Size Jitter 100%
Angle Jitter 6%
Scatter 100%
Count 1%
Hue Jitter 100%
Purity +100%

ORNAMENT 6

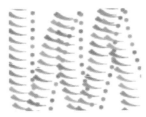

Spacing 100%
Brightness Jitter 33%

Angle 45°
Spacing 100%
Size Jitter 100%
Scatter 50%
Count 1
Brightness Jitter 100%

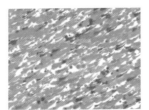

Angle 45°
Size Jitter 100%
Scatter 200%
Count 3
Hue Jitter 50%

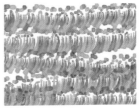

Angle 90°
Size Jitter 100%
Hue Jitter 100%
Wet Edges

SETTINGS

Angle 45°
Spacing 75%

Angle 90°
Spacing 75%
Angle Jitter 10%
Brightness Jitter 100%

Spacing 75%
Size Jitter 100%
Count 1

Angle 60°
Spacing 75%
Scatter 100%
Count 2
Brightness Jitter 100%

Angle 60°
Spacing 75%
Scatter 100%
Count 2
Hue Jitter 50%
Purity +30%

Angle 60°; Spacing 75%
Angle Jitter 30%
Scatter 100%
Count 2; Saturation
Jitter 50%; Brightness
Jitter 100%; Purity +100%

Angle 60°
Spacing 75%
Angle Jitter 30%
Saturation Jitter 50%
Brightness Jitter 100%
Wet Edges

Angle 90°
Spacing 100%
Size Jitter 100%
Hue Jitter 100%
Purity +100%

Angle 90°
Spacing 100%
Size Jitter 100%
Hue Jitter 100%
Brightness Jitter 100%
Purity +100%

Angle 135°
Spacing 50%
Hue Jitter 70%
Purity +100%

ORNAMENT 7

Angle 90°
Spacing 50%
Size Jitter 100%
Hue Jitter 12%
Purity +100%

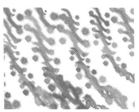

Angle 135°
Spacing 50%
Size Jitter 100%
Brightness Jitter 70%
Purity +100%
Wet Edges

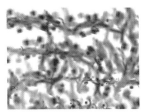

Angle 135°
Spacing 25%
Size Jitter 100%
Angle Jitter 20%
Hue Jitter 100%
Purity +100%

Angle 5°
Spacing 150%
Angle Jitter 5%
Count 3
Hue Jitter 100%
Purity +100%

SETTINGS

Hue Jitter 100%
Brightness Jitter 100%

Angle 90°
Spacing 25%
Brightness Jitter 100%

Angle 135°
Spacing 25%
Scatter 100%
Count 1
Brightness Jitter 100%

Angle 60°
Spacing 33%
Angle Jitter 20%
Hue Jitter 50%
Brightness Jitter 100%

Spacing 33%
Angle Jitter 20%
Hue Jitter 50%
Purity +100%
Flow Jitter 100%

Spacing 20%
Hue Jitter 50%
Purity +100%

Spacing 33%
Angle Jitter 20%
Scatter 150%
Count 1
Hue Jitter 50%
Purity +100%

Spacing 50%
Angle Jitter 50%
Scatter 225%
Count 2
Hue Jitter 100

Spacing 50%
Angle Jitter 50%
Scatter 225%; Count 3
Saturation Jitter 20%
Brightness Jitter 100%
Purity +50%
Wet Edges

Spacing 200%
Size Jitter 100%
Angle Jitter 50%
Count 6
Hue Jitter 100%
Brightness Jitter 50%
Purity +50%

ORNAMENT 8

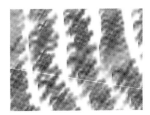

Size Jitter 100%
Foreground/Background Jitter 100%
Purity +100%

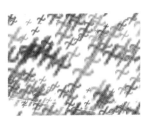

Size Jitter 100%
Scatter 350%
Count 2
Foreground/Background Jitter 100%
Purity +100%

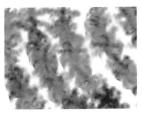

Size Jitter 100%
Angle Jitter 30%
Count 2
Foreground/Background Jitter 25%
Hue Jitter 50%
Purity +100%

Angle 90°
Spacing 66%
Count 2
Hue Jitter 100%
Purity +50%

SETTINGS

Angle 90°
Spacing 66%
Count 2
Hue Jitter 100%
Purity +50%
Wet Edges

Size Jitter 100%
Angle Jitter 5%

Size Jitter 100%
Angle Jitter 5%
Hue Jitter 100%

Size Jitter 50%
Angle Jitter 20%
Hue Jitter 70%
Purity +100%

Angle Jitter 20%
Count 2
Hue Jitter 70%
Purity +100%

Angle Jitter 20%
Count 2
Hue Jitter 70%
Purity +50%
Wet Edges

Angle Jitter 135%
Spacing 100%
Scatter 25%; Count 3
Foreground/Background
Jitter 100%
Purity +100%
Opacity Jitter 50%

Spacing 50%
Scatter 200%
Count 3
Foreground/Background
Jitter 50%
Hue Jitter 20%
Purity +100%

Spacing 50%
Scatter 90%; Count 3
Foreground/Background
Jitter 50%
Hue Jitter 20%
Opacity Jitter 65%
Wet Edges

Spacing 50%
Scatter 300%
Count 2
Foreground/Background
Jitter 50%
Hue Jitter 100%
Purity +100%

SNOWFLAKE

Spacing 100%
Size Jitter 90%
Hue Jitter 70%
Purity +50%

Spacing 50%
Angle Jitter 30%
Foreground/Background Jitter 100%
Brightness Jitter 50%

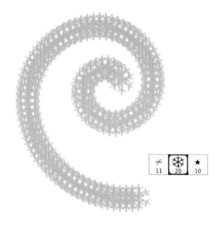

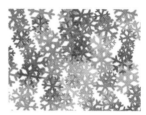

Spacing 50%; Size Jitter 50%
Angle Jitter 30%
Scatter 50%
Count 1
Foreground/Background Jitter 100%
Hue Jitter 15%
Purity +100%
Wet Edges

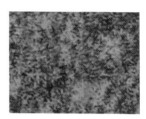

Spacing 2%
Angle Jitter 30%
Scatter 150%
Count 1
Hue Jitter 100%
Purity +50%

SETTINGS

Scatter 150%
Count 1

Scatter 100%
Count 1
Foreground/Background
Jitter 100%

Scatter 100%
Count 2
Foreground/Background
Jitter 100%
Purity +100%

Scatter 150%
Count 2
Foreground/Background
Jitter 100%
Hue Jitter 100%
Purity +100%

Scatter 150%
Count 1
Foreground/Background
Jitter 50%
Hue Jitter 100%

Spacing 50%
Scatter 150%
Count 1
Hue Jitter 100%

Spacing 50%
Scatter 150%
Count 3
Hue Jitter 100%
Wet Edges

Spacing 33%
Scatter 300%
Count 2
Hue Jitter 100%
Purity +100%

Spacing 1%
Size Jitter 100%
Scatter 190%
Count 1
Hue Jitter 50%
Purity +50%
Opacity Jitter 100%

Spacing 105%
Hue Jitter 100%
Saturation Jitter 50%
Purity +100%

STAR SMALL

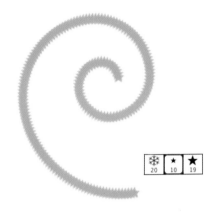

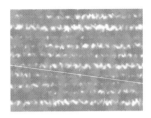

Angle 26°
Roundness 84%
Size Jitter 100%
Angle Jitter 10%
Foreground/Background Jitter 20%

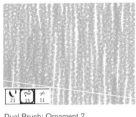

Dual Brush: Ornament 7

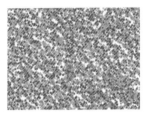

Spacing 65%
Scatter 300%
Count 8
Hue Jitter 100%

Scatter 600%
Count 16
Count Jitter 100%
Opacity Jitter 100%

SETTINGS

Dual Brush: Dashed
Circle 2
Saturation Jitter 100%
Purity +100%

Foreground/Background
Jitter 100%
Hue Jitter 100%
Purity +100%

Spacing 10%
Size Jitter 100%
Scatter 50%
Count 1
Count Jitter 100%

Roundness 25%
Brightness Jitter 100%
Purity +50%

Spacing 2%
Roundness Jitter 100%
Scatter 20%
Foreground/Background
Jitter 100%
Hue Jitter 100%

Spacing 30%
Scatter 60%
Count 5
Saturation Jitter 100%
Opacity Jitter 100%
Flow Jitter 100%

Size Jitter 100%
Roundness Jitter 100%
Scatter 30%
Count 3
Flow Jitter 100%

Spacing 80%
Dual Brush: Circle 2
Hue Jitter 100%
Saturation Jitter 100%

Count 8
Count Jitter 100%
Foreground/Background
Jitter 100%
Brightness Jitter 100%

Spacing 45%
Flow Jitter 100%

STAR LARGE

Spacing 100%
Size Jitter 100%
Scatter 150%
Count 1
Foreground/Background Jitter 100%
Opacity Jitter 25%

Spacing 50%; Size Jitter 100%
Scatter 100% ; Count 2
Foreground/Background Jitter 50%
Purity +100%; Wet Edges

Angle 30°
Spacing 50%
Size Jitter 50%
Hue Jitter 45%
Brightness Jitter 50%

Angle 30°
Spacing 50%
Scatter 205%
Count 1
Hue Jitter 100%
Purity +100%

SETTINGS

Angle 30°
Spacing 50%
Opacity Jitter 50%

Scatter 100%
Count 1
Opacity Jitter 50%

Scatter 100%
Count 1
Foreground/Background
Jitter 100%
Flow Jitter 50%

Spacing 100%
Scatter 50%
Count 2
Foreground/Background
Jitter 100%
Purity +100%
Flow Jitter 50%

Spacing 100%
Scatter 20%
Count 1
Foreground/Background
Jitter 100%
Purity +100%
Flow Jitter 50%

Angle 45°
Spacing 66%
Scatter 30%
Count 1
Hue Jitter 20%

Angle 45°
Spacing 66%
Scatter 150%
Count 2
Hue Jitter 75%

Angle 45°
Scatter 150%
Count 2
Foreground/Background
Jitter 100%
Brightness Jitter 50%
Wet Edges

Angle 45°
Size Jitter 100%
Scatter 150%
Count 2
Foreground/Background
Jitter 90%
Brightness Jitter 50%

Size Jitter 100%
Angle Jitter 25%
Scatter 75%; Count 2
Foreground/Background
Jitter 100%
Hue Jitter 100%
Brightness Jitter 50%

STARBURST SMALL

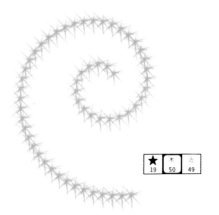

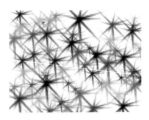

Size Jitter 100%
Foreground/Background Jitter 100%
Brightness Jitter 100%

Size Jitter 100%
Angle Jitter 45%
Scatter 100%
Count 1
Foreground/Background Jitter 100%
Purity +100%

Angle Jitter 45%
Scatter 100%
Count 1
Hue Jitter 100%
Purity +100%
Flow Jitter 100%

Size Jitter 60%
Angle Jitter 40%
Scatter 50%
Count 2
Hue Jitter 100%
Purity +100%
Wet Edges

SETTINGS

Size Jitter 60%
Angle Jitter 40%
Scatter 50%
Count 2
Hue Jitter 100%
Purity +100%
Wet Edges

Size Jitter 60%
Angle Jitter 45%
Count 2
Hue Jitter 100%
Purity +100%

Size Jitter 60%
Angle Jitter 45%
Scatter 100%
Count 2
Hue Jitter 100%

Spacing 10%
Scatter 50%
Count 2
Foreground/Background
Jitter 50%
Wet Edges

Spacing 10%
Scatter 50%
Count 2; Foreground/
Background Jitter 50%
Hue Jitter 50%
Saturation Jitter 100%
Wet Edges

Spacing 10; Scatter 75%
Count 2; Foreground/
Background Jitter 50%
Hue Jitter 50%
Saturation Jitter 100%
Brightness
Jitter 50%; Noise

Spacing 10%
Scatter 150%
Count 2
Foreground/Background
Jitter 50%
Hue Jitter 50%

Spacing 35%
Foreground/Background
Jitter 50%
Hue Jitter 75%

Spacing 35%
Scatter 50%
Count 4
Foreground/Background
Jitter 50%
Hue Jitter 75%
Purity +100%

Spacing 35%; Count 3
Foreground/Background
Jitter 50%
Hue Jitter 75%
Saturation Jitter 25%
Purity +100%
Wet Edges

STARBURST LARGE

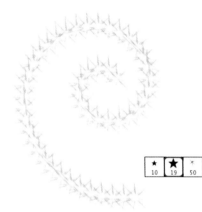

Spacing 12%
Foreground/Background Jitter 50%
Brightness Jitter 50%

Spacing 1%
Foreground/Background Jitter 50%
Brightness Jitter 100%

Spacing 7%
Scatter 100%
Count 1
Foreground/Background Jitter 50%
Hue Jitter 55%
Brightness Jitter100%

Spacing 7%
Scatter 75%
Count 2
Foreground/Background Jitter 50%
Hue Jitter 50%
Brightness Jitter 100%
Purity +100%

SETTINGS

Spacing 10%
Foreground/Background
Jitter 100%
Flow Jitter 50%

Spacing 55%
Foreground/Background
Jitter 50%
Hue Jitter 50%
Purity +100%

Spacing 35%
Size Jitter 100%
Count 2
Foreground/Background
Jitter 50%
Hue Jitter 50%
Purity +100%

Spacing 35%
Size Jitter 100%
Count 2
Hue Jitter 50%
Purity +100%
Wet Edges

Spacing 35%
Size Jitter 50%
Angle Jitter 20%
Count 4
Hue Jitter 20%
Brightness Jitter 25%
Purity +100%

Spacing 10%
Size Jitter 50%
Angle Jitter 20%
Scatter 100%
Count 3
Hue Jitter 75%
Purity +75%

Spacing 30%
Scatter 100%
Count 5
Hue Jitter 33%
Saturation Jitter 40%
Purity +100%

Spacing 30%
Scatter 100%; Count 5
Foreground/Background
Jitter 33%; Hue
Jitter 33%; Saturation
Jitter 100%; Purity +100%
Wet Edges

Spacing 50%
Angle Jitter 35%
Foreground/Background
Jitter 20%; Foreground/
Background Jitter 100%
Hue Jitter 100%
Purity +100%

Spacing 1%
Angle Jitter 35%
Foreground/Background
Jitter 20%; Foreground/
Background Jitter 100%
Hue Jitter 100%
Purity +100%

TEXTURE 1

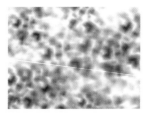

Size Jitter 50%; Angle Jitter 10%
Scatter 100%; Count 1
Foreground/Background Jitter 100%
Hue Jitter 100%
Saturation Jitter 50%

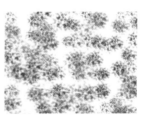

Spacing 75%; Size Jitter 50%
Angle Jitter 10%; Scatter 80%
Count 3; Count Jitter 20%
Foreground/Background Jitter 100%
Hue Jitter 50%

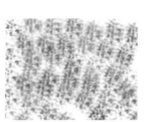

Spacing 75%
Scatter 50%
Count 3
Hue Jitter 100%

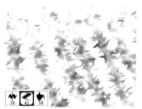

Dual Brush: Ornament 3
Spacing 75%
Scatter 50%
Count 3
Hue Jitter 100%

SETTINGS

Hue Jitter 20%

Angle Jitter 10%
Foreground/Background
Jitter 10%
Hue Jitter 50%

Spacing 50%
Size Jitter 50%
Angle Jitter 20%
Hue Jitter 50%

Spacing 50%
Size Jitter 50%
Angle Jitter 20%
Hue Jitter 50%
Purity +100%
Wet Edges

Spacing 50%
Size Jitter 100%
Angle Jitter 20%
Hue Jitter 100%
Purity +100%

Spacing 50%
Size Jitter 100%
Angle Jitter 20%
Scatter 100%
Count 2
Hue Jitter 100%
Purity +50%

Spacing 25%
Size Jitter 100%
Angle Jitter 20%
Scatter 100%
Count 2
Hue Jitter 100%
Wet Edges

Spacing 25%; Size
Jitter 100%; Angle
Jitter 20%; Scatter 150%
Count 3
Foreground/Background
Jitter 50%
Hue Jitter 50%

Size Jitter 100%
Angle Jitter 20%
Scatter 150%
Count 4
Foreground/Background
Jitter 100%
Hue Jitter 33%

Spacing 60%
Angle Jitter 20%
Foreground/Background
Jitter 100%
Hue Jitter 33%
Purity +100%

TEXTURE 2

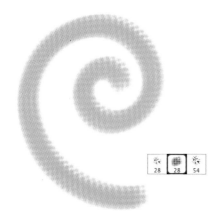

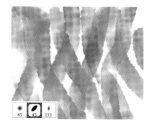

Dual Brush: Hard Elliptical 45
Size Jitter 50%
Scatter 100%
Count 1
Hue Jitter 100%

Size Jitter 50%
Scatter 100%
Count 1
Hue Jitter 100%
Wet Edges

Size Jitter 50%
Scatter 100%
Count 1
Hue Jitter 50%
Purity +100%
Noise

Spacing 50%
Size Jitter 50%
Scatter 50%
Count 3
Foreground/Background Jitter 100%
Purity +100%
Flow Jitter 50%

SETTINGS

Spacing 75%
Scatter 30%
Count 2
Foreground/Background
Jitter 100%
Purity +100%

Spacing 75%
Scatter 30%
Count 2
Foreground/Background
Jitter 100%
Hue Jitter 50%
Purity +100%

Spacing 50%
Scatter 30%
Count 2
Foreground/Background
Jitter 100%
Hue Jitter 50%
Purity +100%; Wet Edges

Scatter 100%
Count 3
Foreground/Background
Jitter 100%
Hue Jitter 50%
Purity +100%

Scatter 150%
Count 2
Foreground/Background
Jitter 100%
Hue Jitter 50%
Purity +50%
Wet Edges

Size Jitter 100%
Scatter 150%
Count 2
Hue Jitter 50%
Purity +50%
Wet Edges

Spacing 1%
Size Jitter 100%
Scatter 300%
Count 2
Hue Jitter 100%
Purity +100%

Spacing 1%
Size Jitter 100%
Scatter 300%
Count 8
Hue Jitter 100%
Purity +100%

Spacing 15%
Scatter 200%
Count 5
Foreground/Background
Jitter 75%
Saturation Jitter 50%
Purity +100%

Spacing 150%
Scatter 200%; Count 16
Foreground/Background
Jitter 75%
Hue Jitter 50%
Saturation Jitter 50%
Purity +100%

TEXTURE 3

Hue Jitter 100%

Spacing 10%
Scatter 100%
Count 2
Foreground/Background Jitter 100%

Spacing 10%
Size Jitter 100%
Scatter 100%
Count 3
Foreground/Background Jitter 100%
Hue Jitter 50%
Purity +25%

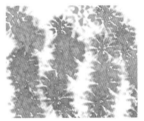

Spacing 55%
Size Jitter 100%
Count 6
Hue Jitter 100%
Wet Edges

SETTINGS

Spacing 55%
Size Jitter 100%
Count 6
Hue Jitter 100%

Spacing 55%
Size Jitter 100%
Count 6
Hue Jitter 100%
Saturation Jitter 50%
Purity +100%

Spacing 1%
Foreground/Background
Jitter 100%
Hue Jitter 100%
Purity +100%

Spacing 1%
Foreground/Background
Jitter 100%
Purity +100%

Spacing 15%
Foreground/Background
Jitter 100%
Hue Jitter 50%
Purity +100%

Spacing 33%
Scatter 30%
Count 1
Foreground/Background
Jitter 50%
Hue Jitter 20%

Spacing 33%
Scatter 30%
Count 1
Foreground/Background
Jitter 100%
Hue Jitter 50%

Spacing 45%
Count 3
Foreground/Background
Jitter 100%
Hue Jitter 50%

Spacing 45%
Scatter 50%
Count 4
Hue Jitter 50%
Saturation Jitter 100%
Wet Edges

Spacing 80%
Scatter 50%
Count 4
Hue Jitter 100%
Saturation Jitter 100%
Purity +20%
Noise

TEXTURE 4

Spacing 90%
Scatter 50%
Count 1
Foreground/Background Jitter 95%
Purity +100%

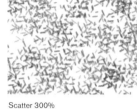

Scatter 300%
Count 3
Foreground/Background Jitter 100%
Hue Jitter 33%
Saturation Jitter 100%
Purity +100%

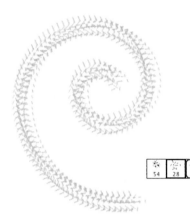

Spacing 10%
Size Jitter 100%
Angle Jitter 15%
Count 2
Hue Jitter 20%
Saturation Jitter 100%
Purity +100%

Spacing 10%
Size Jitter 100%
Angle Jitter 15%
Count 2
Hue Jitter 20%
Purity +100%
Wet Edges

SETTINGS

Spacing 33%
Count 2
Hue Jitter 20%
Purity +50%
Wet Edges

Spacing 100%
Scatter 100%
Count 4
Hue Jitter 20%
Purity +50%
Wet Edges

Spacing 50%
Scatter 120%
Count 4
Hue Jitter 100%
Purity +100%

Spacing 50%
Scatter 200%
Count 1
Hue Jitter 100%
Purity +100%

Spacing 50%
Scatter 120%
Count 4
Foreground/Background
Jitter 20%
Hue Jitter 20%
Purity +100%; Wet Edges

Spacing 50%
Scatter 200%
Count 3
Hue Jitter 100%
Purity +100%
Wet Edges

Spacing 50%
Scatter 200%
Count 5
Foreground/Background
Jitter 50%
Hue Jitter 100%
Purity +100%

Spacing 25%
Scatter 200%
Count 5
Foreground/Background
Jitter 50%
Hue Jitter 100%
Purity +100%

Spacing 5%

Spacing 5%
Scatter 10%
Count 1
Hue Jitter 100%

TEXTURE 5

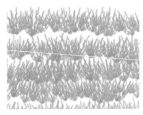

Angle -90°
Spacing 25%
Size Jitter 100%
Angle Jitter 10%
Foreground/Background Jitter 10%
Hue Jitter 10%

Hue Jitter 100%
Wet Edges

Angle 45°
Spacing 25%
Angle Jitter 5%
Scatter 45%
Count 2
Hue Jitter 55%
Purity +50%
Wet Edges

Angle 90°
Spacing 20%
Size Jitter 50%
Scatter 100%
Count 8
Foreground/Background Jitter 100%
Purity +50%

SETTINGS

Angle 90°
Spacing 20%
Size Jitter 100%
Scatter 100%
Count 3
Foreground/Background
Jitter 100%; Purity +50%

Spacing 20%
Size Jitter 100%
Count 2
Foreground/Background
Jitter 100%
Purity +100%
Wet Edges

Angle 45°; Spacing 20%
Size Jitter 100%
Angle Jitter 50%
Scatter 100%; Count 2
Foreground/Background
Jitter 100%
Purity +100%

Angle 45°
Foreground/Background
Jitter 100%
Purity +100%

Angle 90°
Spacing 55%
Hue Jitter 50%
Purity +100%

Angle 90°
Spacing 55%
Hue Jitter 50%
Wet Edges

Angle 135°
Angle Jitter 50%
Hue Jitter 50%

Angle 135°
Angle Jitter 25%
Scatter 100%; Count 3
Foreground/Background
Jitter 30%
Hue Jitter 30%
Purity +25%

Angle -90°
Spacing 100%
Size Jitter 100%; Count 3
Foreground/Background
Jitter 100%
Purity +100%
Flow Jitter 100%

Roundness 50%
Spacing 35%
Foreground/Background
Jitter 25%
Hue Jitter 75%

TEXTURE 6

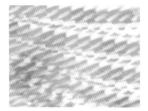

Angle 45°
Spacing 50%
Hue Jitter 50%
Flow Jitter 50%
Wet Edges

Angle 45°
Spacing 25%
Angle Jitter 17%
Hue Jitter 100%
Flow Jitter 50%

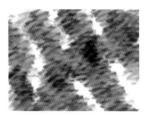

Angle 45°
Spacing 20%
Scatter 100%
Count 2
Foreground/Background Jitter 50%
Purity +100%

Spacing 20%
Scatter 75%
Count 1
Foreground/Background Jitter 50%
Hue Jitter 100%
Purity +100%
Noise

SETTINGS

Spacing 20%
Scatter 75%
Count 1
Foreground/Background
Jitter 50%
Hue Jitter 100%
Purity +100%; Wet Edges

Spacing 35%
Count 3
Hue Jitter 100%

Spacing 35%
Count 3
Hue Jitter 100%
Purity +100%
Wet Edges

Spacing 135%
Scatter 70%
Count 4
Hue Jitter 100%
Purity +100%

Spacing 100%
Angle Jitter 45%
Scatter 75%
Count 4; Foreground/
Background Jitter 10%
Hue Jitter 100%
Purity +100%

Angle 45°; Spacing 70%
Size Jitter 100%
Scatter 75%; Count 4
Foreground/Background
Jitter 100%
Hue Jitter 10%
Purity +100%; Wet Edges

Spacing 50%; Size Jitter
100%; Scatter 100%
Count 2; Foreground/
Background Jitter 10%
Hue Jitter 10%
Brightness Jitter 100%
Purity +100%; Noise

Spacing 15%
Size Jitter 100%
Scatter 100%; Count 2
Foreground/Background
Jitter 100%
Hue Jitter 100%
Purity -50%

Size Jitter 100%
Scatter 200%
Count 2
Hue Jitter 100%
Purity -25%

Spacing 90%
Size Jitter 50%
Scatter 115%
Count 10
Hue Jitter 100%
Purity -75%

TRIANGLE

Spacing 50%
Scatter 100%
Count 2
Hue Jitter 50%

Spacing 50%; Size Jitter 100%
Angle Jitter 100%; Scatter 100%
Count 2; Hue Jitter 50%; Purity -50%

Spacing 20%
Size Jitter 50%
Angle Jitter 50%
Scatter 100%
Count 1
Foreground/Background Jitter 100%
Purity +100%

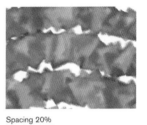

Spacing 20%
Size Jitter 50%
Angle Jitter 50%
Count 3
Foreground/Background Jitter 100%
Hue Jitter 100%
Purity -33%
Noise; Wet Edges

SETTINGS

Spacing 20%
Size Jitter 50%
Angle Jitter 50%
Count 3
Hue Jitter 100%
Brightness Jitter 100%
Purity -33%; Wet Edges

Spacing 20%
Size Jitter 50%
Angle Jitter 50%
Count 3; Foreground/
Background Jitter 100%
Hue Jitter 100%
Purity -70%

Angle 15°
Spacing 45%
Size Jitter 50%
Count 3; Foreground/
Background Jitter 100%
Hue Jitter 100%
Purity +100%

Angle 15°
Spacing 45%
Size Jitter 50%
Scatter 250%
Count 3
Hue Jitter 100%
Purity +100%

Spacing 10%
Size Jitter 100%
Scatter 115%
Count 1
Foreground/Background
Jitter 95%
Purity +100%

Angle Jitter 50%
Roundness Jitter 100%
Scatter 115%; Count 1
Foreground/Background
Jitter 100%
Brightness Jitter 100%
Purity +100%

Angle Jitter 50%
Roundness Jitter 100%
Scatter 115%; Count 1
Foreground/Background
Jitter 100%; Hue Jitter 25%
Brightness Jitter 100%
Purity +100%; Wet Edges

Angle Jitter 50%
Roundness Jitter 100%
Scatter 100%; Count 1
Foreground/Background
Jitter 100%; Hue Jitter
100%; Brightness Jitter
100%; Purity +100%

Angle Jitter 50%
Roundness Jitter 100%
Scatter 200%
Count 3
Foreground/Background
Jitter 100%
Purity +100%

Spacing 100%
Scatter 275%
Count 4
Hue Jitter 22%

TRIANGLE DOTS

Spacing 100%
Size Jitter 100%
Scatter 30%
Count 1
Hue Jitter 100%

Spacing 45%
Size Jitter 50%
Count 3
Hue Jitter 100%

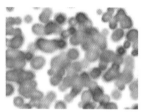

Spacing 45%
Size Jitter 50%
Scatter 50%
Count 3
Hue Jitter 100%
Purity +100%
Wet Edges

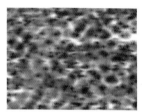

Spacing 5%
Roundness Jitter 100%
Scatter 100%
Count 1
Foreground/Background Jitter 50%
Hue Jitter 100%
Purity +100%
Noise

SETTINGS

Spacing 20%
Foreground/Background
Jitter 50%
Hue Jitter 100%
Purity +100%
Wet Edges

Scatter 80%
Count 1
Foreground/Background
Jitter 100%
Saturation Jitter 95%

Scatter 100%
Count 2
Foreground/Background
Jitter 100%
Brightness Jitter 100%
Purity +50%

Spacing 50%
Foreground/Background
Jitter 100%
Hue Jitter 50%
Brightness Jitter 100%
Purity +50%
Wet Edges

Count 5
Foreground/Background
Jitter 100%
Hue Jitter 50%
Brightness Jitter 100%
Purity +100%

Spacing 50%
Scatter 60%
Count 5
Foreground/Background
Jitter 50%
Brightness Jitter 100%
Purity +100%

Spacing 50%
Scatter 150%
Count 6
Foreground/Background
Jitter 50%
Hue Jitter 50%
Purity +100%
Wet Edges

Scatter 200%
Count 1
Foreground/Background
Jitter 50%
Hue Jitter 50%
Purity +100%

Spacing 1%
Scatter 100%
Count 1
Hue Jitter 100%
Purity -10%
Wet Edges

Spacing 10%
Size Jitter 33%
Angle Jitter 50%
Hue Jitter 33%
Purity +100%
Wet Edges

NEW DP SWIRL

Spacing 35%
Scatter 75%
Foreground/Background Jitter 100%

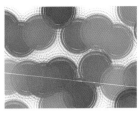

Spacing 35%
Scatter 75%
Foreground/Background Jitter 100%
Hue Jitter 100%
Wet Edges

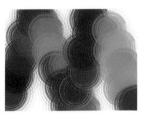

Spacing 35%
Scatter 35%
Count 2
Foreground/Background Jitter 50%
Hue Jitter 100%
Purity +100%

Roundness 50%
Spacing 35%
Size Jitter 78%
Roundness Jitter 100%
Scatter 250%
Count 1
Hue Jitter 100%
Purity +100%

SETTINGS

Spacing 65%
Roundness Jitter 100%
Hue Jitter 100%
Saturation Jitter 100%

Spacing 40%
Roundness Jitter 100%
Hue Jitter 100%
Purity +100%

Spacing 40%
Scatter 50%; Count 2
Roundness Jitter 100%
Foreground/Background
Jitter 100%
Hue Jitter 100%
Purity +100%

Spacing 40%
Scatter 50%; Count 2
Roundness Jitter 100%
Foreground/Background
Jitter 100%; Hue
Jitter 100%; Purity -25%
Wet Edges

Size Jitter 100%
Roundness Jitter 50%

Size Jitter 100%
Roundness Jitter 50%
Foreground/Background
Jitter 100%
Hue Jitter 100%
Wet Edges

Spacing 65%
Size Jitter 100%
Roundness Jitter 50%
Foreground/Background
Jitter 100%
Hue Jitter 100%

Spacing 65%
Size Jitter 100%
Roundness Jitter 50%
Foreground/Background
Jitter 100%
Hue Jitter 100%
Purity +100%; Wet Edges

Spacing 65%; Scatter
125%; Count 2; Size Jitter
100%; Roundness Jitter
50%; Foreground/
Background Jitter 100%
Hue Jitter 100%
Purity +100%; Wet Edges

Spacing 66%
Size Jitter 75%
Foreground/Background
Jitter 100%
Purity -20%
Wet Edges

DP WHEEL 1

504 488 495

Spacing 48%
Roundness Jitter 100%
Hue Jitter 100%
Brightness Jitter 60%
Purity +100%

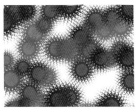

Roundness Jitter 50%
Foreground/Background Jitter 100%
Brightness Jitter 100%
Wet Edges

Size Jitter 100%
Roundness Jitter 50%
Foreground/Background Jitter 100%
Hue Jitter 100%
Wet Edges

Roundness Jitter 100%
Scatter 10%
Count 2
Hue Jitter 100%
Brightness Jitter 20%
Purity +100%

SETTINGS

Roundness Jitter 100%
Scatter 10%
Count 2
Hue Jitter 100%
Brightness Jitter 20%
Purity +100%
Wet Edges

Roundness Jitter 100%
Scatter 66%
Count 2
Hue Jitter 100%
Brightness Jitter 20%
Purity +100%

Size Jitter 100%
Roundness Jitter 100%
Scatter 66%
Count 2
Foreground/Background
Jitter 50%
Hue Jitter 100%
Purity +100%

Spacing 50%
Size Jitter 100%
Roundness Jitter 100%
Scatter 66%; Count 1
Foreground/Background
Jitter 100%
Hue Jitter 45%
Purity +50%; Wet Edges

Spacing 50%
Size Jitter 100%
Roundness Jitter 100%
Scatter 66%; Count 2
Foreground/Background
Jitter 100%
Hue Jitter 45%
Purity +50%

Spacing 50%
Scatter 66%
Count 4
Brightness Jitter 40%
Purity +10%

Spacing 50%
Scatter 66%
Count 8
Hue Jitter 75%
Purity +100%

Spacing 50%
Scatter 66%
Count 8
Hue Jitter 75%
Purity +100%
Wet Edges

Spacing 72%
Scatter 66%
Count 3
Hue Jitter 75%
Purity -55%

Spacing 72%
Scatter 66%
Count 3
Hue Jitter 75%
Purity +100%
Wet Edges

DP WHEEL 2

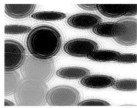

Size Jitter 50%
Roundness Jitter 100%
Scatter 20%
Count 2
Hue Jitter 100%
Brightness Jitter 15%

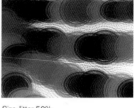

Size Jitter 50%
Roundness Jitter 100%
Scatter 100%
Count 1
Brightness Jitter 100%

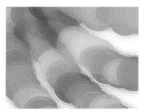

Size Jitter 50%
Count 2
Hue Jitter 100%
Brightness Jitter 15%
Wet Edges

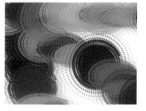

Size Jitter 50%
Angle Jitter 50%
Scatter 100%
Count 1
Foreground/Background Jitter 100%

SETTINGS

Size Jitter 50%
Angle Jitter 50%
Scatter 100%
Count 1
Foreground/Background
Jitter 100%
Wet Edges

Size Jitter 50%
Angle Jitter 50%
Scatter 100%
Count 1
Foreground/Background
Jitter 100%
Hue Jitter 100%

Spacing 66%
Hue Jitter 100%
Saturation Jitter 33%

Spacing 66%
Scatter 36%
Count 1
Foreground/Background
Jitter 50%
Hue Jitter 15%
Saturation Jitter 33%

Spacing 66%
Scatter 36%
Count 1
Brightness Jitter 50%

Spacing 35%
Size Jitter 25%
Angle Jitter 50%
Roundness Jitter 100%
Count 2; Foreground/
Background Jitter 50%
Brightness Jitter 50%

Spacing 70%
Roundness Jitter 100%
Scatter 0%; Count 3
Foreground/Background
Jitter 50%
Hue Jitter 100%
Purity +100%

Spacing 70%
Roundness Jitter 100%
Scatter 0%; Count 3
Foreground/Background
Jitter 50%
Hue Jitter 100%
Purity +100%

Roundness 75%
Spacing 70%
Roundness Jitter 100%
Count 2
Hue Jitter 100%

Spacing 70%
Roundness Jitter 100%
Count 3
Hue Jitter 100%
Purity +100%
Wet Edges

DP FLOWER

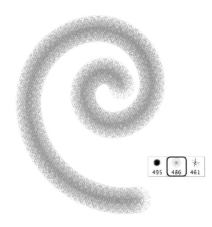

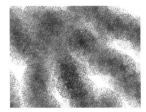

Scatter 66%
Count 2
Hue Jitter 75%
Brightness Jitter 15%
Purity +100%

Scatter 120%
Count 2
Hue Jitter 30%
Brightness Jitter 45%
Purity +100%
Wet Edges

Size Jitter 100%
Roundness Jitter 100%
Scatter 120%
Count 2
Hue Jitter 100%
Purity +100%

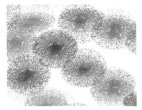

Spacing 75%
Roundness Jitter 100%
Scatter 25%
Count 4
Hue Jitter 100%
Purity +100%

SETTINGS

Spacing 75%
Roundness Jitter 100%
Scatter 25%
Count 4
Hue Jitter 100%
Purity +100%

Size Jitter 100%
Hue Jitter 100%
Purity +100%

Spacing 50%
Size Jitter 100%
Hue Jitter 100%
Purity +100%
Wet Edges

Spacing 50%
Size Jitter 100%
Roundness Jitter 50%
Scatter 0%
Count 3
Hue Jitter 100%
Purity +100%

Hue Jitter 100%
Saturation Jitter 100%
Purity +100%

Scatter 150%
Count 2
Brightness Jitter 100%

Spacing 15%
Size Jitter 100%
Roundness Jitter 50%
Foreground/Background
Jitter 50%
Saturation Jitter 100%
Purity +100%

Spacing 85%
Size Jitter 100%
Roundness Jitter 50%
Scatter 30%; Count 3
Foreground/Background
Jitter 100%; Hue Jitter
10%; Purity +100%

Spacing 85%; Size Jitter
100%; Roundness Jitter
50%; Scatter 30%
Count 3; Foreground/
Background Jitter 100%
Hue Jitter 100%; Purity
+100%; Wet Edges

Spacing 120%
Scatter 0%
Count 7
Foreground/Background
Jitter 100%
Hue Jitter 100%
Purity +100%

DP CRACKLE

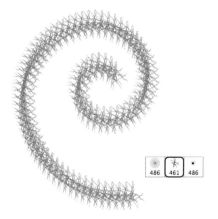

Size Jitter 100%
Scatter 75%
Count 4
Foreground/Background Jitter 100%
Brightness Jitter 100%; Purity +100%

Size Jitter 100%; Scatter 0%
Count 2; Foreground/Background
Jitter 100%; Hue Jitter 30%
Brightness Jitter 100%; Wet Edges

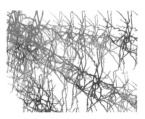

Size Jitter 100%
Foreground/Background Jitter 100%
Hue Jitter 100%

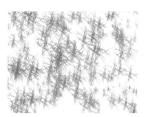

Size Jitter 100%
Scatter 300%
Count 3
Hue Jitter 45%
Saturation Jitter 100%
Purity -50%

486 | 461 | 486

SETTINGS

Size Jitter 100%
Roundness Jitter 100%

Size Jitter 100%
Roundness Jitter 100%
Foreground/Background
Jitter 50%
Hue Jitter 45%
Saturation Jitter 100%

Size Jitter 100%
Roundness Jitter 100%
Foreground/Background
Jitter 50%
Hue Jitter 100%
Saturation Jitter 100%
Wet Edges

Scatter 0%
Count 3
Foreground/Background
Jitter 50%
Hue Jitter 100%
Saturation Jitter 100%

Spacing 60%
Scatter 66%
Count 3
Foreground/Background
Jitter 50%
Hue Jitter 100%

Spacing 60%
Scatter 66%; Count 3
Foreground/Background
Jitter 100%
Hue Jitter 100%
Purity +100%
Wet Edges

Spacing 100%
Size Jitter 100%
Roundness Jitter 100%
Foreground/Background
Jitter 50%
Hue Jitter 100%
Purity +100%

Spacing 1%
Size Jitter 100%
Roundness Jitter 100%
Foreground/Background
Jitter 50%
Hue Jitter 100%
Purity +100%

Spacing 1%
Size Jitter 100%
Roundness Jitter 100%
Foreground/Background
Jitter 50%
Hue Jitter 15%
Purity +100%

Spacing 1%
Size Jitter 100%
Roundness Jitter 100%
Foreground/Background
Jitter 50%
Hue Jitter 15%
Purity +100%

DP STAR

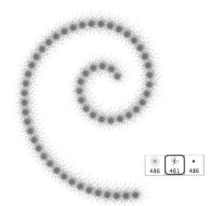

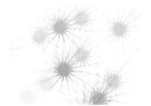

Opacity Jitter 100%
Flow Jitter 100%

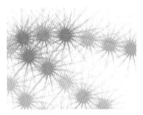

Hue Jitter 100%
Opacity Jitter 50%
Flow Jitter 50%

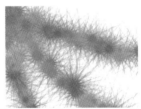

Spacing 15%
Size Jitter 100%
Angle Jitter 35%
Scatter 15%
Count 2
Hue Jitter 100%

Spacing 15%
Size Jitter 100%
Angle Jitter 35%
Scatter 15%
Count 2
Hue Jitter 100%
Purity +100%
Wet Edges

SETTINGS

Spacing 15%
Size Jitter 100%
Angle Jitter 35%
Scatter 15%; Count 2
Hue Jitter 100%
Purity +100%
Wet Edges

Scatter 15%
Count 2
Hue Jitter 100%
Purity +100%

Scatter 15%
Count 2
Purity +100%

Spacing 55%
Scatter 50%
Count 7
Hue Jitter 20%
Purity +100%

Spacing 55%
Hue Jitter 20%
Purity +100%

Spacing 55%
Size Jitter 100%
Hue Jitter 100%
Purity +100%

Spacing 33%
Size Jitter 100%
Hue Jitter 100%
Purity +10%

Spacing 15%
Scatter 40%
Count 2; Foreground/
Background Jitter 20%
Hue Jitter 100%
Opacity Jitter 100%
Wet Edges

Foreground/Background
Jitter 20%
Hue Jitter 100%
Purity +35%
Opacity Jitter 100%

Scatter 0%
Count 3
Foreground/Background
Jitter 20%
Hue Jitter 100%
Purity +35%
Opacity Jitter 100%

PASTEL ON CHARCOAL PAPER

Default Brush

Scatter 350%

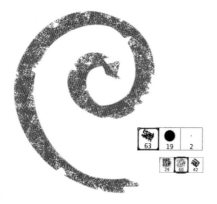

Dual Brush: Pastel Medium Tip
Spacing 85%

Foreground/Background Jitter 100%

SCATTERING

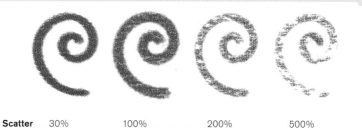

Scatter	30%	100%	200%	500%

COLOR DYNAMICS

Foreground/Background Jitter	100%	0%	0%	100%
Hue Jitter	0%	50%	100%	100%

BRUSH TIP SHAPE • SHAPE DYNAMICS

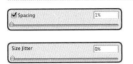

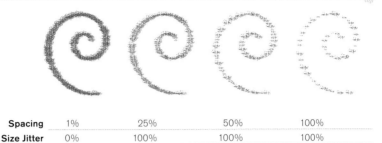

Spacing	1%	25%	50%	100%
Size Jitter	0%	100%	100%	100%

BRUSH TIP SHAPE

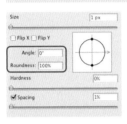

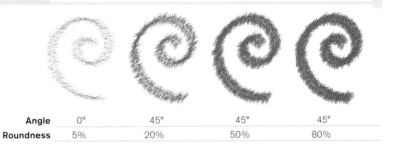

Angle	0°	45°	45°	45°
Roundness	5%	20%	50%	80%

BRUSH TIP SHAPE • COLOR DYNAMICS

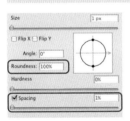

Roundness	20%	20%	20%	20%
Spacing	24%	24%	100%	100%
Hue Jitter	0%	50%	100%	100%

DUAL BRUSH

Dual Brush:
Hard Round

Spacing	20%	70%	160%	250%

PASTEL ROUGH TEXTURE

Default Brush

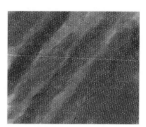

Size Jitter 100%

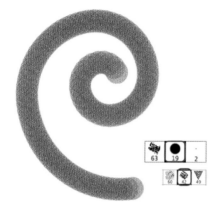

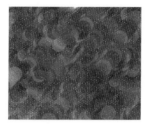

Hue Jitter 50%

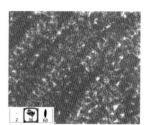

Dual Brush: Chalk
Spacing 100%

SCATTERING

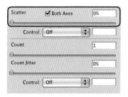

Scatter	100%	200%	500%	800%

BRUSH TIP SHAPE

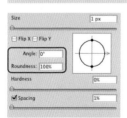

Angle	0°	45°	45°	45°
Roundness	5%	20%	50%	80%

COLOR DYNAMICS

Foreground/Background Jitter	100%	0%	0%	100%
Hue Jitter	0%	50%	100%	100%

DUAL BRUSH

Dual Brush: Chalk

Size	90 px	90 px	90 px	90 px
Spacing	105%	50%	80%	120%

BRUSH TIP SHAPE • COLOR DYNAMICS

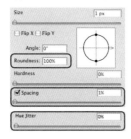

Dual Brush: Chalk

Roundness	20%	20%	20%	20%
Spacing	24%	24%	50%	150%
Hue Jitter	0%	50%	100%	100%

BRUSH TIP SHAPE • TRANSFER

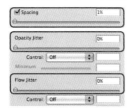

Spacing	20%	20%	20%	50%
Opacity Jitter	100%	100%	100%	100%
Flow Jitter	0%	50%	100%	100%

SOFT OIL PASTEL

Default Brush

Dual Brush: Scatter 500%

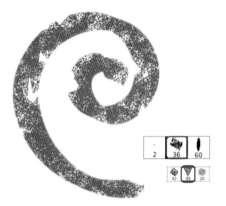

Hue Jitter 70%

Spacing 100%

SCATTERING

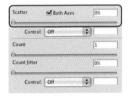

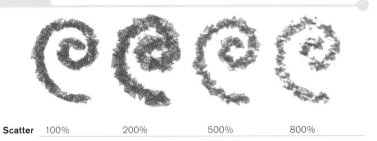

Scatter	100%	200%	500%	800%

COLOR DYNAMICS

Foreground/Background Jitter	100%	0%	0%	100%
Hue Jitter	0%	50%	100%	100%

BRUSH TIP SHAPE • SHAPE DYNAMICS

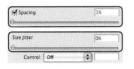

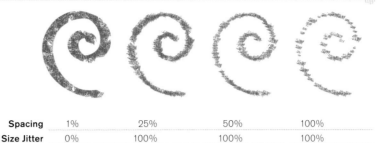

Spacing	1%	25%	50%	100%
Size Jitter	0%	100%	100%	100%

BRUSH TIP SHAPE

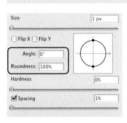

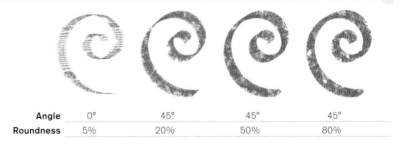

Angle	0°	45°	45°	45°
Roundness	5%	20%	50%	80%

DUAL BRUSH

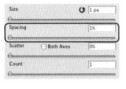

Dual Brush: Chalk

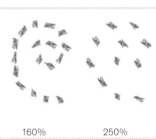

Spacing	20%	70%	160%	250%

BRUSH TIP SHAPE • SHAPE DYNAMICS • COLOR DYNAMICS

Spacing	24%	24%	100%	100%
Angle Jitter	0%	0%	14%	40%
Hue Jitter	0%	50%	100%	100%

SOFT PASTEL LARGE

Default Brush

Spacing 100%

Foreground/Background Jitter 100%

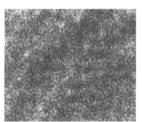

Dual Brush: Spacing 100%

DUAL BRUSH

Size		1 px
Spacing		1%
Scatter	Both Axes	0%
Count		1

Dual Brush:
Hard Round

| **Spacing** | 20% | 70% | 160% | 250% |

BRUSH TIP SHAPE • TRANSFER

Angle:	0°
Roundness:	100%
Hardness	0%
☑ Spacing	1%
Foreground/Background Jitter	0%
Control:	Off

Roundness	20%	20%	20%	20%
Spacing	24%	24%	100%	100%
Foreground/Background Jitter	100%	100%	100%	100%

BRUSH TIP SHAPE

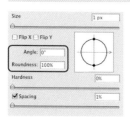
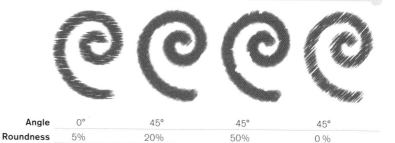

Angle	0°	45°	45°	45°
Roundness	5%	20%	50%	0%

BRUSH TIP SHAPE • SHAPE DYNAMICS

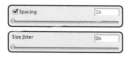
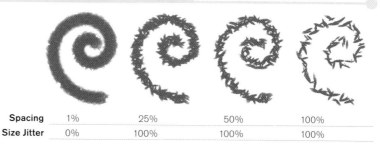

Spacing	1%	25%	50%	100%
Size Jitter	0%	100%	100%	100%

COLOR DYNAMICS

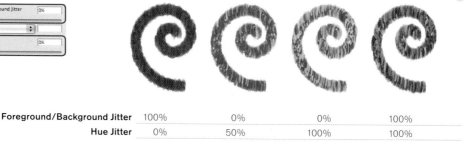

Foreground/Background Jitter	100%	0%	0%	100%
Hue Jitter	0%	50%	100%	100%

SCATTERING

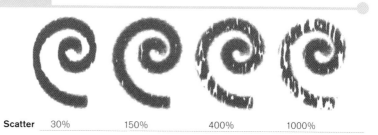

Scatter	30%	150%	400%	1000%

LARGE GRAPHITE HEAVY FLOW

Default Brush

Spacing 100%

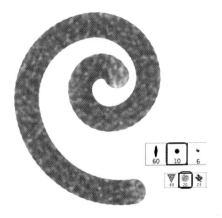

Opacity Jitter 100%

Dual Brush: Sampled Tip

SCATTERING

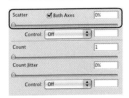

Scatter	30%	100%	200%	500%

COLOR DYNAMICS

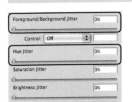

Foreground/Background Jitter	100%	0%	0%	100%
Hue Jitter	0%	50%	100%	100%

BRUSH TIP SHAPE • SHAPE DYNAMICS

 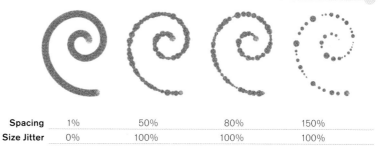

Spacing	1%	50%	80%	150%
Size Jitter	0%	100%	100%	100%

TRANSFER

 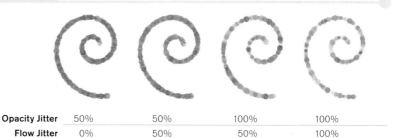

Opacity Jitter	50%	50%	100%	100%
Flow Jitter	0%	50%	50%	100%

BRUSH TIP SHAPE • COLOR DYNAMICS

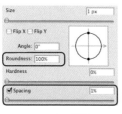 

Roundness	20%	20%	20%	20%
Spacing	24%	200%	300%	500%
Foreground/Background Jitter	100%	100%	100%	100%

DUAL BRUSH

Dual Brush: Default

Spacing	40%	70%	160%	250%

PENCILS

Conté

Charcoal

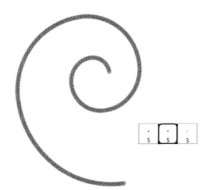

4H Hard

Wax

NUMBER 2–SCATTERING

Scatter   0%   100%   500%   1000%

WAX–SCATTERING

Scatter   30%   100%   500%   1000%

4H HARD—SCATTERING

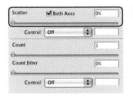
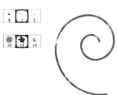

Scatter   0%   100%   500%   1000%

CHARCOAL—SCATTERING

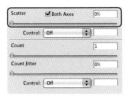

Scatter   0%   100%   500%   1000%

CONTÉ—SCATTERING

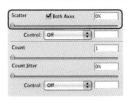

Scatter   0%   100%   500%   1000%

GRAPHITE—SCATTERING

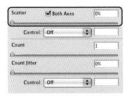

Scatter   0%   100%   500%   1000%

WAXY CRAYON

Default Brush

Spacing 50%

Foreground/Background Jitter 100%

Scatter 450%

DUAL BRUSH

Size	↻	1 px
Spacing		1%
Scatter	☐ Both Axes	0%
Count		1

Dual Brush:
Default

| Scatter | 1% | 40% | 80% | 120% |

BRUSH TIP SHAPE • COLOR DYNAMICS

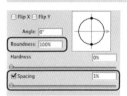

☐ Flip X ☐ Flip Y
Angle: 0°
Roundness: 100%
Hardness   0%
☑ Spacing   1%

Foreground/Background Jitter   0%

Roundness	20%	20%	20%	20%
Spacing	5%	30%	60%	100%
Foreground/Background Jitter	100%	100%	100%	100%

TRANSFER

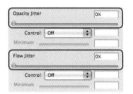

Opacity Jitter	50%	50%	100%	100%
Flow Jitter	0%	50%	50%	100%

BRUSH TIP SHAPE • SHAPE DYNAMICS

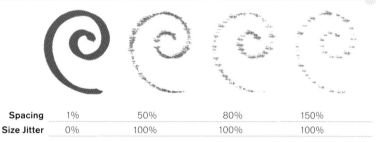

Spacing	1%	50%	80%	150%
Size Jitter	0%	100%	100%	100%

COLOR DYNAMICS

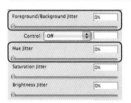

Foreground/Background Jitter	100%	0%	0%	100%
Hue Jitter	0%	50%	100%	100%

SCATTERING

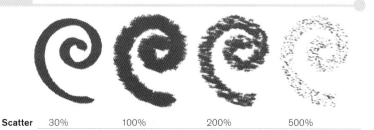

Scatter	30%	100%	200%	500%

PERMANENT MARKER

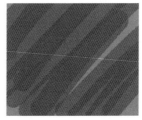

Default Brush

Foreground/Background Jitter 100%

Spacing 150%

Wet Edges

TRANSFER

Opacity Jitter	10%	50%	100%	100%
Flow Jitter	0%	0%	0%	100%

COLOR DYNAMICS

Foreground/Background Jitter	100%	0%	0%	100%
Hue Jitter	0%	50%	100%	100%

SCATTERING

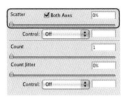

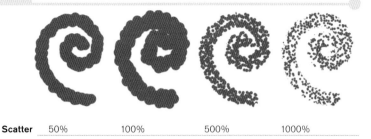

Scatter	50%	100%	500%	1000%

BRUSH TIP SHAPE • SHAPE DYNAMICS

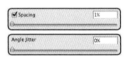

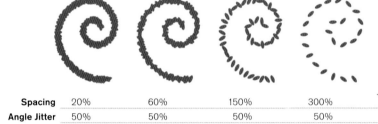

Spacing	20%	60%	150%	300%
Angle Jitter	50%	50%	50%	50%

DUAL BRUSH

Dual Brush:
Sampled Tip

Spacing	20%	60%	100%	120%

SHAPE DYNAMICS

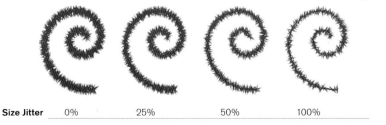

Size Jitter	0%	25%	50%	100%

CHARCOAL SCRAPING PAPER

Default Brush

Hue Jitter 100%

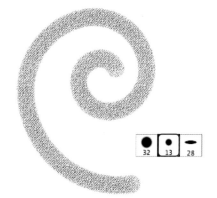

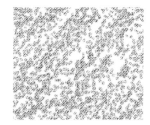

Scatter 700%

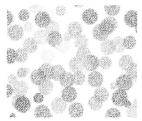

Spacing 1000%

DUAL BRUSH

Dual Brush:
Sampled Tip

Scatter	0%	100%	200%	500%

DUAL BRUSH

Dual Brush:
Sampled Tip

Spacing	20%	60%	100%	120%

BRUSH TIP SHAPE • SHAPE DYNAMICS

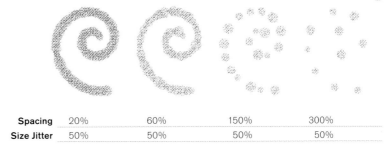

Spacing	20%	60%	150%	300%
Size Jitter	50%	50%	50%	50%

SCATTERING

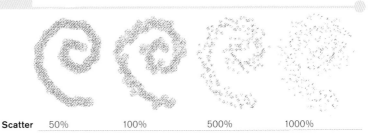

Scatter	50%	100%	500%	1000%

SCATTER • COLOR DYNAMICS

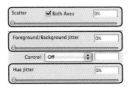

Scatter	200%	200%	200%	200%
Foreground/Background Jitter	100%	0%	0%	100%
Hue Jitter	0%	50%	100%	100%

TRANSFER

Opacity Jitter	10%	50%	100%	100%
Flow Jitter	0%	0%	0%	100%

CHARCOAL FLAT

Default Brush

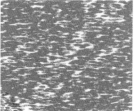
Scatter 700%

13 | 28 | 20

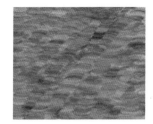
Hue Jitter 100%

Flow Jitter 100%

BRUSH TIP SHAPE • SHAPE DYNAMICS

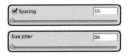

Spacing	20%	60%	150%	300%
Size Jitter	50%	50%	50%	50%

SCATTERING

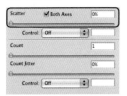

Scatter	50%	100%	500%	1000%

COLOR DYNAMICS

Foreground/Background Jitter	100%	0%	0%	100%
Hue Jitter	0%	50%	100%	100%

SHAPE DYNAMICS

 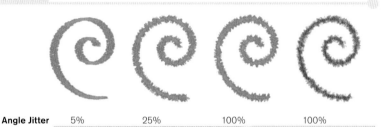

Angle Jitter	5%	25%	100%	100%
Wet Edges	on	on	on	off

DUAL BRUSH

Dual Brush:
Sampled Tip

Spacing	20%	60%	80%	100%

TRANSFER

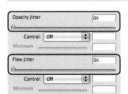 

Opacity Jitter	10%	50%	100%	100%
Flow Jitter	0%	0%	0%	100%

HEAVY SMEAR WAX CRAYON

Default Brush

Scatter 1000%

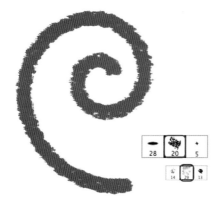

Foreground/Background Jitter 100%

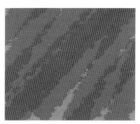

Wet Edges

COLOR DYNAMICS

Foreground/Background Jitter	100%	0%	0%	100%
Hue Jitter	0%	50%	100%	100%

TRANSFER

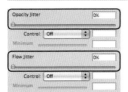

Opacity Jitter	10%	50%	100%	100%
Flow Jitter	0%	0%	0%	100%

SCATTERING

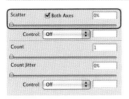

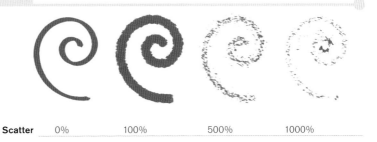

Scatter	0%	100%	500%	1000%

BRUSH TIP SHAPE • SHAPE DYNAMICS

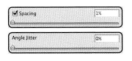

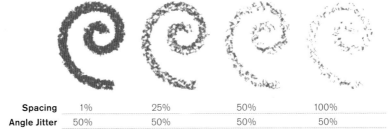

Spacing	1%	25%	50%	100%
Angle Jitter	50%	50%	50%	50%

SHAPE DYNAMICS

Size Jitter	10%	50%	100%	100%
Angle Jitter	0%	0%	0%	100%

DUAL BRUSH • WET EDGES

Dual Brush:
Default
Sampled Tip

Size	1 px	25 px	50 px	70 px
Wet Edges	off	off	off	on

HARD CHARCOAL EDGE

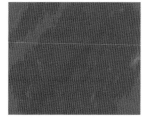

Default Brush

Wet Edges

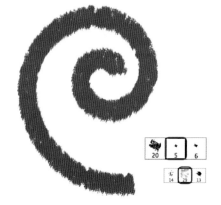

Spacing 60%

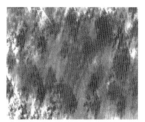

Opacity Jitter 100%

TRANSFER

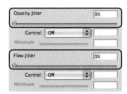

Opacity Jitter	10%	50%	100%	100%
Flow Jitter	0%	0%	0%	100%

COLOR DYNAMICS

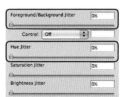

Foreground/Background Jitter	100%	0%	0%	100%
Hue Jitter	0%	50%	100%	100%

SCATTERING

 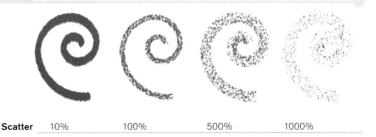

| Scatter | 10% | 100% | 500% | 1000% |

BRUSH TIP SHAPE • SHAPE DYNAMICS

 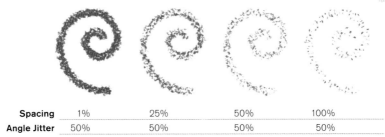

| Spacing | 1% | 25% | 50% | 100% |
| Angle Jitter | 50% | 50% | 50% | 50% |

DUAL BRUSH • WET EDGES

Dual Brush:
Default
Sampled Tip

| Spacing | 20% | 60% | 100% | 120% |
| Wet Edges | off | off | off | on |

SHAPE DYNAMICS • WET EDGES

 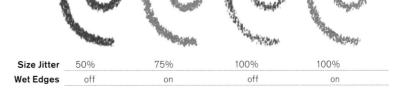

| Size Jitter | 50% | 75% | 100% | 100% |
| Wet Edges | off | on | off | on |

PASTEL
MEDIUM TIP

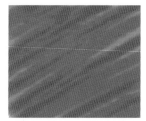

Default Brush

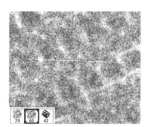

Dual Brush: Sampled Tip

Hue Jitter 40%

Wet Edges

SHAPE DYNAMICS • WET EDGES

Size Jitter	50%	75%	100%	100%
Wet Edges	off	on	off	on

DUAL BRUSH

Dual Brush:
Sampled Tip

Spacing	20%	60%	100%	120%

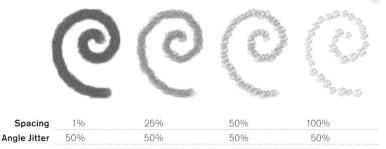
BRUSH TIP SHAPE • SHAPE DYNAMICS

Spacing	1%	25%	50%	100%
Angle Jitter	50%	50%	50%	50%

SCATTERING

Scatter	10%	100%	500%	1000%

COLOR DYNAMICS

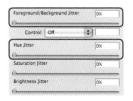

Foreground/Background Jitter	100%	0%	0%	100%
Hue Jitter	0%	50%	100%	100%

TRANSFER

Opacity Jitter	10%	50%	100%	100%
Flow Jitter	0%	0%	0%	100%

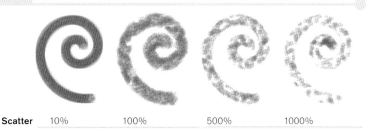

MESH SMALL

Spacing 25%

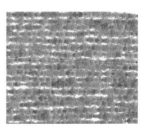

Size Jitter 100%
Angle Jitter 50%
Hue Jitter 10%
Purity +50%

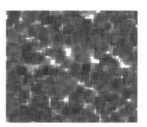

Spacing 30%
Dual Brush: Stencil Brush Dry

Scatter 150%
Count 3
Count Jitter 100%
Foreground/Background Jitter 50%

SETTINGS

Angle 30°
Roundness 50%
Spacing 60%

Dual Brush: Mesh Large

Foreground/Background
Jitter 50%
Saturation Jitter 100%
Purity -50%

Size Jitter 100%
Angle Jitter 50%
Opacity Jitter 50%
Flow Jitter 50%

Scatter 50%
Count 1
Count Jitter 100%
Noise

Hue Jitter 100%
Saturation Jitter 100%
Purity +100%

Size Jitter 50%
Angle Jitter 10%
Foreground/Background
Jitter 100%
Hue Jitter 5%
Saturation Jitter 100%
Purity +50%

Spacing 25%
Hue Jitter 25%
Brightness Jitter 10%

Flow 25%
Scatter 100%
Count 3
Foreground/Background
Jitter 25%
Purity +25%
Flow Jitter 100%

Size Jitter 50%
Angle Jitter 50%
Roundness Jitter 50%
Foreground/Background
Jitter 25%
Brightness Jitter 100%
Purity +50%

MESH LARGE

Default Brush

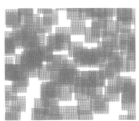

Scatter 600%

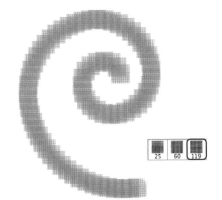

Dual Brush: Veining Feather
Brightness Jitter 100%

Size Jitter 50%
Angle Jitter 50%
Opacity Jitter 50%
Flow Jitter 50%

SETTINGS

Angle 31°
Roundness 20%

Size Jitter 100%
Scatter 100%

Size Jitter 50%
Angle Jitter 50%

Angle Jitter 50%
Scatter 100%

Foreground/Background
Jitter 80%
Brightness Jitter 20%
Wet Edges

Spacing 80%
Roundness 80%
Size Jitter 100%

Spacing 20%
Foreground/Background
Jitter 100%
Wet Edges

Scatter 50%
Count 4
Count Jitter 100%

Scatter 50%
Count 4
Count Jitter 100%

Angle 45°
Roundness 50%
Spacing 125%
Wet Edges

PLASTIC WRAP DARK

Hue Jitter 20%
Wet Edges

Angle 20°
Roundness 40%
Spacing 1%

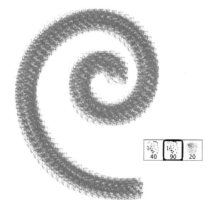

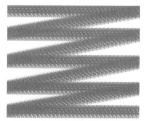

Default Brush

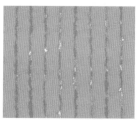

Size Jitter 100%
Roundness Jitter 50%
Wet Edges

SETTINGS

Scatter 100%

Dual Brush: Texture
Comb 2
Brightness Jitter 80%

Count 2
Brightness Jitter 50%

Angle 90°
Brightness Jitter 30%
Flow Jitter 50%

Roundness Jitter 100%
Scatter 10%
Foreground/Background
Jitter 50%

Dual Brush: Veining
Feather 1
Saturation Jitter 100%

Angle 50°
Roundness 30%
Spacing 20%
Angle Jitter 50%

Foreground/Background
Jitter 100%
Saturation Jitter 50%
Wet Edges

Spacing 80%
Angle Jitter 100%
Roundness Jitter 100%
Hue Jitter 50%

Spacing 80%
Angle Jitter 80%

PLASTIC WRAP LIGHT

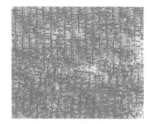

Scatter 100%
Count 5

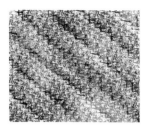

Foreground/Background Jitter 100%
Brightness Jitter 80%
Wet Edges

Angle Jitter 100%
Flow Jitter 50%
Opacity Jitter 50%

Angle 30°
Roundness 30%
Spacing 10%

SETTINGS

Hue Jitter 30%

Scatter 100%
Count 3

Angle 40°
Roundness 20%
Spacing 4%
Saturation Jitter 30%
Wet Edges

Spacing 5%
Saturation Jitter 20%

Scatter 100%
Count 8
Count Jitter 100%
Saturation Jitter 50%

Roundness 70%
Spacing 40%
Angle Jitter 80%

Size Jitter 50%
Foreground/Background
Jitter 20%
Flow Jitter 50%
Wet Edges

Spacing 30%

Size Jitter 50%
Angle Jitter 50%
Roundness Jitter 50%
Hue Jitter 50%

Spacing 20%
Angle Jitter 100%
Opacity Jitter 50%
Wet Edges

ROLLED RAG COTTON

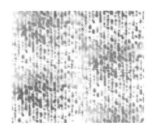

Spacing 80%
Foreground/Background Jitter 50%
Wet Edges

Dual Brush: Sea Sponge 1
Foreground/Background Jitter 100%

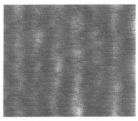

Scatter 70%
Count 4
Foreground/Background Jitter 20%

Roundness 50%
Spacing 50%

SETTINGS

Scatter 10%
Count 4
Count Jitter 100%

Hue Jitter 20%
Saturation Jitter 20%

Angle Jitter 50%
Brightness Jitter 50%

Angle 90°
Roundness 60%
Spacing 50%

Spacing 20%
Saturation Jitter 50%
Opacity Jitter 50%
Wet Edges

Spacing 100%
Scatter 100%
Count 10
Dual Brush: Soft Round
Foreground/Background
Jitter 100%

Size Jitter 50%
Foreground/Background
Jitter 100%

Scatter 0%
Count 4
Brightness Jitter 40%

Angle 100°
Roundness Jitter 100%
Opacity Jitter 50%

Angle 33°
Spacing 50%
Size Jitter 100%
Angle Jitter 100%

ROLLED RAG TERRY

Spacing 50%
Scatter 1%
Hue Jitter 20%

Spacing 100%
Hue Jitter 50%

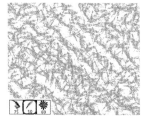

Dual Brush: Veining Feather 2

Angle Jitter 33%
Roundness Jitter 100%
Flow Jitter 80%

SETTINGS

Angle 30°
Roundness 30%
Spacing 10%

Angle 30°
Roundness 30%
Spacing 100%
Angle Jitter 100%

Saturation Jitter 100%
Wet Edges

Foreground/Background
Jitter 100%
Hue Jitter 25%

Angle 25°
Roundness 50%
Scatter 50%
Count 3

Spacing 50%
Size Jitter 100%
Angle Jitter 100%

Spacing 50%
Roundness Jitter 50%
Noise
Wet Edges

Size Jitter 50%
Foreground/Background
Jitter 50%

Spacing 50%
Angle Jitter 50%
Roundness Jitter 50%
Hue Jitter 20%

Scatter 75%
Foreground/Background
Jitter 20%
Hue Jitter 20%
Brightness Jitter 20%
Flow Jitter 50%

SEA SPONGE 1

Default Brush

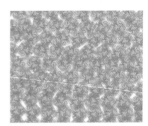

Spacing 100%
Angle Jitter 100%

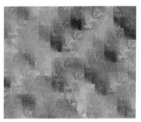

Scatter 80%
Count 5
Count Jitter 100%
Hue Jitter 10%

Brightness Jitter 50%
Wet Edges

SETTINGS

Spacing 100%
Angle Jitter 100%

Saturation Jitter 50%
Flow Jitter 50%
Wet Edges

Dual Brush: Texture Comb
Hue Jitter 10%

Roundness 50%
Angle Jitter 50%
Saturation Jitter 50%

Dual Brush: Mesh

Angle 50°
Roundness 50%
Hue Jitter 20%
Saturation Jitter 20%

Spacing 70%
Wet Edges

Scatter 50%

Angle Jitter 50%
Opacity Jitter 50%
Flow Jitter 50%

Roundness Jitter 50%
Saturation Jitter 50%
Wet Edges

SEA SPONGE 2

Foreground/Background Jitter 100%

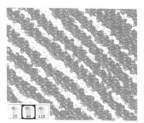

Dual Brush: Rolled Rag
Spacing 45%

Saturation Jitter 80%

Size Jitter 50%
Foreground/Background Jitter 100%
Wet Edges

SETTINGS

Roundness Jitter 100%

Hue Jitter 50%
Brightness Jitter 50%

Angle 30°
Roundness 80%
Spacing 100%
Saturation Jitter 100%

Hue Jitter 50%
Flow Jitter 50%

Scatter 200%
Count 2
Count Jitter 100%

Spacing 50%
Angle Jitter 50%
Brightness Jitter 50%
Wet Edges

Roundness 50%
Spacing 10%
Brightness Jitter 30%

Size Jitter 50%
Hue Jitter 10%
Saturation Jitter 50%
Opacity Jitter 50%
Flow Jitter 50%

Spacing 50%
Angle Jitter 80%
Brightness Jitter 50%
Wet Edges
Noise

Spacing 80%
Angle Jitter 60%

STENCIL SPONGE DRY

Spacing 100%
Size Jitter 100%
Angle Jitter 100%

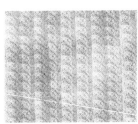

Foreground/Background Jitter 100%
Flow Jitter 50%

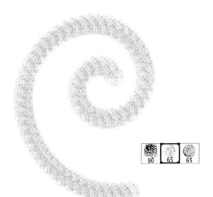

Spacing 10%
Angle Jitter 50%
Opacity Jitter 50%

Spacing 10%
Scatter 100%
Count 2
Hue Jitter 50%
Wet Edges

SETTINGS

Angle Jitter 100%
Roundness Jitter 100%

Roundness 50%
Hue Jitter 50%
Saturation Jitter 50%

Size Jitter 50%
Angle Jitter 50%
Flow Jitter 20%
Wet Edges

Spacing 10%
Foreground/Background
Jitter 100%

Spacing 10%
Size Jitter 100%

Spacing 50%
Brightness Jitter 100%
Wet Edges

Scatter 0%
Count 10
Count Jitter 100%

Angle 60°
Roundness 30%
Spacing 30%

Size Jitter 100%
Saturation Jitter 50%
Brightness Jitter 50%

Foreground/Background
Jitter 100%
Wet Edges

STENCIL SPONGE TWIRL

Default Brush

Spacing 100%
Hue Jitter 50%
Wet Edges

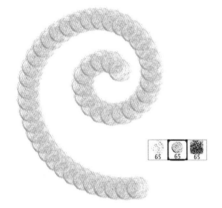

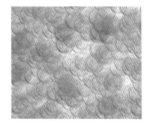

Roundness 50%

Scatter 200%
Count 5
Count Jitter 50%
Hue Jitter 10%

SETTINGS

Spacing 80%
Size Jitter 50%
Angle Jitter 50%

Spacing 30%
Size Jitter 50%
Angle Jitter 50%

Angle Jitter 50%
Roundness Jitter 100%
Brightness Jitter 50%
Purity +50%

Spacing 10%
Size Jitter 50%
Flow Jitter 50%

Scatter 60%
Noise
Wet Edges

Dual Brush:
Texture Comb 2

Angle 30°
Roundness 50%
Spacing 80%
Hue Jitter 20%

Spacing 25%
Size Jitter 50%
Roundness Jitter 50%
Flow Jitter 50%

Angle Jitter 100%
Hue Jitter 100%
Wet Edges

Spacing 100%
Size Jitter 50%
Scattering 0%

STENCIL
SPONGE WET

Hue Jitter 50%
Saturation Jitter 50%
Purity +50%

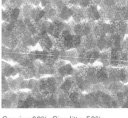

Spacing 60%; Size Jitter 50%
Angle Jitter 50%
Roundness Jitter 50%
Hue Jitter 5%
Brightness Jitter 15%

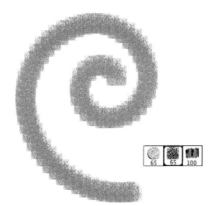

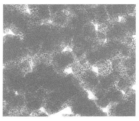

Size Jitter 50%
Angle Jitter 50%
Scatter 200%
Count 2

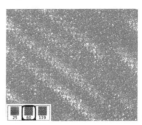

Dual Brush: Mesh

SETTINGS

Scatter 100%

Angle Jitter 50%
Hue Jitter 20%

Spacing 80%
Wet Edges

Angle 30°
Roundness 80%

Spacing 25%
Brightness Jitter 25%

Spacing 100%
Size Jitter 50%
Angle Jitter 100%
Wet Edges

Scatter 20%
Saturation Jitter 50%
Noise

Roundness Jitter 50%
Scatter 0%
Flow Jitter 100%

Spacing 60%
Angle Jitter 50%
Hue Jitter 50%

Spacing 20%
Scatter 150%
Brightness Jitter 10%

TEXTURE COMB 1

Angle 30°
Spacing 100%

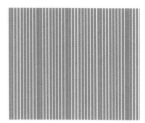

Default Brush

Scatter 200%
Foreground/Background Jitter 100%

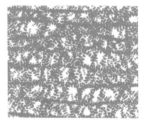

Spacing 50%
Size Jitter 50%
Angle Jitter 100%

SETTINGS

Hue Jitter 20%

Angle 30°
Spacing 25%
Brightness Jitter 20%
Wet Edges

Opacity Jitter 50%

Size Jitter 50%
Scatter 10%
Count 5
Count Jitter 100%
Foreground/Background
Jitter 50%

Angle Jitter 50%
Roundness Jitter 50%
Saturation Jitter 50%

Angle 20°
Angle Jitter 50%

Scatter 50%
Opacity Jitter 50%

Roundness 50%
Spacing 25%
Hue Jitter 20%

Roundness 50%
Spacing 50%

Roundness 80%
Spacing 200%
Brightness Jitter 100%

TEXTURE COMB 2

Angle 30°
Roundness 50%

Hue Jitter 25%
Purity +25%
Noise
Wet Edges

Scatter 100%
Foreground/Background Jitter 100%
Hue Jitter 20%
Opacity Jitter 100%
Wet Edges

Angle 50°
Spacing 25%
Size Jitter 50%
Saturation Jitter 50%
Purity +50%

SETTINGS

Angle 30°
Noise
Wet Edges

Roundness 80%
Spacing 10%
Scatter 50%

Scatter 50%
Foreground/Background
Jitter 100%

Angle Jitter 50%
Opacity Jitter 10%

Roundness 90%
Roundness Jitter 50%
Brightness Jitter 50%
Flow Jitter 80%

Foreground/Background
Jitter 100%

Dual Brush: Soft Round

Dual Brush: Mesh
Spacing 50%
Scatter 25%

Spacing 50%
Angle Jitter 50%
Count 2

Dual Brush: Hard Round
Spacing 70%
Scatter 50%
Wet Edges

TEXTURE COMB 3

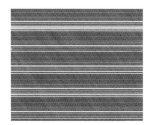

Scatter 0%
Count 2
Foreground/Background Jitter 50%

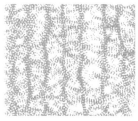

Spacing 10%
Angle Jitter 50%
Wet Edges

Angle 90°
Roundness 30%

Scatter 200%
Hue Jitter 30%

SETTINGS

Dual Brush:
Veining Feather 2

Spacing 50%
Hue Jitter 25%

Angle 50°
Scatter 0%
Flow Jitter 50%
Noise

Spacing 100%
Angle Jitter 80%

Count 10
Count Jitter 100%

Dual Brush: Soft Round
Spacing 60%
Scatter 60%
Hue Jitter 50%

Scatter 50%
Flow Jitter 50%

Dual Brush:
Texture Comb 1
Spacing 60%
Foreground/Background
Jitter 100%

Saturation Jitter 50%
Noise
Wet Edges

Angle Jitter 100%
Roundness Jitter 100%
Minimum Roundness 1%

VEINING FEATHER 1

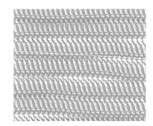

Spacing 50%
Wet Edges

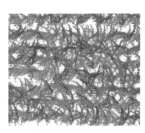

Angle Jitter 25%
Brightness Jitter 20%

Angle 30°
Roundness 80%
Foreground/Background Jitter 50%
Hue Jitter 50%

Roundness Jitter 50%
Scatter 100%
Count 3
Brightness Jitter 20%

SETTINGS

Angle 35°
Roundness 80%

Saturation Jitter 20%
Brightness Jitter 20%

Spacing 100%
Angle Jitter 50%

Dual Brush: Mesh
Scatter 400%
Hue Jitter 10%
Wet Edges

Angle 30°
Roundness 50%
Roundness Jitter 50%

Angle 133°
Size Jitter 100%
Roundness Jitter 50%

Angle 75°
Opacity Jitter 80%

Dual Brush: Soft Round
Spacing 100%
Noise
Wet Edges

Spacing 1%
Angle Jitter 100%
Foreground/Background
Jitter 80%

Saturation Jitter 100%
Brightness Jitter 100%

VEINING FEATHER 2

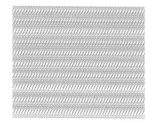

Default

Angle 85°
Spacing 10%
Angle Jitter 25%
Foreground/Background Jitter 50%

Size Jitter 100%
Angle Jitter 50%
Roundness Jitter 100%
Saturation Jitter 50%

Angle Jitter 100%
Scatter 100%
Count 10
Foreground/Background Jitter 100%

SETTINGS

Scatter 80%
Count 5

Spacing 10%
Angle Jitter 50%
Hue Jitter 20%

Count 10
Count Jitter 50%

Spacing 50%
Size Jitter 60%
Foreground/Background
Jitter 50%

Angle Jitter 100%
Scatter 50%
Count 5
Count Jitter 50%

Spacing 1%
Angle Jitter 20%
Hue Jitter 10%

Scatter 50%
Count 5
Count Jitter 50%

Saturation Jitter 50%
Brightness Jitter 50%
Opacity Jitter 100%

Angle 25°
Spacing 5%
Noise

Roundness 80%
Count 5
Brightness Jitter 50%

CROSSHATCH GESTURE

Dual Brush: Size 210px
Spacing 44%; Scatter 400%
Count 2
Hue Jitter 100%
Brightness Jitter 100%
Purity +100%

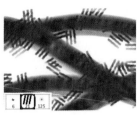

Dual Brush: Size 46px
Spacing 81%; Scatter 332%
Count 1
Hue Jitter 100%
Brightness Jitter 100%
Purity +100%

Dual Brush: Size 53px
Spacing 81%
Scatter 332%
Count 1
Wet Edges

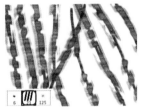

Dual Brush: Size 53px
Spacing 81%
Scatter 332%
Count 3
Hue Jitter 100%
Brightness Jitter 100%
Purity +100%
Wet Edges

SETTINGS

Dual Brush: Size 47px
Spacing 44%
Scatter 400%
Count 2
Hue Jitter 100%
Brightness Jitter 100%
Purity +100%
Wet Edges

Dual Brush: Size 47px
Spacing 44%
Scatter 400%
Count 2
Hue Jitter 100%
Wet Edges

Dual Brush: Size 53px
Spacing 81%
Scatter 332%
Count 1
Foreground/Background
Jitter 100%
Brightness Jitter 60%

Angle Jitter 100%
Dual Brush: Size 53px
Spacing 81%
Scatter 332%; Count 1
Foreground/Background
Jitter 100%
Brightness Jitter 60%
Wet Edges

Dual Brush: Size 53px
Spacing 81%
Scatter 332%
Count 2
Foreground/Background
Jitter 100%

Dual Brush: Size 53px
Spacing 81%
Scatter 600%; Count 3
Foreground/Background
Jitter 100%
Hue Jitter 100%
Purity -26%; Wet Edges

Dual Brush: Size 14px
Spacing 81%
Scatter 200%
Count 3
Hue Jitter 100%
Purity +100%

Dual Brush: Size 9px
Spacing 81%
Scatter 200%
Count 2
Hue Jitter 100%
Purity +100%

Dual Brush: Size 22px
Spacing 110%
Scatter 800%
Count 4
Hue Jitter 100%
Purity +100%

Dual Brush: Size 36px
Spacing 400%
Scatter 20%
Count 1
Hue Jitter 100%
Purity +100%
Wet Edges

BIG FUZZY

Scatter 31%
Dual Brush: Size 446px
Spacing 264%; Scatter 0%; Count 1
Hue Jitter 50%
Purity +100%
Wet Edges

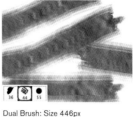

Dual Brush: Size 446px
Spacing 264%; Scatter 0%
Count 11
Hue Jitter 50%
Purity +100%
Wet Edges

Angle Jitter 100%
Dual Brush: Size 893px
Spacing 62%; Scatter 0%; Count 2
Hue Jitter 100%
Purity +100%
Wet Edges

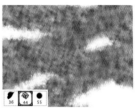

Scatter 82%
Dual Brush: Size 298px
Spacing 14%; Scatter 97%; Count 2
Hue Jitter 100%
Purity +100%
Wet Edges

SETTINGS

Scatter 82%
Dual Brush: Size 298px
Spacing 14%
Scatter 97%
Count 2
Hue Jitter 100%
Purity +100%
Wet Edges

Dual Brush: Size 134px
Spacing 264%
Scatter 0%
Count 1
Foreground/Background
Jitter 100%
Purity +50%

Scatter 83%
Dual Brush: Size 134px
Spacing 264%
Scatter 0%
Count 1
Foreground/Background
Jitter 100%
Purity +50%

Scatter 83%; Count 3
Dual Brush: Size 134px
Spacing 264%
Scatter 0%; Count 1
Foreground/Background
Jitter 100%
Purity +50%

Dual Brush: Size 134px
Spacing 264%
Scatter 0%
Count 1
Purity +100%

Size Jitter 100%
Dual Brush: Size 134px
Spacing 264%
Scatter 0%
Count 1
Hue Jitter 30%
Purity +100%

Size Jitter 100%
Dual Brush: Size 134px
Spacing 264%
Scatter 0%
Count 1
Hue Jitter 75%
Purity +100%

Size Jitter 100%
Dual Brush: Size 134px
Spacing 264%
Scatter 0%; Count 1
Foreground/Background
Jitter 100%; Hue Jitter
75%; Purity +100%

Dual Brush: Size 134px
Spacing 264%
Scatter 0%; Count 1
Foreground/Background
Jitter 100%
Hue Jitter 75%
Purity +35%

Dual Brush: Size 134px
Spacing 264%
Scatter 0%; Count 1
Hue Jitter 75%
Purity +100%
Opacity Jitter 100%
Wet Edges

DRY BRUSH

Foreground/Background Jitter 57%
Hue Jitter 100%

Foreground/Background Jitter 57%
Hue Jitter 100%
Brightness Jitter 100%
Purity +100%

Spacing 20%
Foreground/Background Jitter 57%
Hue Jitter 100%

Foreground/Background Jitter 100%
Hue Jitter 100%
Purity +100%
Opacity Jitter 35%

SETTINGS

Foreground/Background
Jitter 100%
Hue Jitter 100%
Purity +100%
Opacity Jitter 35%

Foreground/Background
Jitter 40%
Hue Jitter 100%

Size Jitter 100%
Foreground/Background
Jitter 100%
Hue Jitter 100%

Size Jitter 100%
Dual Brush: Size 60px
Spacing 81%
Scatter 0%; Count 3
Foreground/Background
Jitter 100%
Hue Jitter 100%

Size Jitter 100%
Dual Brush: Size 60px
Spacing 81%
Scatter 0%
Count 3
Hue Jitter 100%
Purity +100%

Dual Brush: Size 60px
Spacing 81%
Scatter 0%
Count 3
Hue Jitter 100%
Purity +100%

Dual Brush: Size 60px
Spacing 81%
Scatter 0%
Count 6
Foreground/Background
Jitter 100%
Brightness Jitter 100%

Dual Brush: Size 60px
Spacing 81%
Scatter 0%; Count 10
Foreground/Background
Jitter 100%
Hue Jitter 20%
Brightness Jitter 100%

Dual Brush: Size 300px
Spacing 81%; Scatter 0%
Count 2; Foreground/
Background Jitter 100%
Hue Jitter 20%
Brightness Jitter 100%
Wet Edges

Dual Brush: Size 31px
Spacing 81%
Scatter 0%
Count 2
Foreground/Background
Jitter 100%
Hue Jitter 20%

CHALK BRUSH

Purity +100%

Hue Jitter 50%
Purity +100%
Wet Edges

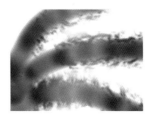

Dual Brush: Size 337px
Spacing 48%
Scatter 350%
Count 1
Foreground/Background Jitter 100%
Hue Jitter 50%

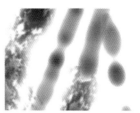

Dual Brush: Size 337px
Spacing 48%
Scatter 350%; Count 1
Foreground/Background Jitter 100%
Hue Jitter 100%
Flow Jitter 100%

SETTINGS

Hue Jitter 100%
Purity +100%

Hue Jitter 100%
Purity +40%
Wet Edges

Foreground/Background
Jitter 50%
Hue Jitter 50%
Purity +40%

Dual Brush: Size 90px
Spacing 100%
Scatter 0%; Count 1
Foreground/Background
Jitter 50%
Hue Jitter 12%
Flow Jitter 100%

Dual Brush: Size 90px
Spacing 100%
Scatter 400%; Count 3
Foreground/Background
Jitter 50%
Hue Jitter 12%
Flow Jitter 100%

Scatter 120%
Count 2
Hue Jitter 75%

Scatter 200%
Count 2
Foreground/Background
Jitter 100%
Hue Jitter 75%
Wet Edges

Scatter 200%
Count 2
Foreground/Background
Jitter 100%
Hue Jitter 75%

Scatter 75%
Count 2
Foreground/Background
Jitter 100%
Brightness Jitter 75%
Flow Jitter 100%

Scatter 75%
Count 3
Foreground/Background
Jitter 100%
Hue Jitter 25%
Brightness Jitter 75%
Flow Jitter 100%

SQUARE CHAR

Scatter 120%
Count 1
Hue Jitter 20%

Hue Jitter 20%

Foreground/Background Jitter 100%
Hue Jitter 20%
Brightness Jitter 100%

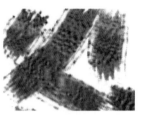

Foreground/Background Jitter 100%
Hue Jitter 100%
Brightness Jitter 50%

SETTINGS

Foreground/Background
Jitter 100%
Hue Jitter 100%
Brightness Jitter 50%
Wet Edges

Scatter 150%
Foreground/Background
Jitter 100%
Hue Jitter 100%
Brightness Jitter 50%

Scatter 150%
Count 2
Opacity Jitter 100%

Scatter 150%
Count 2
Hue Jitter 50%
Brightness Jitter 50%
Opacity Jitter 100%

Foreground/Background
Jitter 25%
Hue Jitter 25%
Purity -25%

Scatter 300%
Count 1
Foreground/Background
Jitter 25%
Hue Jitter 25%
Purity -25%

Scatter 300%
Count 1
Foreground/Background
Jitter 25%
Hue Jitter 100%
Purity +100%

Size Jitter 100%
Foreground/Background
Jitter 25%
Hue Jitter 100%
Purity +100%

Size Jitter 100%
Foreground/Background
Jitter 25%
Hue Jitter 100%
Purity -50%

Size Jitter 100%
Foreground/Background
Jitter 25%
Hue Jitter 50%
Purity +50%

CLOSE
CROSSHATCH

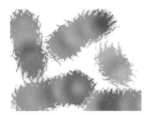

Hue Jitter 30%

Scatter 50%
Count 2
Hue Jitter 30%
Brightness Jitter 50%

Hue Jitter 100%

Foreground/Background Jitter 100%
Hue Jitter 33%
Wet Edges

SETTINGS

Foreground/Background
Jitter 100%
Hue Jitter 33%

Scatter 200%
Count 1
Foreground/Background
Jitter 100%
Hue Jitter 33%

Scatter 20%
Count 1
Foreground/Background
Jitter 100%
Hue Jitter 15%
Purity +100%

Dual Brush:
Spacing 125%

Dual Brush: Size 35px
Spacing 125%
Scatter 0%
Count 1

Dual Brush: Size 35px
Spacing 125%
Scatter 0%
Count 1
Foreground/Background
Jitter 100%
Purity +100%

Saturation Jitter 100%
Purity +50%

Hue Jitter 45%
Saturation Jitter 100%
Purity +50%

Hue Jitter 45%
Saturation Jitter 100%
Purity +50%
Wet Edges

Hue Jitter 80%
Brightness Jitter 100%
Purity +50%
Wet Edges

CROSSHATCH

Brightness Jitter 100%

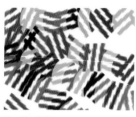
Hue Jitter 60%
Brightness Jitter 60%

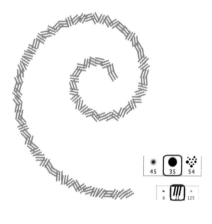

Dual Brush: Size 90px
Spacing 35%
Scatter 0%
Count 1
Hue Jitter 60%

Dual Brush: Size 156px
Spacing 81%
Scatter 0%
Count 1
Wet Edges

SETTINGS

Hue Jitter 100%

Dual Brush: Size 27px
Spacing 15%
Scatter 0%
Count 1
Foreground/Background
Jitter 100%
Hue Jitter 100%

Dual Brush: Size 27px
Spacing 15%
Scatter 0%
Count 1
Foreground/Background
Jitter 20%
Hue Jitter 20%
Purity +100%

Dual Brush: Size 21px
Spacing 200%
Scatter 0%
Count 3
Foreground/Background
Jitter 100%
Opacity Jitter 100%
Wet Edges

Dual Brush: Size 21px
Spacing 200%
Scatter 100%
Count 3
Hue Jitter 100%
Flow Jitter 100%
Wet Edges

Dual Brush: Size 21px
Spacing 200%
Scatter 100%
Count 3
Hue Jitter 100%
Flow Jitter 100%

Dual Brush: Size 21px
Spacing 150%
Scatter 100%
Count 4
Hue Jitter 60%
Purity +100%

Dual Brush: Size 21px
Spacing 60%
Scatter 100%
Count 2
Hue Jitter 30%
Purity +100%

Dual Brush: Size 21px
Spacing 60%
Scatter 100%; Count 2
Hue Jitter 30%
Brightness Jitter 100%
Purity +100%
Wet Edges

Dual Brush: Size 21px
Spacing 20%
Scatter 100%
Count 1
Hue Jitter 30%
Brightness Jitter 100%

FROSTED GLASS

Hue Jitter 15%

Dual Brush: Size 125px
Spacing 60%; Scatter 0%; Count 1
Foreground/Background Jitter 100%

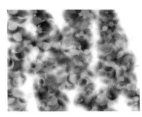

Dual Brush: Size 125px
Spacing 60%; Scatter 0%; Count 1
Foreground/Background Jitter 100%
Hue Jitter 33%
Purity +100%

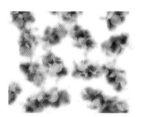

Dual Brush: Size 125px
Spacing 85%; Scatter 0%; Count 1
Foreground/Background Jitter 100%
Hue Jitter 100%
Purity +100%

SETTINGS

Dual Brush: Size 38px
Spacing 85%
Scatter 0%
Count 1
Foreground/Background
Jitter 100%
Hue Jitter 100%
Purity +100%

Dual Brush: Size 29px
Spacing 60%
Scatter 90%
Count 2
Foreground/Background
Jitter 100%
Hue Jitter 100%
Purity +100%

Dual Brush: Size 29px
Spacing 60%
Scatter 90%; Count 2
Foreground/Background
Jitter 100%
Hue Jitter 25%
Purity +100%
Wet Edges

Dual Brush: Size 29px
Spacing 30%
Scatter 60%
Count 1
Hue Jitter 25%
Purity +100%

Dual Brush: Size 29px
Spacing 30%
Scatter 60%
Count 1
Hue Jitter 25%

Dual Brush: Size 29px
Spacing 10%
Scatter 60%
Count 1
Hue Jitter 25%
Wet Edges

Dual Brush: Size 29px
Spacing 75%
Scatter 60%
Count 3
Foreground/Background
Jitter 100%
Brightness Jitter 100%

Dual Brush: Size 29px
Spacing 75%
Scatter 60%; Count 3
Foreground/Background
Jitter 100%; Hue
Jitter 100%; Brightness
Jitter 100%; Purity -33%

Dual Brush: Size 33px
Spacing 75%
Scatter 150%
Count 1
Hue Jitter 50%

Dual Brush: Size 33px
Spacing 75%
Scatter 150%
Count 1
Hue Jitter 100%
Purity +100%

FUZZY CLUSTER LOOSE

Dual Brush: Size 167px
Spacing 40%; Scatter 250%; Count 3
Hue Jitter 55%

Dual Brush: Size 167px
Spacing 50%; Scatter 250%; Count 2
Hue Jitter 100%
Purity +100%

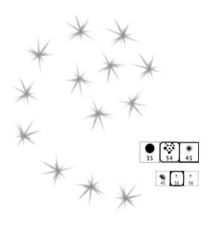

Dual Brush: Size 167px
Spacing 25%; Scatter 50%; Count 1
Hue Jitter 100%
Brightness Jitter 50%
Purity +40%

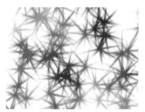

Dual Brush: Size 167px
Spacing 20%; Scatter 50%; Count 1
Foreground/Background Jitter 100%
Hue Jitter 30%
Purity +40%
Wet Edges

SETTINGS

Dual Brush: Size 56px
Spacing 20%
Scatter 50%; Count 1
Foreground/Background
Jitter 100%
Hue Jitter 30%
Purity +40%
Wet Edges

Dual Brush: Size 56px
Spacing 20%
Scatter 50%
Count 1
Hue Jitter 30%
Purity +40%
Wet Edges

Dual Brush: Size 67px
Spacing 85%
Scatter 0%
Count 1
Foreground/Background
Jitter 80%
Purity +30%

Dual Brush: Size 67px
Spacing 85%
Scatter 0%
Count 3
Foreground/Background
Jitter 80%
Hue Jitter 60%
Purity +30%

Dual Brush: Size 67px
Spacing 60%
Scatter 0%; Count 3
Foreground/Background
Jitter 80%
Hue Jitter 60%
Purity +30%
Wet Edges

Dual Brush: Size 67px
Spacing 45%
Scatter 0%; Count 2
Foreground/Background
Jitter 80%
Hue Jitter 100%
Purity +30%

Dual Brush: Size 67px
Spacing 45%
Scatter 90%
Count 2
Hue Jitter 100%
Purity +30%

Dual Brush: Size 50px
Spacing 50%
Scatter 180%; Count 3
Hue Jitter 100%
Saturation Jitter 100%
Brightness Jitter 100%
Wet Edges

Dual Brush: Size 33px
Spacing 25%
Scatter 100%
Count 3
Hue Jitter 100%
Saturation Jitter 100%
Wet Edges

Dual Brush: Size 67px
Spacing 60%
Scatter 0%; Count 1
Foreground/Background
Jitter 100%; Hue
Jitter 100%; Saturation
Jitter 60%; Wet Edges

FUZZY CLUSTER TIGHT

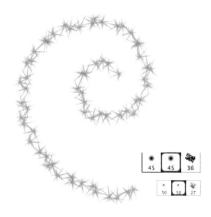

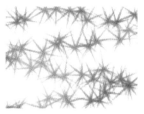

Dual Brush: Size 50px
Spacing 25%; Scatter 0%; Count 1
Foreground/Background Jitter 40%
Hue Jitter 100%
Noise

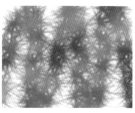

Dual Brush: Size 167px
Spacing 25%; Scatter 0%; Count 5
Foreground/Background Jitter 40%
Hue Jitter 100%

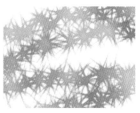

Dual Brush: Size 167px
Spacing 25%; Scatter 0%; Count 1
Hue Jitter 100%
Wet Edges

Dual Brush: Size 100px
Spacing 25%; Scatter 125%; Count 4
Hue Jitter 100%
Purity +100%

SETTINGS

Dual Brush: Size 100px
Spacing 25%
Scatter 125%
Count 4
Hue Jitter 100%
Purity +100%

Dual Brush: Size 50px
Spacing 25%
Scatter 0%
Count 1
Hue Jitter 100%
Purity +100%

Dual Brush: Size 50px
Spacing 25%
Scatter 0%
Count 3
Hue Jitter 100%
Purity +100%

Dual Brush: Size 50px
Spacing 15%
Scatter 0%
Count 3
Hue Jitter 100%
Purity +35%
Wet Edges

Dual Brush: Size 50px
Spacing 15%
Scatter 0%
Count 3
Hue Jitter 100%

Dual Brush: Size 50px
Spacing 15%
Scatter 0%
Count 2
Foreground/Background
Jitter 100%
Hue Jitter 40%

Scatter 250%
Dual Brush: Size 44px
Spacing 15%
Scatter 0%; Count 2
Foreground/Background
Jitter 100%
Hue Jitter 40%

Scatter 0%; Count 16
Dual Brush: Size 44px
Spacing 15%
Scatter 0%; Count 2
Foreground/Background
Jitter 100%
Hue Jitter 40%

Scatter 0%
Count 16
Dual Brush: Size 44px
Spacing 15%
Scatter 50%
Count 6
Brightness Jitter 40%

Dual Brush: Size 44px
Spacing 15%
Scatter 50%
Count 6
Brightness Jitter 40%
Wet Edges

WASH WITH BLEEDS

Scatter 600%
Dual Brush: Size 68px
Spacing 5%; Scatter 37%; Count 3

Scatter 600%
Dual Brush: Size 68px
Spacing 5%; Scatter 37%; Count 3
Foreground/Background Jitter 100%
Purity +100%

Scatter 600%
Dual Brush: Size 68px
Spacing 5%; Scatter 37%; Count 3
Hue Jitter 100%
Foreground/Background Jitter 100%
Purity +100%

Dual Brush: Size 68px
Spacing 100%; Scatter 37%; Count 3
Hue Jitter 50%
Purity +100%

SETTINGS

Dual Brush: Size 68px
Spacing 100%
Scatter 37%
Count 3
Hue Jitter 50%
Purity +100%
Wet Edges

Scatter 600%
Dual Brush: Size 68px
Spacing 5%
Scatter 37%
Count 3

Scatter 600%
Dual Brush: Size 68px
Spacing 5%
Scatter 37%
Count 3
Hue Jitter 50%

Scatter 600%
Dual Brush: Size 27px
Spacing 80%
Scatter 37%; Count 3
Foreground/Background
Jitter 50%
Hue Jitter 50%
Wet Edges

Dual Brush: Size 34px
Spacing 50%
Scatter 37%
Count 1
Foreground/Background
Jitter 50%
Hue Jitter 50%
Brightness Jitter 25%

Dual Brush: Size 28px
Spacing 120%
Scatter 10%
Count 4
Foreground/Background
Jitter 25%
Hue Jitter 75%

Dual Brush: Size 28px
Spacing 120%
Scatter 300%; Count 4
Foreground/Background
Jitter 25%
Hue Jitter 75%
Wet Edges

Dual Brush: Size 28px
Spacing 120%
Scatter 200%; Count 4
Foreground/Background
Jitter 25%
Hue Jitter 75%
Purity +100%; Wet Edges

Dual Brush: Size 28px
Spacing 75%
Scatter 200%; Count 4
Foreground/Background
Jitter 25%
Hue Jitter 75%
Purity +100%

Dual Brush: Size 28px
Spacing 60%
Scatter 100%; Count 3
Foreground/Background
Jitter 25%
Hue Jitter 75%
Purity +100%

INK ON ROUGH

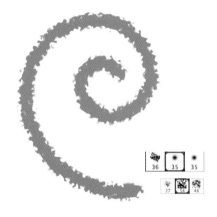

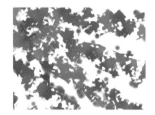

Scatter 200%
Dual Brush: Size 77px
Spacing 80%; Scatter 0%; Count 1
Foreground/Background Jitter 50%
Purity +100%

Dual Brush: Size 135px
Spacing 100%; Scatter 0%; Count 1
Foreground/Background Jitter 50%
Hue Jitter 20%
Purity +15%

Dual Brush: Size 135px
Spacing 100%; Scatter 0%; Count 1
Foreground/Background Jitter 50%
Hue Jitter 100%
Purity +15%
Wet Edges

Dual Brush: Size 135px
Spacing 120%; Scatter 0%; Count 3
Foreground/Background Jitter 50%
Hue Jitter 100%
Purity +15%
Wet Edges
Noise

SETTINGS

Dual Brush: Size 39px
Spacing 100%
Scatter 0%
Count 1

Dual Brush: Size 39px
Spacing 100%
Scatter 0%
Count 1
Foreground/Background
Jitter 50%
Brightness Jitter 100%

Scatter 200%
Dual Brush: Size 39px
Spacing 100%
Scatter 0%
Count 1
Foreground/Background
Jitter 50%
Brightness Jitter 100%

Scatter 200%
Dual Brush: Size 39px
Spacing 100%
Scatter 0%; Count 1
Foreground/Background
Jitter 50%
Hue Jitter 100%
Brightness Jitter 100%

Dual Brush: Size 39px
Spacing 100%
Scatter 0%
Count 1
Foreground/Background
Jitter 50%
Hue Jitter 100%
Purity +100%

Dual Brush: Size 39px
Spacing 100%
Scatter 0%; Count 1
Foreground/Background
Jitter 50%
Hue Jitter 100%
Purity -33%; Wet Edges

Dual Brush: Size 39px
Spacing 100%
Scatter 300%
Count 2
Foreground/Background
Jitter 50%
Hue Jitter 100%

Dual Brush: Size 39px
Spacing 100%
Scatter 300%
Count 1
Hue Jitter 100%
Purity +100%

Dual Brush: Size 39px
Spacing 145%
Scatter 135%
Count 1
Hue Jitter 100%
Purity +100%

Dual Brush: Size 39px
Spacing 145%
Scatter 135%
Count 1
Hue Jitter 100%
Purity +100%
Wet Edges

GRANITE

Dual Brush: Size 123px
Spacing 43%; Scatter 0%; Count 1
Foreground/Background Jitter 100%
Brightness Jitter 15%
Purity -55%

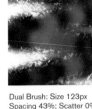

Dual Brush: Size 123px
Spacing 43%; Scatter 0%; Count 1
Foreground/Background Jitter 100%
Brightness Jitter 80%
Purity +100%

Dual Brush: Size 123px
Spacing 43%; Scatter 0%; Count 1
Foreground/Background Jitter 25%
Brightness Jitter 25%
Purity +50%

Size Jitter 100%
Dual Brush: Size 206px
Spacing 100%; Scatter 0%; Count 1
Foreground/Background Jitter 25%
Hue Jitter 100%
Noise

SETTINGS

Scatter 550%
Count 1
Dual Brush: Size 10px
Spacing 43%
Scatter 0%
Count 1

Scatter 235%
Count 1
Dual Brush: Size 10px
Spacing 43%
Scatter 0%
Count 1
Foreground/Background
Jitter 100%

Dual Brush: Size 34px
Spacing 43%
Scatter 75%; Count 2
Foreground/Background
Jitter 100%
Hue Jitter 55%
Opacity Jitter 100%
Wet Edges

Dual Brush: Size 34px
Spacing 43%
Scatter 75%
Count 2
Foreground/Background
Jitter 55%
Hue Jitter 55%
Opacity Jitter 100%

Dual Brush: Size 48px
Spacing 43%
Scatter 300%
Count 1
Foreground/Background
Jitter 55%
Hue Jitter 55%
Opacity Jitter 100%

Dual Brush: Size 48px
Spacing 65%
Scatter 300%; Count 1
Foreground/Background
Jitter 100%
Hue Jitter 55%
Opacity Jitter 100%

Dual Brush: Size 48px
Spacing 65%
Scatter 175%; Count 1
Foreground/Background
Jitter 100%
Hue Jitter 55%
Opacity Jitter 60%

Dual Brush: Size 48px
Spacing 65%
Scatter 175%; Count 1
Foreground/Background
Jitter 100%; Hue
Jitter 55%; Opacity
Jitter 60%; Wet Edges

Dual Brush: Size 48px
Spacing 50%
Scatter 600%; Count 2
Foreground/Background
Jitter 100%; Hue
Jitter 100%; Purity +100%
Opacity Jitter 25%

Dual Brush: Size 48px
Spacing 20%
Scatter 240%
Count 1
Hue Jitter 100%
Purity +25%
Opacity Jitter 25%

HYPNO LINE

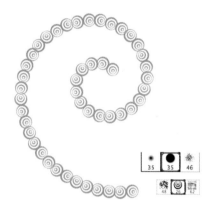

Dual Brush: Size 93px
Spacing 85%; Scatter 0%; Count 1
Hue Jitter 100%
Purity +25%
Wet Edges

Dual Brush: Size 93px
Spacing 46%; Scatter 0%; Count 1
Hue Jitter 100%
Purity +100%

Dual Brush: Size 93px
Spacing 46%; Scatter 0%; Count 1
Hue Jitter 100%
Purity +100%
Opacity Jitter 100%

Dual Brush: Size 93px
Spacing 46%; Scatter 56%; Count 4
Hue Jitter 50%
Purity +50%
Opacity Jitter 100%
Wet Edges

SETTINGS

Dual Brush: Size 26px
Spacing 46%
Scatter 56%
Count 4
Hue Jitter 50%
Purity +50%
Opacity Jitter 100%

Dual Brush: Size 26px
Spacing 46%
Scatter 56%; Count 4
Foreground/Background
Jitter 100%
Hue Jitter 50%
Purity +50%
Opacity Jitter 50%

Dual Brush: Size 26px
Spacing 33%
Scatter 56%
Count 1
Foreground/Background
Jitter 100%
Hue Jitter 50%
Opacity Jitter 50%

Dual Brush: Size 26px
Spacing 100%
Scatter 56%
Count 1
Foreground/Background
Jitter 100%
Hue Jitter 50%

Dual Brush: Size 26px
Spacing 100%
Scatter 0%
Count 3
Foreground/Background
Jitter 25%
Hue Jitter 100%

Dual Brush: Size 26px
Spacing 100%
Scatter 50%; Count 3
Foreground/Background
Jitter 25%
Hue Jitter 100%
Wet Edges

Dual Brush: Size 26px
Spacing 100%
Scatter 50%; Count 3
Hue Jitter 100%
Purity +100%
Opacity Jitter 50%
Wet Edges

Dual Brush: Size 26px
Spacing 65%
Scatter 420%
Count 2
Hue Jitter 100%
Purity +100%

Dual Brush: Size 24px
Spacing 160%
Scatter 0%
Count 9
Hue Jitter 100%
Purity +100%
Wet Edges

Dual Brush: Size 33px
Spacing 160%
Scatter 0%; Count 3
Foreground/Background
Jitter 100%
Hue Jitter 15%
Purity +100%

JUMBLE GRID

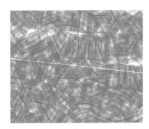

Scatter 200%

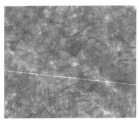

Size Jitter 100%
Angle Jitter 50%
Roundness Jitter 100%
Hue Jitter 50%

Scatter 550%
Dual Brush: Size 94 px
Spacing 43%; Scatter 0%; Count 2
Hue Jitter 100%
Purity +100%
Noise

Dual Brush: Size 94 px
Spacing 43%; Scatter 0%; Count 2
Hue Jitter 100%
Purity +100%

SETTINGS

Scatter 550%
Dual Brush: Size 94 px
Spacing 43%
Scatter 0%
Count 2
Hue Jitter 100%
Purity +100%
Wet Edges

Dual Brush: Size 27 px
Spacing 110%
Scatter 0%
Count 2
Hue Jitter 100%
Purity +100%

Dual Brush: Size 40 px
Spacing 110%
Scatter 0%
Count 2
Foreground/Background
Jitter 100%
Hue Jitter 100%

Dual Brush: Size 40 px
Spacing 110%
Scatter 300%
Count 2
Foreground/Background
Jitter 100%
Hue Jitter 100%
Purity +100%

Dual Brush: Size 40 px
Spacing 110%
Scatter 200%; Count 2
Foreground/Background
Jitter 100%
Hue Jitter 100%
Purity +100%
Opacity Jitter 50%

Dual Brush: Size 40 px
Spacing 150%
Scatter 0%
Count 5
Hue Jitter 100%
Purity +100%

Scatter 66%
Dual Brush: Size 40 px
Spacing 1%
Scatter 550%
Count 2
Hue Jitter 100%
Purity +100%

Scatter 550%
Dual Brush: Size 27 px
Spacing 7%
Scatter 0%
Count 1
Hue Jitter 100%
Purity +100%

Scatter 550%
Dual Brush: Size 27 px
Spacing 7%
Scatter 0%; Count 1
Hue Jitter 100%
Brightness Jitter 100%
Purity -30%; Wet Edges

Dual Brush: Size 27 px
Spacing 7%
Scatter 0%
Count 1
Hue Jitter 100%
Brightness Jitter 100%
Purity -30%

LEAF WITH TILT AND COLOR

Size Jitter 100%
Scatter 100%
Count 1
Foreground/Background Jitter 100%

Size Jitter 100%
Scatter 100%
Count 6
Foreground/Background Jitter 100%
Saturation Jitter 100%

Size Jitter 100%; Scatter 100%
Count 6; Count Jitter 33%
Foreground/Background Jitter 100%
Saturation Jitter 100%; Wet Edges

Size Jitter 100%; Scatter 100%
Count 3; Count Jitter 33%
Foreground/Background Jitter 100%
Hue Jitter 50%; Saturation Jitter 100%

SETTINGS

Size Jitter 100%
Angle Jitter 40%
Count 3
Foreground/Background
Jitter 100%
Hue Jitter 50%

Scatter 110%
Size Jitter 100%
Angle Jitter 40%
Count 3
Foreground/Background
Jitter 100%
Hue Jitter 50%
Wet Edges

Angle Jitter 20%
Roundness Jitter 100%
Scatter 40%
Count 4
Foreground/Background
Jitter 50%
Hue Jitter 50%
Purity +100%

Angle Jitter 20%
Roundness Jitter 100%
Scatter 40%
Count 4
Foreground/Background
Jitter 50%
Hue Jitter 100%
Purity +100%

Angle Jitter 20%
Roundness Jitter 100%
Scatter 40%
Count 1
Foreground/Background
Jitter 50%
Hue Jitter 100%
Purity +100%

Brightness Jitter 100%

Hue Jitter 100%
Brightness Jitter 100%
Purity +100%

Spacing 100%
Angle Jitter 100%
Scatter 15%
Count 7; Hue Jitter 100%
Brightness Jitter 100%
Purity +100%
Opacity Jitter 75%

Spacing 100%
Angle Jitter 100%
Scatter 15%
Count 2
Hue Jitter 100%
Brightness Jitter 100%
Purity +100%

Spacing 100%
Angle Jitter 100%
Scatter 15%
Count 7
Brightness Jitter 100%
Purity +100%
Opacity Jitter 75%

HAIRY WITH LIGHT TEXT

Scatter 200%; Count 1
Dual Brush: Size 60 px
Spacing 10%; Scatter 0%; Count 1
Hue Jitter 100%; Brightness
Jitter 100%; Purity +100%

Flow 25%
Dual Brush: Size 104 px
Spacing 30%; Scatter 0%; Count 1

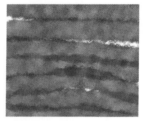

Scatter 800%
Count 3
Dual Brush: Size 60 px
Spacing 30%; Scatter 0%; Count 1
Foreground/Background Jitter 100%
Wet Edges

Dual Brush: Size 60 px
Spacing 10%; Scatter 0%; Count 1
Foreground/Background Jitter 100%
Hue Jitter 80%
Brightness Jitter 50%

SETTINGS

Scatter 370%
Count 1
Dual Brush: Size 3 px
Spacing 93%
Scatter 0%
Count 1

Scatter 370%; Count 1
Dual Brush: Size 33 px
Spacing 93%
Scatter 0%; Count 1
Foreground/Background
Jitter 100%
Brightness Jitter 100%
Purity +100%

Dual Brush: Size 33 px
Spacing 93%
Scatter 0%; Count 1
Foreground/Background
Jitter 100%
Hue Jitter 50%
Brightness Jitter 100%
Purity +100%

Dual Brush: Size 33 px
Spacing 120%
Scatter 0%; Count 6
Foreground/Background
Jitter 100%
Hue Jitter 50%
Brightness Jitter 100%
Purity +100%

Dual Brush: Size 6 px
Spacing 90%
Scatter 0%
Count 3
Hue Jitter 100%
Purity +100%

Dual Brush: Size 46 px
Spacing 90%
Scatter 0%
Count 3
Hue Jitter 100%
Purity +100%
Wet Edges

Size Jitter 100%
Dual Brush: Size 46 px
Spacing 90%
Scatter 0%; Count 12
Hue Jitter 100%
Purity +100%; Opacity
Jitter 100%; Wet Edges

Size Jitter 100%
Dual Brush: Size 60 px
Spacing 90%
Scatter 0%; Count 1
Hue Jitter 100%
Purity +100%
Opacity Jitter 100%

Dual Brush: Size 210 px
Spacing 105%
Scatter 0%
Count 2
Hue Jitter 100%
Purity +100%
Opacity Jitter 50%

Dual Brush: Size 210 px
Spacing 105%
Scatter 0%; Count 2
Hue Jitter 100%
Purity +100%
Flow Jitter 50%
Wet Edges

LOOSE CROSSHATCH

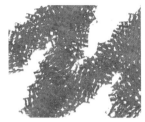

Scatter 370%; Count 1
Dual Brush: Size 93 px
Spacing 59%; Scatter 0%; Count 1
Foreground/Background Jitter 100%
Purity +100%; Wet Edges

Dual Brush: Size 104 px
Spacing 30%; Scatter 0%; Count 1
Foreground/Background Jitter 100%
Purity +100%

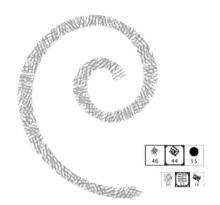

Dual Brush: Size 93 px
Spacing 93%; Scatter 0%; Count 1
Foreground/Background Jitter 50%
Hue Jitter 100%
Purity +50%
Wet Edges

Dual Brush: Size 155 px
Spacing 80%; Scatter 0%; Count 3
Foreground/Background Jitter 50%
Hue Jitter 100%
Purity +50%

SETTINGS

Dual Brush: Size 36 px
Spacing 80%
Scatter 0%
Count 3
Foreground/Background
Jitter 50%
Hue Jitter 100%
Purity +50%

Scatter 133%; Count 1
Dual Brush: Size 36 px
Spacing 80%
Scatter 0%; Count 1
Foreground/Background
Jitter 50%
Hue Jitter 100%
Purity +50%

Scatter 133%; Count 3
Dual Brush: Size 26 px
Spacing 80%
Scatter 0%; Count 1
Foreground/Background
Jitter 50%
Hue Jitter 100%
Purity +50%; Wet Edges

Scatter 133%
Count 11
Dual Brush: Size 26 px
Spacing 80%
Scatter 0%; Count 3
Foreground/Background
Jitter 100%
Brightness Jitter 100%

Dual Brush: Size 26 px
Spacing 75%
Scatter 200%
Count 1
Hue Jitter 80%
Brightness Jitter 70%
Purity +100%

Dual Brush: Size 40 px
Spacing 40%
Scatter 200%
Count 1
Hue Jitter 80%
Brightness Jitter 70%
Purity +100%

Scatter 133%; Count 1
Dual Brush: Size 16 px
Spacing 40%
Scatter 200%; Count 1
Hue Jitter 80%
Brightness Jitter 70%
Purity +100%; Wet Edges

Scatter 133%; Count 1
Dual Brush: Size 16 px
Spacing 40%
Scatter 200%; Count 8
Hue Jitter 80%
Brightness Jitter 70%
Purity +100%

Scatter 133%
Count 1
Dual Brush: Size 16 px
Spacing 40%
Scatter 200%; Count 8
Hue Jitter 15%
Purity +100%

Dual Brush: Size 36 px
Spacing 40%
Scatter 1000%
Count 4
Hue Jitter 15%
Purity +100%

ROUGH WASH

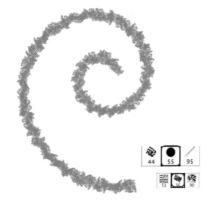

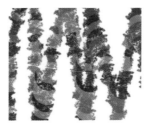

Dual Brush: Size 54 px
Spacing 43%; Scatter 0%; Count 1
Foreground/Background Jitter 100%

Dual Brush: Size 82 px
Spacing 43%; Scatter 0%; Count 1
Foreground/Background Jitter 100%
Purity +100%
Wet Edges

Dual Brush: Size 82 px
Spacing 43%; Scatter 200%; Count 1
Foreground/Background Jitter 60%
Hue Jitter 20%
Purity +100%

Dual Brush: Size 82 px
Spacing 43%; Scatter 200%; Count 1
Foreground/Background Jitter 60%
Hue Jitter 100%
Purity -20%

SETTINGS

Dual Brush: Size 82 px
Spacing 43%
Scatter 200%; Count 1
Foreground/Background
Jitter 60%
Hue Jitter 100%
Purity -20%
Wet Edges

Dual Brush: Size 82 px
Spacing 43%
Scatter 200%
Count 2
Foreground/Background
Jitter 60%
Hue Jitter 100%
Purity +55%

Dual Brush: Size 23 px
Spacing 116%
Scatter 0%
Count 2
Foreground/Background
Jitter 60%
Hue Jitter 100%
Purity +55%

Dual Brush: Size 33 px
Spacing 116%
Scatter 0%
Count 1
Foreground/Background
Jitter 60%
Hue Jitter 100%
Purity +55%

Dual Brush: Size 33 px
Spacing 116%
Scatter 0%
Count 1
Foreground/Background
Jitter 50%
Hue Jitter 50%
Purity +100%

Dual Brush: Size 33 px
Spacing 10%
Scatter 50%
Count 1
Hue Jitter 50%
Purity +100%

Dual Brush: Size 33 px
Spacing 23%
Scatter 0%
Count 1
Hue Jitter 15%
Purity +100%
Opacity Jitter 100%

Dual Brush: Size 33 px
Spacing 23%
Scatter 0%; Count 1
Hue Jitter 15%
Purity +100%
Opacity Jitter 100%
Wet Edges

Dual Brush: Size 33 px
Spacing 23%
Scatter 0%; Count 1
Hue Jitter 40%
Brightness Jitter 100%
Purity +100%
Opacity Jitter 100%

Dual Brush: Size 33 px
Spacing 23%
Scatter 0%; Count 1
Hue Jitter 40%
Brightness Jitter 40%
Purity +40%
Opacity Jitter 100%

ROUGH COMB WITH DIRECTION

Dual Brush: Size 76 px
Spacing 43%; Scatter 0%; Count 1
Foreground/Background Jitter 100%
Purity +50%

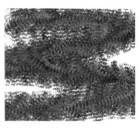

Angle Jitter 50%
Dual Brush: Size 90 px
Spacing 43%; Scatter 0%; Count 1
Foreground/Background Jitter 100%
Hue Jitter 25%; Purity +50%

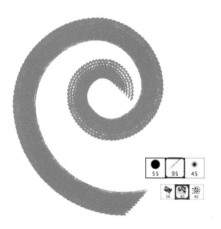

Dual Brush: Size 90 px
Spacing 43%; Scatter 0%; Count 1
Foreground/Background Jitter 100%
Hue Jitter 25%
Purity +50%

Dual Brush: Size 76 px
Spacing 90%; Scatter 0%; Count 1
Foreground/Background Jitter 100%
Hue Jitter 100%

SETTINGS

Dual Brush: Size 38 px
Spacing 90%
Scatter 0%
Count 3
Hue Jitter 100%

Size Jitter 100%
Angle Jitter 20%
Dual Brush: Size 38 px
Spacing 90%
Scatter 0%
Count 3
Hue Jitter 60%
Purity +50%

Size Jitter 100%
Angle Jitter 20%
Dual Brush: Size 38 px
Spacing 90%
Scatter 0%; Count 3
Foreground/Background
Jitter 100%; Hue Jitter
60%; Purity +50%

Size Jitter 100%
Angle Jitter 10%
Dual Brush: Size 38 px
Spacing 90%
Scatter 145%; Count 3
Foreground/Background
Jitter 100%; Hue
Jitter 60%; Purity +50%

Dual Brush: Size 38 px
Spacing 90%
Scatter 145%
Count 3
Foreground/Background
Jitter 100%
Hue Jitter 60%
Purity +50%

Dual Brush: Size 38 px
Spacing 22%
Scatter 0%
Count 1
Hue Jitter 60%
Purity +50%

Angle Jitter 10%
Dual Brush: Size 28 px
Spacing 1%
Scatter 0%
Count 1
Hue Jitter 60%
Purity +50%

Angle Jitter 10%
Scatter 300%
Dual Brush: Size 28 px
Spacing 1%
Scatter 0%; Count 1
Hue Jitter 100%
Purity +100%

Angle Jitter 10%
Scatter 300%
Dual Brush: Size 28 px
Spacing 1%
Scatter 0%; Count 1
Hue Jitter 100%
Wet Edges

Scatter 300%
Dual Brush: Size 28 px
Spacing 1%
Scatter 0%; Count 1
Hue Jitter 100%
Brightness Jitter 100%
Purity +100%

PEBBLED

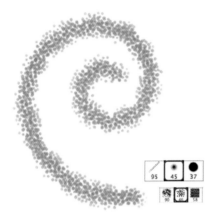

Dual Brush: Size 128 px
Spacing 55%; Scatter 0%; Count 1
Foreground/Background Jitter 100%
Hue Jitter 100%
Brightness Jitter 100%

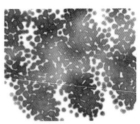

Dual Brush: Size 128 px
Spacing 55%; Scatter 0%; Count 1
Foreground/Background Jitter 100%
Hue Jitter 100%
Brightness Jitter 100%; Wet Edges

Dual Brush: Size 128 px
Spacing 55%; Scatter 0%; Count 3
Foreground/Background Jitter 100%
Brightness Jitter 100%
Wet Edges

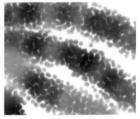

Dual Brush: Size 128 px
Spacing 55%; Scatter 0%; Count 3
Foreground/Background Jitter 100%
Brightness Jitter 100%

SETTINGS

Dual Brush: Size 128 px
Spacing 55%
Scatter 0%; Count 3
Foreground/Background
Jitter 100%
Brightness Jitter 100%
Wet Edges

Dual Brush: Size 31 px
Spacing 55%
Scatter 100%
Count 1
Foreground/Background
Jitter 50%
Brightness Jitter 50%

Dual Brush: Size 31 px
Spacing 55%
Scatter 100%
Count 1
Hue Jitter 100%
Brightness Jitter 50%

Dual Brush: Size 31 px
Spacing 55%
Scatter 0%
Count 4
Hue Jitter 100%
Brightness Jitter 50%

Dual Brush: Size 46 px
Spacing 50%
Scatter 0%
Count 1
Hue Jitter 100%

Dual Brush: Size 46 px
Spacing 50%
Scatter 170%
Count 2
Hue Jitter 100%

Dual Brush: Size 46 px
Spacing 50%
Scatter 170%
Count 2
Brightness Jitter 100%
Wet Edges

Dual Brush: Size 46 px
Spacing 50%
Scatter 170%
Count 2
Hue Jitter 100%
Brightness Jitter 50%
Purity +100%

Dual Brush:
Size 46 px
Spacing 50%
Scatter 170%; Count 16
Hue Jitter 100%
Brightness Jitter 100%
Purity +100%

Dual Brush: Size 46 px
Spacing 50%
Scatter 170%; Count 16
Hue Jitter 100%
Brightness Jitter 100%
Purity -50%
Wet Edges

SNAKESKIN

Dual Brush: Size 94 px
Spacing 80%; Scatter 0%; Count 1
Hue Jitter 100%

Dual Brush: Size 140 px
Spacing 80%; Scatter 0%; Count 1
Hue Jitter 100%
Brightness Jitter 50%
Opacity Jitter 100%

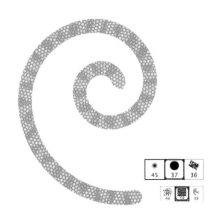

Scatter 100%
Dual Brush: Size 125 px
Spacing 80%; Scatter 0%; Count 1
Foreground/Background Jitter 100%
Brightness Jitter 50%

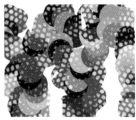

Scatter 100%; Dual Brush:
Size 125 px; Spacing 80%
Scatter 0%; Count 1
Foreground/Background Jitter 100%
Hue Jitter 50%; Brightness Jitter 50%
Purity +100%

SETTINGS

Dual Brush: Size 58 px
Spacing 80%
Scatter 0%
Count 1
Hue Jitter 50%

Size Jitter 100%
Roundness Jitter 100%
Dual Brush: Size 58 px
Spacing 80%
Scatter 0%
Count 1
Hue Jitter 50%

Size Jitter 100%
Roundness Jitter 100%
Dual Brush: Size 58 px
Spacing 80%
Scatter 0%; Count 1
Foreground/Background
Jitter 100%; Hue
Jitter 50%; Wet Edges

Size Jitter 100%
Roundness Jitter 100%
Dual Brush: Size 78 px
Spacing 80%
Scatter 0%; Count 3
Foreground/Background
Jitter 100%
Hue Jitter 50%

Dual Brush: Size 58 px
Spacing 80%
Scatter 0%
Count 1
Brightness Jitter 100%
Opacity Jitter 100%

Dual Brush: Size 58 px
Spacing 80%
Scatter 0%
Count 3
Brightness Jitter 100%
Opacity Jitter 100%

Dual Brush: Size 58 px
Spacing 100%
Scatter 0%
Count 1
Hue Jitter 100%
Brightness Jitter 33%

Dual Brush: Size 58 px
Spacing 100%
Scatter 0%
Count 1
Hue Jitter 100%
Brightness Jitter 33%
Purity +100%

Dual Brush: Size 58 px
Spacing 100%
Scatter 0%; Count 3
Hue Jitter 100%
Brightness Jitter 33%
Purity +100%
Opacity Jitter 100%

Size 100 px
Dual Brush: Size 58 px
Spacing 70%
Scatter 0%
Count 1
Hue Jitter 100%
Purity +100%

SOFT TEXTURE

Dual Brush: Size 95 px
Spacing 25%; Scatter 37%; Count 3
Foreground/Background Jitter 100%

Spacing 65%
Dual Brush: Size 95 px
Spacing 25%; Scatter 37%; Count 3
Foreground/Background Jitter 100%

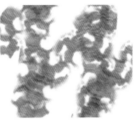

Dual Brush: Size 132 px
Spacing 60%; Scatter 37%; Count 1
Foreground/Background Jitter 100%
Hue Jitter 100%

Dual Brush: Size 95 px
Spacing 60%; Scatter 0%; Count 2
Foreground/Background Jitter 25%
Hue Jitter 100%
Brightness Jitter 95%

SETTINGS

Dual Brush: Size 46 px
Spacing 60%
Scatter 0%; Count 2
Foreground/Background
Jitter 25%
Hue Jitter 100%
Brightness Jitter 95%
Wet Edges

Spacing 50%
Dual Brush: Size 36 px
Spacing 25%
Scatter 37%
Count 3
Brightness Jitter 50%

Spacing 50%
Dual Brush: Size 36 px
Spacing 25%
Scatter 37%
Count 3
Hue Jitter 50%

Spacing 50%
Angle Jitter 50%
Dual Brush: Size 36 px
Spacing 25%
Scatter 37%
Count 3
Hue Jitter 50%
Purity +100%

Spacing 50%
Angle Jitter 50%
Dual Brush: Size 36 px
Spacing 25%
Scatter 37%; Count 3
Hue Jitter 100%
Purity +100%
Wet Edges

Spacing 50%
Scatter 30%; Count 5
Dual Brush: Size 36 px
Spacing 25%
Scatter 37%; Count 3
Hue Jitter 100%
Purity +100%

Spacing 80%
Dual Brush: Size 36 px
Spacing 25%
Scatter 37%
Count 3
Hue Jitter 100%
Purity +100%

Spacing 80%
Dual Brush: Size 36 px
Spacing 25%
Scatter 37%; Count 3
Hue Jitter 100%
Purity +100%
Opacity Jitter 100%

Spacing 22%
Dual Brush: Size 28 px
Spacing 25%
Scatter 133%; Count 2
Foreground/Background
Jitter 100%; Hue Jitter
25%; Purity +100%
Opacity Jitter 100%

Spcng 22%; Scttr 280%
Count 5; Dual Brush:
Size 26 px; Spacing 25%
Scatter 133%; Count 2
Fgnd/Bgnd Jitter 100%
Hue Jitter 25%; Purity
+100%; Opacity Jitter
100%; Wet Edges

ROUGH GRAPHITE

Dual Brush: Size 77 px
Spacing 30%; Scatter 0%; Count 1
Hue Jitter 75%

Dual Brush: Size 77 px
Spacing 30%; Scatter 0%; Count 5
Hue Jitter 75%
Purity +100%

Dual Brush: Size 77 px
Spacing 30%; Scatter 0%; Count 3
Foreground/Background Jitter 100%
Brightness Jitter 50%

Dual Brush: Size 77 px
Spacing 100%; Scatter 0%; Count 1
Purity +100%

SETTINGS

Dual Brush: Size 31 px
Spacing 100%
Scatter 0%
Count 1
Purity +100%
Wet Edges

Dual Brush: Size 31 px
Spacing 25%
Scatter 0%
Count 3
Purity +100%
Opacity Jitter 100%

Dual Brush: Size 28 px
Spacing 30%
Scatter 0%
Count 4
Hue Jitter 50%
Brightness Jitter 50%

Dual Brush: Size 28 px
Spacing 30%
Scatter 0%
Count 4
Hue Jitter 50%
Brightness Jitter 50%
Purity +100%
Wet Edges

Dual Brush: Size 28 px
Spacing 30%
Scatter 0%; Count 4
Hue Jitter 50%
Brightness Jitter 50%
Purity +100%
Opacity Jitter 100%
Wet Edges

Dual Brush: Size 28 px
Spacing 30%
Scatter 0%; Count 16
Hue Jitter 50%
Brightness Jitter 50%
Purity +100%
Opacity Jitter 100%

Dual Brush: Size 28 px
Spacing 30%
Scatter 380%; Count 2
Hue Jitter 50%
Brightness Jitter 50%
Purity +100%
Opacity Jitter 100%

Dual Brush: Size 28 px
Spacing 30%
Scatter 380%
Count 2
Hue Jitter 100%
Brightness Jitter 50%
Purity +100%

Dual Brush: Size 28 px
Spacing 30%
Scatter 380%
Count 2
Brightness Jitter 50%
Purity -40%

Dual Brush: Size 28 px
Spacing 30%
Scatter 380%
Count 3
Foreground/Background
Jitter 100%
Hue Jitter 100%

BRUSH 4

Dual Brush: Size 138 px
Spacing 30%; Scatter 0%; Count 1
Brightness Jitter 100%

Dual Brush: Size 138 px
Spacing 30%; Scatter 0%; Count 1
Hue Jitter 100%
Opacity Jitter 100%

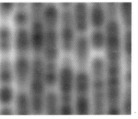

Dual Brush: Size 138 px
Spacing 30%; Scatter 0%; Count 3
Foreground/Background Jitter 100%
Purity +50%
Flow Jitter 100%

Size Jitter 100%
Angle Jitter 20%
Roundness Jitter 100%
Dual Brush: Size 138 px
Spacing 30%; Scatter 330%; Count 3

SETTINGS

Dual Brush: Size 55 px
Spacing 30%
Scatter 330%
Count 3
Hue Jitter 60%
Purity +100%
Opacity Jitter 100%
Wet Edges

Dual Brush: Size 5 px
Spacing 30%
Scatter 0%
Count 1
Hue Jitter 60%
Purity +100%
Opacity Jitter 100%

Scatter 270%
Count 1
Dual Brush: Size 33 px
Spacing 30%
Scatter 0%
Count 1

Scatter 270%
Count 2
Dual Brush: Size 33 px
Spacing 30%
Scatter 0%; Count 1
Foreground/Background
Jitter 100%
Hue Jitter 50%

Scatter 270%; Count 2
Dual Brush: Size 33 px
Spacing 30%
Scatter 0%; Count 3
Foreground/Background
Jitter 100%
Hue Jitter 50%
Wet Edges

Scatter 120%; Count 2
Dual Brush: Size 21 px
Spacing 30%
Scatter 220%; Count 2
Foreground/Background
Jitter 100%
Hue Jitter 50%

Scatter 120%
Count 2
Dual Brush: Size 21 px
Spacing 30%
Scatter 220%; Count 2
Hue Jitter 50%
Purity +100%

Scatter 120%; Count 2
Dual Brush: Size 21 px
Spacing 30%
Scatter 220%; Count 2
Hue Jitter 100%
Purity +100%
Opacity Jitter 100%

Scatter 200%
Count 1
Dual Brush: Size 21 px
Spacing 30%
Scatter 220%; Count 2
Hue Jitter 100%
Purity +100%

Size Jitter 100%
Dual Brush: Size 55 px
Spacing 30%
Scatter 220%
Count 2
Hue Jitter 100%
Purity +100%

SLIGHT BLEED

Dual Brush: Size 48 px
Spacing 58%; Scatter 37%; Count 3
Opacity Jitter 100%
Flow Jitter 100%

Dual Brush: Size 48 px
Spacing 58%; Scatter 390%; Count 3
Saturation Jitter 100%
Purity +25%

Dual Brush: Size 58 px
Spacing 1%; Scatter 0%; Count 1
Foreground/Background Jitter 100%
Purity +25%

Dual Brush: Size 58 px
Spacing 10%; Scatter 0%; Count 1
Foreground/Background Jitter 100%
Hue Jitter 50%
Purity +25%

SETTINGS

Dual Brush: Size 33 px
Spacing 10%
Scatter 0%
Count 1
Foreground/Background
Jitter 100%
Hue Jitter 50%
Purity +25%

Dual Brush: Size 33 px
Spacing 50%
Scatter 0%
Count 2
Foreground/Background
Jitter 100%
Hue Jitter 50%
Purity +25%

Dual Brush: Size 33 px
Spacing 50%
Scatter 0%
Count 1
Foreground/Background
Jitter 100%
Hue Jitter 100%
Purity -20%

Dual Brush: Size 33 px
Spacing 7%
Scatter 0%
Count 7
Foreground/Background
Jitter 100%
Hue Jitter 100%

Dual Brush: Size 33 px
Spacing 30%
Scatter 0%
Count 7
Foreground/Background
Jitter 100%
Hue Jitter 20%
Opacity Jitter 100%

Dual Brush: Size 33 px
Spacing 100%
Scatter 0%; Count 7
Foreground/Background
Jitter 100%; Hue
Jitter 20%; Opacity
Jitter 50%; Wet Edges

Dual Brush: Size 33 px
Spacing 100%
Scatter 0%
Count 7
Hue Jitter 20%
Opacity Jitter 50%

Dual Brush: Size 23 px
Spacing 130%
Scatter 100%
Count 4
Hue Jitter 100%

Dual Brush: Size 23 px
Spacing 130%
Scatter 100%
Count 4
Hue Jitter 100%
Brightness Jitter 100%
Purity +100%

Dual Brush: Size 23 px
Spacing 1%
Scatter 0%
Count 4
Hue Jitter 100%
Brightness Jitter 100%
Purity +100%

ROUGH CHARCOAL

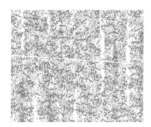

Size Jitter 100%
Angle Jitter 30%

Dual Brush: Size 100 px
Spacing 67%; Scatter 0%; Count 4
Foreground/Background Jitter 100%
Hue Jitter 100%
Purity +100%

Dual Brush: Size 100 px
Spacing 67%; Scatter 0%; Count 4
Opacity Jitter 100%
Flow Jitter 100%

Dual Brush: Size 100 px
Spacing 67%; Scatter 200%; Count 1
Foreground/Background Jitter 20%
Hue Jitter 100%
Purity +100%

SETTINGS

Dual Brush: Size 40 px
Spacing 30%
Scatter 350%
Count 1
Hue Jitter 100%
Purity +100%

Dual Brush: Size 40 px
Spacing 30%
Scatter 350%
Count 3
Hue Jitter 100%
Purity +100%

Scatter 435%
Count 1
Dual Brush: Size 40 px
Spacing 30%
Scatter 350%
Count 3
Hue Jitter 100%
Purity +100%

Scatter 200%
Count 1
Dual Brush: Size 40 px
Spacing 30%
Scatter 0%; Count 3
Hue Jitter 100%
Brightness Jitter 60%
Purity +100%

Scatter 33%
Count 1
Dual Brush: Size 33 px
Spacing 110%
Scatter 0%; Count 3
Hue Jitter 100%
Brightness Jitter 60%
Purity +100%

Scatter 33%; Count 1
Dual Brush: Size 33 px
Spacing 110%
Scatter 0%; Count 3
Hue Jitter 100%
Brightness Jitter 100%
Wet Edges

Scatter 800%; Count 1
Dual Brush: Size 33 px
Spacing 110%
Scatter 0%; Count 7
Foreground/Background
Jitter 100%; Brightness
Jitter 100%; Wet Edges

Scatter 800%; Count 1
Dual Brush: Size 33 px
Spacing 110%
Scatter 0%; Count 5
Fgnd/Bgnd Jitter 100%
Hue Jitter 100%
Brightness Jitter 100%

Spacing 90%
Dual Brush: Size 44 px
Spacing 110%
Scatter 0%; Count 5
Fgnd/Bgnd Jitter 100%
Hue Jitter 100%
Brightness Jitter 100%

Angle 45°; Spacing 90%
Dual Brush: Size 44 px
Spacing 110%
Scatter 0%; Count 5
Fgnd/Bgnd Jitter 100%
Hue Jitter 100%
Brightness Jitter 100%

SUMI 2

Count 3
Opacity Jitter 100%
Flow Jitter 100%

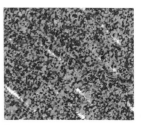

Scatter 50%
Count 1%
Hue Jitter 100%
Purity +100%

Size Jitter 100%
Scatter 500%
Count 1

Dual Brush: Size 100 px
Spacing 80%; Scatter 0%; Count 2
Hue Jitter 25%
Brightness Jitter 100%

SETTINGS

Dual Brush: Size 45 px
Spacing 80%
Scatter 0%
Count 2
Hue Jitter 25%
Brightness Jitter 100%
Wet Edges

Dual Brush: Size 45 px
Spacing 80%
Scatter 0%
Count 2
Hue Jitter 100%
Purity +50%

Dual Brush: Size 45 px
Spacing 80%
Scatter 0%
Count 2
Hue Jitter 20%
Purity -20%

Dual Brush: Size 45 px
Spacing 80%
Scatter 0%
Count 1
Hue Jitter 20%
Purity +1000%

Dual Brush: Size 36 px
Spacing 80%
Scatter 50%
Count 7
Hue Jitter 20%
Purity +1000%

Dual Brush: Size 36 px
Spacing 80%
Scatter 0%
Count 7
Hue Jitter 20%
Purity +100%

Dual Brush: Size 36 px
Spacing 80%
Scatter 50%
Count 7
Foreground/Background
Jitter 100%
Purity +100%

Dual Brush: Size 36 px
Spacing 80%
Scatter 30%
Count 2
Saturation Jitter 100%
Brightness Jitter 50%

Dual Brush: Size 33 px
Spacing 15%
Scatter 0%
Count 1
Hue Jitter 30%
Brightness Jitter 50%
Purity +100%

Dual Brush: Size 33 px
Spacing 1%
Scatter 900%
Count 1
Foreground/Background
Jitter 100%
Hue Jitter 10%

TARMAC

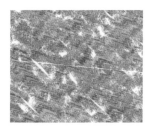

Dual Brush: Size 67 px
Spacing 100%; Scatter 100%
Count 1
Hue Jitter 100%

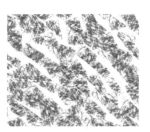

Dual Brush: Size 67 px
Spacing 100%; Scatter 100%
Count 1
Foreground/Background Jitter 100%
Saturation Jitter 100%

Scatter 640%
Dual Brush: Size 67 px
Spacing 70%; Scatter 0%; Count 1
Hue Jitter 60%
Brightness Jitter 100%

Scatter 640%
Count 3
Dual Brush: Size 67 px
Spacing 1%; Scatter 0%; Count 1
Opacity Jitter 100%

SETTINGS

Scatter 300%
Dual Brush: Size 67 px
Spacing 1%
Scatter 0%
Count 1
Hue Jitter 100%
Brightness Jitter 100%

Scatter 300%
Dual Brush: Size 67 px
Spacing 1%
Scatter 0%
Count 1
Hue Jitter 100%
Brightness Jitter 100%
Wet Edges

Dual Brush: Size 67 px
Spacing 1%
Scatter 0%
Count 1
Hue Jitter 100%
Brightness Jitter 50%
Purity +15%

Angle Jitter 50%
Dual Brush: Size 30 px
Spacing 70%
Scatter 0%; Count 1
Foreground/Background
Jitter 100%
Hue Jitter 100%
Brightness Jitter 50%

Angle Jitter 50%
Dual Brush: Size 30 px
Spacing 70%
Scatter 0%; Count 2
Foreground/Background
Jitter 100%
Hue Jitter 100%
Brightness Jitter 50%

Angle Jitter 50%
Dual Brush: Size 30 px
Spacing 70%
Scatter 230%; Count 2
Foreground/Background
Jitter 100%
Hue Jitter 100%

Angle Jitter 50%
Dual Brush: Size 30 px
Spacing 110%
Scatter 230%; Count 2
Foreground/Background
Jitter 100%; Hue Jitter
100%; Purity +100%

Angle Jitter 50%
Dual Brush: Size 30 px
Spacing 110%
Scatter 230%; Count 4
Foreground/Background
Jitter 100%; Hue Jitter
20%; Purity +100%

Spacing 55%; Angle
Jitter 50%. Dual Brush:
Size 30 px; Spacing
110%; Scatter 230%
Count 4; Fgnd/Bgnd
Jitter 100%; Hue
Jitter 20%; Purity +100%

Spacing 55%
Angle Jitter 50%
Dual Brush: Size 30 px
Spacing 110%
Scatter 230%; Count 4
Hue Jitter 20%
Opacity Jitter 100%

TRIANGLE JUMBLE

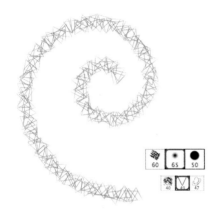

Default Brush

Dual Brush: Size 75 px
Spacing 80%; Scatter 50%; Count 2
Hue Jitter 20%
Brightness Jitter 50%
Purity +100%

Dual Brush: Size 75 px
Spacing 10%; Scatter 5%; Count 3
Foreground/Background Jitter 50%

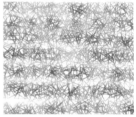

Dual Brush: Size 47 px
Spacing 10%; Scatter 100%
Hue Jitter 100%
Purity +50%

SETTINGS

Dual Brush: Size 26 px
Spacing 80%
Scatter 0%
Count 4
Hue Jitter 100%
Brightness Jitter 100%
Purity +100%
Wet Edges

Dual Brush: Size 34 px
Spacing 25%
Scatter 0%
Count 1
Hue Jitter 100%
Brightness Jitter 100%

Dual Brush: Size 34 px
Spacing 25%
Scatter 200%
Count 1
Hue Jitter 100%
Brightness Jitter 100%

Dual Brush: Size 34 px
Spacing 25%
Scatter 200%
Count 6
Hue Jitter 100%
Brightness Jitter 100%
Wet Edges

Dual Brush: Size 85 px
Spacing 25%
Angle Jitter 63%
Scatter 200%
Count 1
Hue Jitter 100%
Brightness Jitter 100%

Dual Brush: Size 30 px
Spacing 62%
Scatter 0%
Count 8

Dual Brush: Size 30 px
Spacing 62%
Scatter 0%; Count 8
Foreground/Background
Jitter 100%
Brightness Jitter 50%
Purity +100%

Dual Brush: Size 30 px
Spacing 62%
Scatter 0%; Count 3
Foreground/Background
Jitter 100%
Brightness Jitter 50%
Purity +100%; Wet Edges

Dual Brush: Size 30 px
Spacing 62%
Scatter 0%; Count 1
Foreground/Background
Jitter 100%
Brightness Jitter 100%
Purity +100%

Dual Brush: Size 34 px
Spacing 150%
Scatter 0%; Count 1
Foreground/Background
Jitter 100%
Brightness Jitter 100%
Purity +100%; Wet Edges

TUMBLE PLANET

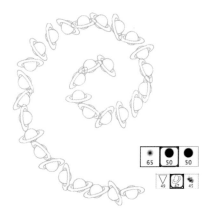

Dual Brush: Size 85 px
Spacing 127%; Scatter 0%; Count 1
Foreground/Background Jitter 100%
Purity +25%

Dual Brush: Size 85 px
Spacing 55%; Scatter 0%; Count 1
Hue Jitter 100%
Brightness Jitter 100%
Wet Edges

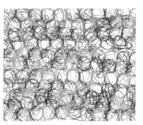

Dual Brush: Size 85 px
Spacing 90%; Scatter 0%; Count 2
Foreground/Background Jitter 50%
Hue Jitter 100%
Purity +100%

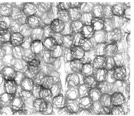

Dual Brush: Size 85 px
Spacing 90%; Scatter 15%; Count 3
Foreground/Background Jitter 50%
Hue Jitter 100%
Purity +100%
Opacity Jitter 100%

SETTINGS

Dual Brush: Size 42 px
Spacing 90%
Scatter 15%; Count 1
Foreground/Background
Jitter 50%
Hue Jitter 100%
Brightness Jitter 100%
Purity +100%

Dual Brush: Size 42 px
Spacing 90%
Scatter 15%
Count 1
Foreground/Background
Jitter 100%
Brightness Jitter 100%
Purity +100%

Dual Brush: Size 33 px
Spacing 90%
Scatter 15%
Count 6
Foreground/Background
Jitter 100%
Brightness Jitter 100%
Purity +100%

Dual Brush: Size 33 px
Spacing 90%
Scatter 15%; Count 6
Foreground/Background
Jitter 20%
Hue Jitter 70%
Brightness Jitter 100%
Purity +100%

Dual Brush: Size 33 px
Spacing 90%
Scatter 100%
Count 2
Foreground/Background
Jitter 20%
Hue Jitter 70%
Purity +100%

Dual Brush: Size 33 px
Spacing 20%
Scatter 0%; Count 2
Foreground/Background
Jitter 20%
Hue Jitter 70%
Purity +100%

Dual Brush: Size 33 px
Spacing 20%
Scatter 0%
Count 2
Foreground/Background
Jitter 100%
Purity +100%

Dual Brush: Size 33 px
Spacing 20%
Scatter 0%; Count 2
Foreground/Background
Jitter 100%
Saturation Jitter 100%
Wet Edges

Dual Brush: Size 33 px
Spacing 33%
Scatter 0%
Count 1
Foreground/Background
Jitter 25%
Hue Jitter 25%

Dual Brush: Size 33 px
Spacing 70%
Scatter 0%; Count 1
Foreground/Background
Jitter 25%
Hue Jitter 100%
Purity +100%

FUZZY

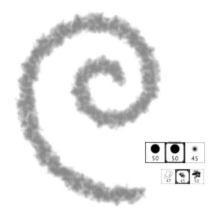

Spacing 20%
Dual Brush: Size 81 px
Spacing 28%; Scatter 0%; Count 1
Foreground/Background Jitter 25%
Hue Jitter 100%; Purity +100%

Spacing 1%
Dual Brush: Size 90 px
Spacing 10%; Scatter 0%; Count 1
Foreground/Background Jitter 25%
Hue Jitter 25%; Purity +100%

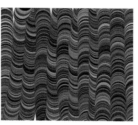

Dual Brush: Size 81 px
Spacing 28%; Scatter 0%; Count 4
Hue Jitter 10%
Brightness Jitter 100%
Purity +15%

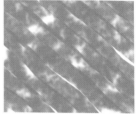

Dual Brush: Size 81 px
Spacing 28%; Scatter 190%; Count 4
Opacity Jitter 100%
Flow Jitter 100%

SETTINGS

Dual Brush: Size 32 px
Spacing 28%
Scatter 190%; Count 4
Hue Jitter 10%
Brightness Jitter 100%
Purity +15%
Opacity Jitter 100%
Wet Edges

Dual Brush: Size 32 px
Spacing 28%
Scatter 0%
Count 4
Hue Jitter 10%
Brightness Jitter 33%
Purity +15%

Dual Brush: Size 45 px
Spacing 28%
Scatter 0%
Count 1
Hue Jitter 100%
Purity +15%

Dual Brush: Size 45 px
Spacing 28%
Scatter 0%
Count 1
Hue Jitter 100%
Purity +15%
Wet Edges

Dual Brush: Size 45 px
Spacing 75%
Scatter 0%
Count 2
Hue Jitter 100%
Purity +100%

Spacing 40%
Dual Brush: Size 45 px
Spacing 75%
Scatter 0%
Count 2
Hue Jitter 100%
Purity +100%

Spacing 40%
Dual Brush: Size 45 px
Spacing 75%
Scatter 45%
Count 1
Hue Jitter 100%
Purity +100%

Spacing 120%
Dual Brush: Size 45 px
Spacing 75%
Scatter 45%
Count 1
Hue Jitter 100%
Purity +100%

Spacing 120%
Dual Brush: Size 45 px
Spacing 75%
Scatter 45%; Count 2
Fgnd/Bgnd Jitter 100%
Hue Jitter 20%; Purity
+100%; Wet Edges

Spacing 25%
Dual Brush: Size 36 px
Spacing 75%
Scatter 45%; Count 2
Fgnd/Bgnd Jitter 100%
Hue Jitter 45%
Purity +100%

WET SPREAD

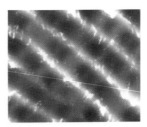

Dual Brush: Size 110 px
Spacing 25%; Scatter 0%; Count 1
Foreground/Background Jitter 100%

Dual Brush: Size 110 px
Spacing 25%; Scatter 100%; Count 2
Hue Jitter 20%
Brightness Jitter 20%

Dual Brush: Size 110 px
Spacing 25%; Scatter 0%; Count 2
Hue Jitter 100%
Brightness Jitter 20%

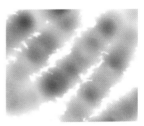

Dual Brush: Size 110 px
Spacing 25%; Scatter 0%; Count 2
Hue Jitter 100%
Brightness Jitter 20%
Opacity Jitter 100%

SETTINGS

Dual Brush: Size 50 px
Spacing 25%
Scatter 0%
Count 2
Hue Jitter 100%
Brightness Jitter 20%
Opacity Jitter 100%
Wet Edges

Dual Brush: Size 50 px
Spacing 25%
Scatter 0%
Count 1
Hue Jitter 100%

Dual Brush: Size 50 px
Spacing 25%
Scatter 0%
Count 1
Foreground/Background
Jitter 100%
Brightness Jitter 100%

Dual Brush: Size 50 px
Spacing 25%
Scatter 0%
Count 1
Foreground/Background
Jitter 100%
Brightness Jitter 100%
Opacity Jitter 100%

Dual Brush: Size 39 px
Spacing 25%
Scatter 133%
Count 1
Foreground/Background
Jitter 100%
Brightness Jitter 100%
Opacity Jitter 100%

Dual Brush: Size 39 px
Spacing 25%
Scatter 0%
Count 6
Foreground/Background
Jitter 20%
Brightness Jitter 100%

Spacing 100%
Dual Brush: Size 39 px
Spacing 25%
Scatter 0%; Count 6
Foreground/Background
Jitter 20%
Brightness Jitter 100%

Spacing 100%
Dual Brush: Size 39 px
Spacing 1%
Scatter 0%; Count 1
Fgnd/Bgnd Jitter 20%
Brightness Jitter 100%
Purity +100%

Spacing 60%
Dual Brush: Size 39 px
Spacing 1%
Scatter 0%; Count 1
Fgnd/Bgnd Jitter 20%
Hue Jitter 100%
Purity +100%; Wet Edges

Spacing 60%
Dual Brush: Size 39 px
Spacing 1%
Scatter 0%; Count 1
Fgnd/Bgnd Jitter 10%
Hue Jitter 35%
Purity +100%; Noise

CROSSHATCH

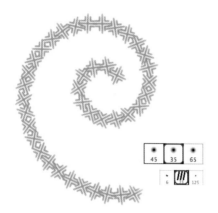

Dual Brush: Size 86 px
Spacing 1%; Scatter 0%; Count 1
Foreground/Background Jitter 100%
Purity +100%; Opacity Jitter 100%
Flow Jitter 100%

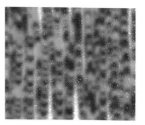

Dual Brush: Size 86 px
Spacing 1%; Scatter 0%; Count 1
Hue Jitter 50%
Brightness Jitter 50%
Noise

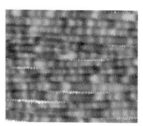

Dual Brush: Size 86 px
Spacing 30%; Scatter 0%; Count 2
Hue Jitter 50%
Brightness Jitter 50%
Wet Edges

Dual Brush: Size 51 px
Spacing 85%; Scatter 150%; Count 2
Hue Jitter 100%
Brightness Jitter 50%
Purity +100%

SETTINGS

Dual Brush: Size 17 px
Spacing 85%
Scatter 150%
Count 2
Hue Jitter 100%
Brightness Jitter 50%
Purity +100%
Noise

Dual Brush: Size 23 px
Spacing 85%
Scatter 0%
Count 1
Hue Jitter 100%
Brightness Jitter 50%
Purity +100%

Dual Brush: Size 23 px
Spacing 120%
Scatter 40%
Count 1
Hue Jitter 100%
Brightness Jitter 50%
Purity +100%

Dual Brush: Size 23 px
Spacing 100%
Scatter 40%
Count 2
Foreground/Background
Jitter 100%
Hue Jitter 100%
Purity +100%

Spacing 100%
Dual Brush: Size 23 px
Spacing 100%
Scatter 40%; Count 2
Foreground/Background
Jitter 100%
Hue Jitter 100%
Purity +100%

Spacing 100%
Dual Brush: Size 23 px
Spacing 100%
Scatter 0%; Count 2
Foreground/Background
Jitter 33%
Hue Jitter 100%

Dual Brush: Size 23 px
Spacing 100%
Scatter 75%
Count 5
Foreground/Background
Jitter 33%
Hue Jitter 100%

Dual Brush: Size 23 px
Spacing 100%
Scatter 75%; Count 5
Foreground/Background
Jitter 33%
Hue Jitter 100%
Wet Edges

Scatter 133%
Dual Brush: Size 23 px
Spacing 100%
Scatter 75%; Count 5
Foreground/Background
Jitter 33%
Hue Jitter 100%

Scatter 133%
Dual Brush: Size 23 px
Spacing 100%
Scatter 75%; Count 5
Fgnd/Bgnd Jitter 33%
Hue Jitter 100%
Opacity Jitter 100%

ZIGZAG JUMBLE

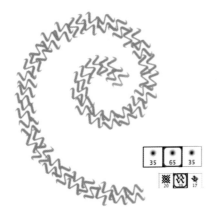

Dual Brush: Size 90 px
Spacing 80%; Scatter 0%; Count 2
Foreground/Background Jitter 100%

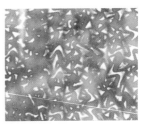

Dual Brush: Size 90 px
Spacing 80%; Scatter 0%; Count 2
Hue Jitter 100%; Purity +100%; Noise
Wet Edges

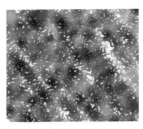

Dual Brush: Size 42 px
Spacing 80%; Scatter 100%; Count 5
Hue Jitter 50%
Brightness Jitter 50%

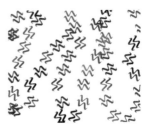

Dual Brush: Size 42 px
Spacing 130%; Scatter 100%
Count 1; Hue Jitter 50%
Brightness Jitter 100%; Purity +100%
Opacity Jitter 100%

Dual Brush: Size 22 px
Spacing 130%
Scatter 100%
Count 1
Hue Jitter 100%
Purity +100%

Dual Brush: Size 29 px
Spacing 80%
Scatter 0%
Count 2
Hue Jitter 100%
Purity +100%

Dual Brush: Size 29 px
Spacing 30%
Scatter 0%
Count 1
Foreground/Background
Jitter 100%
Purity +100%

Dual Brush: Size 29 px
Spacing 100%
Scatter 0%
Count 1
Foreground/Background
Jitter 100%
Brightness Jitter 75%
Purity +100%

Dual Brush: Size 29 px
Spacing 100%
Scatter 0%; Count 1
Foreground/Background
Jitter 100%
Hue Jitter 100%
Brightness Jitter 75%
Purity +100%

Dual Brush: Size 29 px
Spacing 100%
Scatter 0%; Count 3
Fgnd/Bgnd Jitter 100%
Hue Jitter 100%
Brightness Jitter 75%
Purity +100%

Dual Brush: Size 13 px
Spacing 100%
Scatter 210%; Count 2
Foreground/Background
Jitter 100%
Hue Jitter 100%
Brightness Jitter 75%

Dual Brush: Size 29 px
Spacing 100%
Scatter 0%; Count 6
Fgnd/Bnd Jitter 100%
Hue Jitter 100%
Brightness Jitter 75%
Wet Edges

Dual Brush: Size 16 px
Spacing 100%
Scatter 100%
Count 2
Foreground/Background
Jitter 100%
Hue Jitter 100%

Dual Brush: Size 16 px
Spacing 100%
Scatter 100%; Count 2
Fgnd/Bgnd Jitter 100%
Hue Jitter 100%
Brightness Jitter 75%
Opacity Jitter 100%

ROUGH INK WITH SIZE

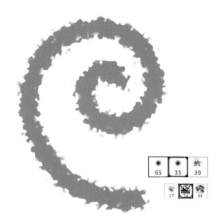

Dual Brush: Size 140 px
Spacing 120%; Scatter 200%
Count 4
Foreground/Background Jitter 100%
Noise

Dual Brush: Size 140 px
Spacing 80%; Scatter 300%
Count 1; Saturation Jitter 100%
Purity +100%; Opacity Jitter 100%
Flow Jitter 100%

Dual Brush: Size 140 px
Spacing 50%; Scatter 0%; Count 1
Hue Jitter 100%
Purity +100%
Noise

Dual Brush: Size 140 px
Spacing 1%; Scatter 0%; Count 1
Hue Jitter 100%
Purity -33%
Wet Edges

SETTINGS

Dual Brush: Size 40 px
Spacing 1%
Scatter 0%
Count 1
Hue Jitter 100%
Opacity Jitter 100%

Dual Brush: Size 140 px
Spacing 40%
Scatter 0%
Count 1
Hue Jitter 100%
Opacity Jitter 100%

Dual Brush: Size 40 px
Spacing 100%
Scatter 0%
Count 1
Foreground/Background
Jitter 100%
Hue Jitter 25%
Brightness Jitter 50%

Dual Brush: Size 46 px
Spacing 100%
Scatter 150%
Count 1
Foreground/Background
Jitter 100%
Hue Jitter 25%
Brightness Jitter 20%

Dual Brush: Size 46 px
Spacing 220%
Scatter 150%
Count 1
Foreground/Background
Jitter 100%
Hue Jitter 25%

Dual Brush: Size 54 px
Spacing 80%
Scatter 0%
Count 1
Opacity Jitter 100%

Dual Brush: Size 54 px
Spacing 150%
Scatter 0%
Count 1
Foreground/Background
Jitter 100%
Opacity Jitter 100%

Spacing 100%
Dual Brush: Size 54 px
Spacing 150%
Scatter 0%; Count 1
Foreground/Background
Jitter 100%
Brightness Jitter 50%

Spacing 100%
Dual Brush: Size 54 px
Spacing 150%
Scatter 0%; Count 1
Fgnd/Bgnd Jitter 100%
Hue Jitter 50%; Purity
+100%; O. Jitter 100%

Dual Brush: Size 54 px
Spacing 80%
Scatter 0%
Count 1
Hue Jitter 100%
Purity +100%

DRY BRUSH

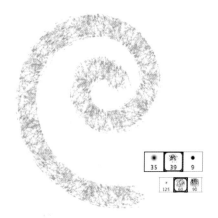

Dual Brush: Size 154 px
Spacing 81%
Scatter 0%; Count 1
Hue Jitter 50%
Purity +50%

Dual Brush: Size 154 px
Spacing 30%; Scatter 0%; Count 1
Hue Jitter 50%
Brightness Jitter 100%
Purity +50%

Dual Brush: Size 154 px
Spacing 30%
Scatter 0%; Count 1
Hue Jitter 100%
Purity +50%
Opacity Jitter 100%

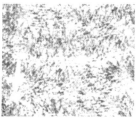

Dual Brush: Size 154 px
Spacing 110%; Scatter 0%; Count 1
Foreground/Background Jitter 100%
Hue Jitter 100%
Purity +50%
Opacity Jitter 100%

SETTINGS

Dual Brush: Size 46 px
Spacing 81%
Scatter 0%
Count 1
Brightness Jitter 100%
Purity +100%

Dual Brush: Size 46 px
Spacing 81%
Scatter 0%
Count 1
Hue Jitter 100%
Brightness Jitter 100%
Purity +100%
Wet Edges

Dual Brush: Size 46 px
Spacing 81%
Scatter 0%
Count 3
Hue Jitter 100%
Brightness Jitter 100%
Purity +100%

Dual Brush: Size 46 px
Spacing 81%
Scatter 0%
Count 3
Hue Jitter 100%
Brightness Jitter 10%
Purity +100%

Dual Brush: Size 54 px
Spacing 81%
Scatter 70%
Count 3
Hue Jitter 100%
Brightness Jitter 10%
Purity +100%

Dual Brush: Size 54 px
Spacing 81%
Scatter 70%
Count 3
Foreground/Background
Jitter 100%
Hue Jitter 100%

Dual Brush: Size 60 px
Spacing 81%
Scatter 0%; Count 3
Hue Jitter 25%
Foreground/Background
Jitter 100%
Opacity Jitter 90%

Dual Brush: Size 60 px
Spacing 10%
Scatter 0%; Count 1
Foreground/Background
Jitter 100%
Hue Jitter 100%
Purity +100%

Dual Brush: Size 60 px
Spacing 10%
Scatter 175%; Count 1
Foreground/Background
Jitter 100%
Hue Jitter 100%
Purity +50%

Dual Brush: Size 60 px
Spacing 10%
Scatter 175%; Count 1
Foreground/Background
Jitter 100%
Hue Jitter 100%
Purity +10%; Wet Edges

ROUGH COMB

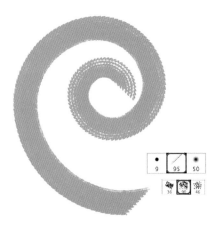

Dual Brush: Size 90 px
Spacing 43%
Scatter 0%
Count 1
Foreground/Background Jitter 100%

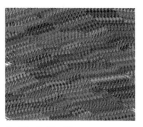

Dual Brush: Size 90 px
Spacing 94%; Scatter 0%; Count 1
Foreground/Background Jitter 60%
Hue Jitter 60%
Brightness Jitter 50%

Angle Jitter 45%
Dual Brush: Size 90 px
Spacing 94%; Scatter 0%; Count 1
Foreground/Background Jitter 60%
Hue Jitter 60%
Brightness Jitter 50%

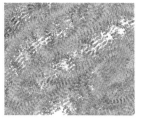

Angle Jitter 45%
Dual Brush: Size 90 px
Spacing 94%; Scatter 0%; Count 1
Foreground/Background Jitter 60%
Hue Jitter 60%; Brightness Jitter 50%
Wet Edges

SETTINGS

Angle Jitter 45%
Dual Brush: Size 38 px
Spacing 43%
Scatter 0%
Count 1

Angle Jitter 45%
Dual Brush: Size 38 px
Spacing 43%
Scatter 0%
Count 1
Hue Jitter 100%

Angle Jitter 45%
Dual Brush: Size 28 px
Spacing 150%
Scatter 0%
Count 1
Hue Jitter 100%

Angle Jitter 45%
Dual Brush: Size 28 px
Spacing 150%
Scatter 0%
Count 4
Hue Jitter 100%
Purity +30%

Dual Brush: Size 28 px
Spacing 150%
Scatter 0%
Count 4
Foreground/Background
Jitter 30%
Hue Jitter 100%
Purity +30%

Dual Brush: Size 28 px
Spacing 75%
Scatter 0%; Count 1
Foreground/Background
Jitter 30%
Hue Jitter 100%
Purity +30%

Angle 45°
Dual Brush: Size 28 px
Spacing 75%;
Scatter 0%; Count 1
Foreground/Background
Jitter 30%; Hue Jitter
100%; Purity +100%

Angle 45°
Dual Brush: Size 28 px
Spacing 1%
Scatter 0%; Count 1
Foreground/Background
Jitter 30%; Hue Jitter
100%; Purity +100%

Dual Brush: Size 28 px
Spacing 1%
Scatter 0%; Count 1
Foreground/Background
Jitter 100%; Hue Jitter
100%; Purity +100%
Opacity Jitter 100%

Dual Brush: Size 28 px
Spacing 125%
Scatter 0%; Count 1
Foreground/Background
Jitter 100%; Hue Jitter
100%; Purity +100%
Opacity Jitter 100%

SOFT ROUND

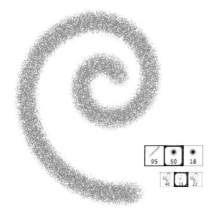

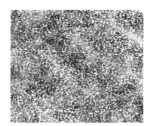

Dual Brush: Size 120 px
Spacing 57%; Scatter 0%; Count 1
Hue Jitter 100%
Brightness Jitter 100%
Purity +100%

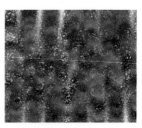

Dual Brush: Size 120 px
Spacing 57%; Scatter 0%; Count 5
Hue Jitter 100%
Brightness Jitter 100%
Purity +100%

Dual Brush: Size 120 px
Spacing 57%
Scatter 0%
Count 5
Hue Jitter 100%
Purity +100%

Dual Brush: Size 120 px
Spacing 57%
Scatter 0%
Count 3
Hue Jitter 100%
Purity +40%

SETTINGS

Dual Brush: Size 46 px
Spacing 57%
Scatter 0%
Count 3
Hue Jitter 100%
Purity +40%
Wet Edges

Dual Brush: Size 40 px
Spacing 20%
Scatter 0%
Count 1
Hue Jitter 100%
Brightness Jitter 30%
Purity +40%

Dual Brush: Size 40 px
Spacing 80%
Scatter 0%
Count 4
Foreground/Background
Jitter 50%
Hue Jitter 100%
Brightness Jitter 30%

Dual Brush: Size 40 px
Spacing 90%
Scatter 50%
Count 6
Foreground/Background
Jitter 50%
Hue Jitter 100%
Purity +100%

Dual Brush: Size 40 px
Spacing 90%
Scatter 0%; Count 6
Foreground/Background
Jitter 50%
Hue Jitter 100%
Purity +100%
Wet Edges

Dual Brush: Size 40 px
Spacing 35%
Scatter 0%; Count 3
Foreground/Background
Jitter 50%; Hue Jitter
100%; Purity +100%
Opacity Jitter 100%

Dual Brush: Size 40 px
Spacing 78%
Scatter 400%
Count 7
Foreground/Background
Jitter 100%
Purity +100%

Dual Brush: Size 40 px
Spacing 49%
Scatter 200%
Count 7
Hue Jitter 100%

Dual Brush: Size 40 px
Spacing 49%
Scatter 200%
Count 7
Hue Jitter 100%
Wet Edges

Dual Brush: Size 40 px
Spacing 49%
Scatter 200%
Count 7
Hue Jitter 100%
Brightness Jitter 100%

SOFT ROUND 18

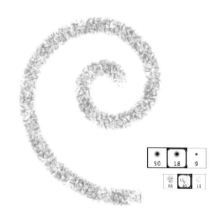

Dual Brush: Size 300 px
Spacing 20%
Scatter 0%
Count 1
Hue Jitter 100%

Dual Brush: Size 133 px
Spacing 40%
Scatter 0%; Count 4
Hue Jitter 100%
Purity -55%

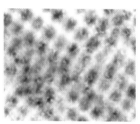

Spacing 95%
Dual Brush: Size 180 px
Spacing 40%; Scatter 0%; Count 4
Hue Jitter 15%
Purity +100%
Wet Edges

Spacing 75%
Dual Brush: Size 180 px
Spacing 1%
Scatter 0%
Count 1
Hue Jitter 95%

SETTINGS

Dual Brush: Size 56 px
Spacing 20%
Scatter 1%
Count 1
Hue Jitter 100%

Dual Brush: Size 56 px
Spacing 60%
Scatter 0%
Count 2
Hue Jitter 100%
Purity +50%

Dual Brush: Size 56 px
Spacing 20%
Scatter 240%
Count 2
Foreground/Background Jitter 33%
Hue Jitter 100%
Purity +50%

Dual Brush: Size 56 px
Spacing 10%
Scatter 240%
Count 3
Foreground/Background Jitter 33%
Hue Jitter 100%
Purity +100%

Dual Brush: Size 56 px
Spacing 55%
Scatter 0%
Count 1
Foreground/Background Jitter 100%
Hue Jitter 100%
Purity +100%

Dual Brush: Size 56 px
Spacing 55%
Scatter 0%; Count 16
Foreground/Background Jitter 100%
Hue Jitter 100%
Purity +100%; Wet Edges

Dual Brush: Size 56 px
Spacing 55%; Scatter 0%; Count 1; Fgnd/Bgnd Jitter 100%; Hue Jitter 100%; Brightness Jitter 100% Purity +100%
Opacity Jitter 100%

Spacing 25%
Dual Brush: Size 67 px
Spacing 20%
Scatter 0%; Count 2
Hue Jitter 100%
Purity +100%
Opacity Jitter 100%

Dual Brush: Size 67 px
Spacing 20%
Scatter 0%; Count 4
Hue Jitter 100%
Purity +100%
Opacity Jitter 100%
Wet Edges

Dual Brush: Size 67 px
Spacing 10%
Scatter 0%
Count 1
Hue Jitter 25%
Purity +100%
Opacity Jitter 100%

SOFT OIL PASTEL

Dual Brush: Size 182 px
Spacing 25%
Scatter 68%
Count 1
Foreground/Background Jitter 100%

Dual Brush: Size 100 px
Spacing 25%
Scatter 60%; Count 2
Foreground/Background Jitter 20%
Hue Jitter 50%; Purity +100%

Scatter 185%
Count 1
Dual Brush: Size 82 px
Spacing 25%; Scatter 68%; Count 2
Foreground/Background Jitter 20%
Hue Jitter 50%

Scatter 85%
Count 1
Dual Brush: Size 82 px
Spacing 25%; Scatter 68%
Count 2
Hue Jitter 100%

SETTINGS

Scatter 85%
Count 1
Dual Brush: Size 34 px
Spacing 25%
Scatter 68%
Count 2
Hue Jitter 100%
Wet Edges

Dual Brush: Size 34 px
Spacing 25%
Scatter 68%
Count 2
Foreground/Background Jitter 100%
Hue Jitter 100%
Purity +100%

Scatter 85%; Count 1
Dual Brush: Size 34 px
Spacing 25%
Scatter 68%; Count 2
Foreground/Background Jitter 100%
Hue Jitter 100%
Purity +100%

Scatter 85%
Count 1
Dual Brush: Size 27 px
Spacing 25%
Scatter 68%
Count 2
Hue Jitter 100%

Angle Jitter 100%
Dual Brush: Size 48 px
Spacing 25%
Scatter 68%
Count 2
Hue Jitter 100%

Angle Jitter 100%
Dual Brush: Size 48 px
Spacing 25%
Scatter 68%
Count 2
Hue Jitter 50%
Purity +100%

Angle Jitter 100%
Dual Brush: Size 48 px
Spacing 25%
Scatter 68%; Count 2
Hue Jitter 50%
Brightness Jitter 100%
Purity +100%

Scatter 240%; Count 1
Dual Brush: Size 20 px
Spacing 25%
Scatter 68%; Count 3
Hue Jitter 50%
Brightness Jitter 50%
Purity +100%

Dual Brush: Size 48 px
Spacing 70%
Scatter 68%
Count 1
Hue Jitter 50%
Brightness Jitter 50%
Purity +100%

Dual Brush: Size 48 px
Spacing 85%
Scatter 120%
Count 1
Foreground/Background Jitter 100%
Purity +100%

SOFT PASTEL LARGE

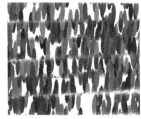

Scatter 500%
Count 1
Dual Brush: Size 60 px
Spacing 10%; Scatter 0%; Count 1
Foreground/Background Jitter 100%

Angle Jitter 100%; Scatter 500%
Count 1; Dual Brush: Size 60 px
Spacing 10%; Scatter 0%; Count 1
Foreground/Background Jitter 100%
Hue Jitter 100%

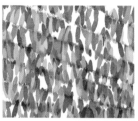

Angle Jitter 5%; Scatter 500%
Count 1
Dual Brush: Size 60 px
Spacing 10%; Scatter 0%; Count 1
Foreground/Background Jitter 100%
Hue Jitter 100%; Wet Edges

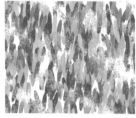

Angle Jitter 5%
Scatter 500%
Count 1
Dual Brush: Size 60 px
Spacing 10%; Scatter 160%; Count 1
Hue Jitter 100%

SETTINGS

Angle Jitter 5%
Scatter 500%
Count 1
Dual Brush: Size 22 px
Spacing 10%
Scatter 85%
Count 1
Hue Jitter 100%

Angle Jitter 5%
Dual Brush: Size 22 px
Spacing 10%
Scatter 85%
Count 1
Hue Jitter 100%

Dual Brush: Size 22 px
Spacing 75%
Scatter 30%
Count 4
Foreground/Background
Jitter 20%
Hue Jitter 100%
Purity +100%

Angle 45°
Dual Brush: Size 22 px
Spacing 110%
Scatter 120%; Count 4
Foreground/Background
Jitter 20%
Hue Jitter 100%
Purity +100%

Angle 5°
Dual Brush: Size 22 px
Spacing 110%
Scatter 120%; Count 4
Foreground/Background
Jitter 20%
Hue Jitter 100%
Purity +100%; Wet Edges

Scatter 50%
Dual Brush: Size 30 px
Spacing 10%
Scatter 0%; Count 1
Foreground/Background
Jitter 100%
Purity +100%

Scatter 500%
Dual Brush: Size 30 px
Spacing 10%
Scatter 0%; Count 1
Foreground/Background
Jitter 100%; Purity +100%
Opacity Jitter 100%

Angle Jitter 20%; Scatter
500%; Dual Brush: Size
30 px; Spacing 10%
Scatter 0%; Count 1
Foreground/Background
Jitter 100%
Hue Jitter 100%
Purity +100%

Angle Jitter 20%; Scatter
500%; Dual Brush: Size
30 px; Spacing 10%
Scatter 0%; Count 1
Foreground/Background
Jitter 100%
Hue Jitter 100%
Purity -20%; Wet Edges

Angle Jitter 20%; Scatter
500%; Dual Brush: Size
30 px; Spacing 10%
Scatter 0%; Count 1
Hue Jitter 100%
Fgnd/Bgnd Jitter 100%
Purity +100%
Opacity Jitter 100%

HEAVY SMEAR
WAX CRAYON

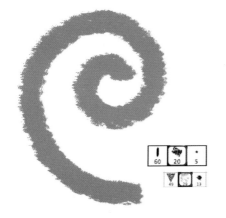

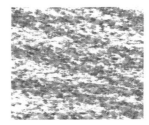

Scatter 500%
Dual Brush: Size 29 px
Spacing 25%
Scatter 0%; Count 1
Hue Jitter 100%

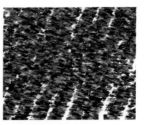

Scatter 190%; Count 1
Dual Brush: Size 44 px
Spacing 25%; Scatter 0%; Count 1
Hue Jitter 100%
Brightness Jitter 100%; Purity +100%

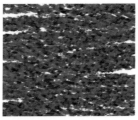

Scatter 190%; Count 1
Dual Brush: Size 44 px
Spacing 25%; Scatter 0%; Count 1
Brightness Jitter 50%
Purity +100%
Wet Edges

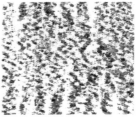

Scatter 200%; Count 1
Dual Brush: Size 44 px
Spacing 1000%
Scatter 0%; Count 1
Hue Jitter 100%
Purity +100%

SETTINGS

Scatter 200%
Count 1
Dual Brush: Size 22 px
Spacing 1000%
Scatter 0%
Count 1
Hue Jitter 100%
Purity +100%

Dual Brush: Size 22 px
Spacing 1000%
Scatter 0%
Count 1
Hue Jitter 100%
Purity +100%

Scatter 35%
Count 1
Dual Brush: Size 22 px
Spacing 1000%
Scatter 0%
Count 1
Hue Jitter 100%
Purity -40%

Scatter 180%
Count 2
Dual Brush: Size 22 px
Spacing 1000%
Scatter 0%; Count 1
Hue Jitter 100%
Brightness Jitter 100%
Purity +20%

Scatter 200%
Count 1
Dual Brush: Size 29 px
Spacing 100%
Scatter 0%; Count 3
Hue Jitter 100%
Brightness Jitter 50%
Purity +20%

Size Jitter 75%
Angle Jitter 35%
Dual Brush: Size 65 px
Spacing 100%; Scatter 0%
Count 1; Foreground/
Background Jitter 100%
Brightness Jitter 50%
Purity +100%

Dual Brush: Size 30 px
Spacing 100%
Scatter 0%; Count 1
Foreground/Background
Jitter 100%
Brightness Jitter 50%
Purity +100%
Opacity Jitter 100%

Dual Brush: Size 33 px
Spacing 100%
Scatter 0%; Count 1
Foreground/Background
Jitter 100%
Hue Jitter 50%
Purity +100%
Opacity Jitter 100%

Scatter 190%; Count 2
Dual Brush: Size 30 px
Spacing 25%
Scatter 0%; Count 1
Brightness Jitter 100%
Purity +100%
Opacity Jitter 100%

Scatter 0%; Count 2
Dual Brush: Size 65 px
Spacing 150%
Scatter 0%; Count 1
Brightness Jitter 100%
Purity +100%
Opacity Jitter 100%

HARD CHARCOAL EDGE

Spacing 20%
Scatter 185%; Count 3
Dual Brush: Size 174 px
Spacing 25%; Scatter 0%; Count 1
Foreground/Background Jitter 100%

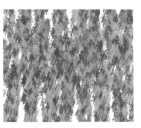

Spacing 20%
Scatter 100%; Count 3
Dual Brush: Size 290 px
Spacing 25%; Scatter 0%
Count 1; Hue Jitter 50%

Scatter 100%
Count 3
Dual Brush: Size 290 px
Spacing 25%
Scatter 0%; Count 1
Hue Jitter 100%

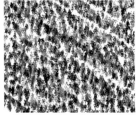

Spacing 22%
Scatter 185%; Count 3
Dual Brush: Size 45 px
Spacing 25%
Scatter 0%; Count 3
Brightness Jitter 100%

SETTINGS

Spacing 22%
Scatter 185%
Count 3
Dual Brush: Size 10 px
Spacing 25%
Scatter 0%; Count 3
Brightness Jitter 100%
Purity +100%

Spacing 22%
Scatter 185%; Count 3
Dual Brush: Size 13 px
Spacing 25%
Scatter 0%; Count 3
Hue Jitter 100%
Brightness Jitter 100%
Purity +100%

Spacing 50%
Scatter 185%; Count 3
Dual Brush: Size 13 px
Spacing 25%
Scatter 0%; Count 3
Hue Jitter 100%
Brightness Jitter 100%
Purity +100%

Scatter 185%
Count 3
Dual Brush: Size 87 px
Spacing 25%
Scatter 0%
Count 3
Hue Jitter 100%
Opacity Jitter 60%

Scatter 70%
Count 1
Dual Brush: Size 145 px
Spacing 25%
Scatter 0%
Count 1
Hue Jitter 100%
Opacity Jitter 60%

Scatter 70%; Count 1
Dual Brush: Size 14 px
Spacing 1%
Scatter 185%; Count 1
Hue Jitter 100%
Purity +100%
Opacity Jitter 50%

Scatter 70%; Count 1
Dual Brush: Size 14 px
Spacing 1%
Scatter 185%; Count 1
Foreground/Background
Jitter 100%; Hue Jitter
100%; Opacity Jitter 50%
Wet Edges

Spacing 70%
Scatter 70%; Count 1
Dual Brush: Size 14 px
Spacing 1%; Scatter 185%
Count 1; Foreground/
Background Jitter 100%
Hue Jitter 100%
Opacity Jitter 50%

Spacing 70%
Dual Brush: Size 14 px
Spacing 1%
Scatter 185%; Count 1
Foreground/Background
Jitter 100%
Hue Jitter 100%
Purity +100%

Scatter 185%; Count 3
Dual Brush: Size 14 px
Spacing 25%; Scatter 0%
Count 1; Fgnd/Bgnd Jitter
10%; Hue Jitter 100%
Brightness Jitter 100%
Purity +100%
Flow Jitter 100%

CHALK DARK

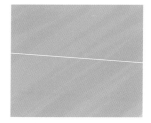

Default Brush

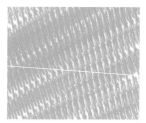

Roundness 50%

Scatter 90%

Hue Jitter 100%

SHAPE DYNAMICS

Size Jitter	0%	50%	50%	100%
Minimum Diameter	0%	0%	50%	0%

SCATTERING

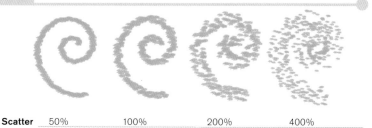

Scatter	50%	100%	200%	400%

COLOR DYNAMICS

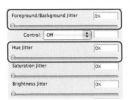

Foreground/Background Jitter	50%	50%	0%	100%
Hue Jitter	0%	50%	50%	100%

TRANSFER

Opacity Jitter	0%	0%	50%	100%
Flow Jitter	0%	50%	0%	100%

BRUSH TIP SHAPE

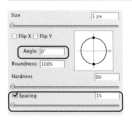

Angle	135°	135°	135°	135°
Spacing	1%	25%	50%	100%

DUAL BRUSH

Dual Brush:
Watercolor 2

Spacing	25%	1%	100%	1000%
Scatter	0%	200%	200%	1000%

CHALK LIGHT

Default Brush

Hue Jitter 100%

Flow Jitter 100%

Scatter 100%

TRANSFER

Opacity Jitter	0%	0%	50%	100%
Flow Jitter	0%	50%	0%	100%

DUAL BRUSH

Chalk Dark

Spacing	25%	1%	100%	400%
Scatter	0%	200%	200%	0%

SHAPE DYNAMICS

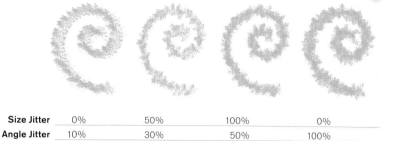

Size Jitter	0%	50%	100%	0%
Angle Jitter	10%	30%	50%	100%

BRUSH TIP SHAPE

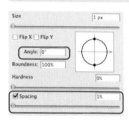

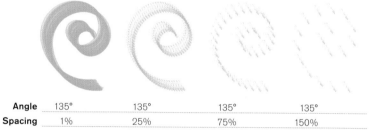

Angle	135°	135°	135°	135°
Spacing	1%	25%	75%	150%

COLOR DYNAMICS

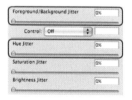

Foreground/Background Jitter	50%	50%	0%	100%
Hue Jitter	0%	50%	50%	100%

SCATTERING

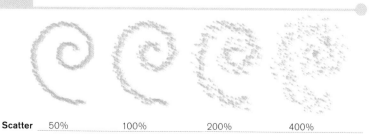

Scatter	50%	100%	200%	400%

DRY BRUSH

Default Brush

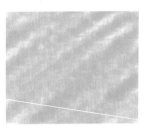

Size Jitter 100%

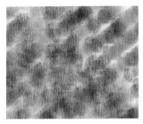

Foreground/Background Jitter 100%

Roundness Jitter 100%

SCATTERING

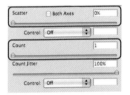

Scatter	50%	50%	150%	150%
Count	1	5	1	10

TRANSFER

Opacity Jitter	0%	0%	50%	100%
Flow Jitter	0%	100%	0%	100%

BRUSH TIP SHAPE

Angle	100°	100°	100°	100°
Spacing	1%	30%	150%	300%

DUAL BRUSH

Dual Brush: Chalk Dark

Spacing	50%	30%	200%	0%
Scatter	0%	200%	0%	1000%

SHAPE DYNAMICS • WET EDGES

Size Jitter	50%	50%	100%	100%
Wet Edges	Off	On	Off	On

COLOR DYNAMICS

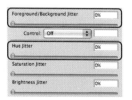 

Foreground/Background Jitter	100%	100%	0%	100%
Hue Jitter	0%	50%	100%	100%

PASTEL DARK

Default Brush

Dual Brush: Chalk Dark

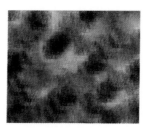

Hue Jitter 50%

Spacing 110%

COLOR DYNAMICS

Foreground/Background Jitter	50%	50%	0%	100%
Hue Jitter	0%	50%	50%	100%

SCATTERING

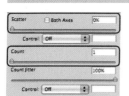

Scatter	50%	50%	200%	200%
Count	1	3	1	3

BRUSH TIP SHAPE

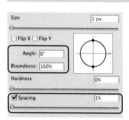

Angle	-125°	-125°	-125°	-125°
Roundness	25%	25%	25%	25%
Spacing	1%	30%	75%	100%

TRANSFER • WET EDGES

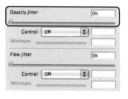

Opacity Jitter	50%	50%	100%	100%
Wet Edges	Off	On	Off	On

SHAPE DYNAMICS

Size Jitter	50%	50%	100%	100%
Minimum Diameter	0%	50%	0%	100%

DUAL BRUSH

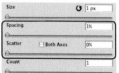

Dual Brush:
Chalk Dark

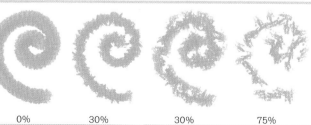

Spacing	0%	30%	30%	75%
Scatter	0%	0%	100%	100%

PASTEL LIGHT

Default Brush

Dual Brush: Pencil Thick

Foreground/Background Jitter 100%   Spacing 40%

TRANSFER • WET EDGES

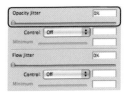

Opacity Jitter	50%	50%	100%	100%
Wet Edges	Off	On	Off	On

DUAL BRUSH

Dual Brush:
Chalk Light

Spacing	20%	20%	100%	100%
Scatter	0%	100%	0%	200%

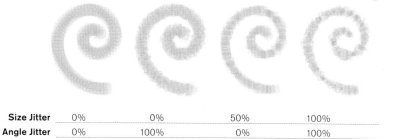

SHAPE DYNAMICS

Size Jitter	0%	0%	50%	100%
Angle Jitter	0%	100%	0%	100%

SCATTERING

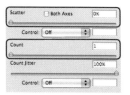

Scatter	100%	100%	300%	300%
Count	1	3	1	3

BRUSH TIP SHAPE

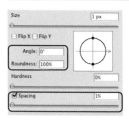

Angle	150°	150°	150°	150°
Roundness	60%	60%	60%	60%
Spacing	25%	45%	75%	100%

COLOR DYNAMICS

Foreground/Background Jitter	0%	0%	50%	100%
Hue Jitter	50%	100%	0%	100%

SWIRL

Default Brush

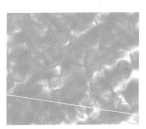

Angle Jitter 80%

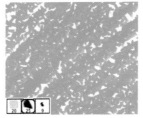

Dual Brush: Pencil Thick

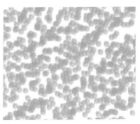

Scatter 300%

BRUSH TIP SHAPE

Angle	45°	45°	45°	45°
Roundness	100%	100%	100%	100%
Spacing	20%	50%	100%	150%

SHAPE DYNAMICS • SCATTERING

Size Jitter	30%	30%	100%	100%
Scatter	0%	100%	0%	200%

DUAL BRUSH

Dual Brush:
Chalk Dark

Spacing	75%	75%	75%	75%
Scatter	0%	100%	0%	100%
Count	1	3	1	3

COLOR DYNAMICS

Hue Jitter	100%	100%	100%	100%
Brightness Jitter	0%	50%	0%	100%
Purity	0%	0%	+50%	+100%

SCATTERING

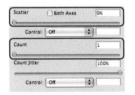

Scatter	100%	100%	300%	300%
Count	3	3	3	3
Wet Edges	Off	On	Off	On

COLOR DYNAMICS • TRANSFER • NOISE

Hue Jitter	100%	100%	100%	100%
Opacity Jitter	0%	0%	100%	100%
Noise	Off	On	Off	On

WATERCOLOR BRUSH 1

Default Brush

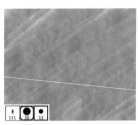

Dual Brush: Hard Round

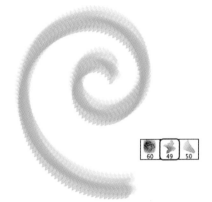

Hue Jitter 50%

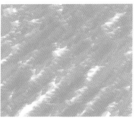

Wet Edges

SCATTERING

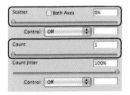

Scatter	50%	50%	100%	100%
Count	1	3	1	3

TRANSFER • NOISE

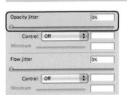

Opacity Jitter	0%	0%	100%	100%
Noise	Off	On	Off	On

BRUSH TIP SHAPE

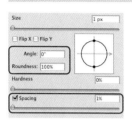

Angle	85°	85°	85°	85°
Roundness	35%	35%	35%	35%
Spacing	25%	50%	75%	150%

SHAPE DYNAMICS • WET EDGES

Size Jitter	100%	100%	100%	100%
Roundness Jitter	50%	50%	100%	100%
Wet Edges	Off	On	Off	On

COLOR DYNAMICS • NOISE

Foreground/Background Jitter	100%	100%	0%	0%
Hue Jitter	0%	0%	100%	100%
Noise	Off	On	Off	On

DUAL BRUSH

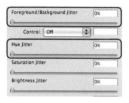

Chalk Dark

Spacing	75%	75%	75%	75%
Scatter	0%	100%	0%	100%
Count	1	3	1	3

WATERCOLOR BRUSH 2

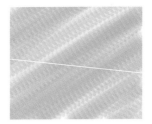

Default Brush

Spacing 30%

Foreground/Background Jitter 50%

Scatter 500%

SHAPE DYNAMICS • SCATTERING

Size Jitter	20%	20%	20%	20%
Roundness Jitter	0%	20%	0%	20%
Scatter	0%	50%	0%	50%

SCATTERING • COLOR DYNAMICS

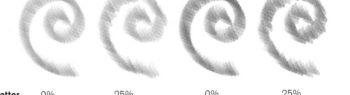

Scatter	0%	25%	0%	25%
Hue Jitter	50%	50%	100%	100%

SCATTERING • WET EDGES

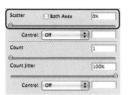

Scatter	50%	50%	100%	100%
Wet Edges	Off	On	Off	On

DUAL BRUSH

Dual Brush:
Watercolor 2

Spacing	25%	25%	50%	50%
Scatter	0%	100%	0%	100%
Count	3	3	3	3

BRUSH TIP SHAPE

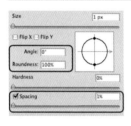

Angle	0°	20°	0°	20°
Roundness	45%	45%	45%	45%
Spacing	25%	25%	50%	50%

COLOR DYNAMICS • TRANSFER

Hue Jitter	0%	50%	0%	50%
Opacity Jitter	10%	10%	100%	100%

WATERCOLOR BRUSH 3

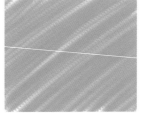

Default Brush

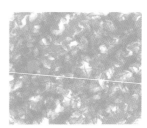

Angle Jitter 50%

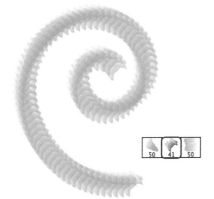

Scatter 150%

Dual Brush: Wet Brush

DUAL BRUSH

Dual Brush:
Dry Brush

Spacing	70%	70%	70%	70%
Count	3	6	9	15

COLOR DYNAMICS • TRANSFER

Purity	0%	+100%	0%	+100%
Opacity Jitter	50%	50%	100%	100%

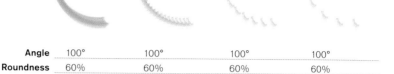

BRUSH TIP SHAPE

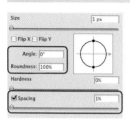

Angle	100°	100°	100°	100°
Roundness	60%	60%	60%	60%
Spacing	10%	30%	75%	130%

SHAPE DYNAMICS

Angle Jitter	10%	50%	10%	50%
Roundness Jitter	30%	30%	100%	100%

SCATTERING

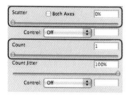

Scatter	10%	10%	100%	100%
Count	4	10	4	10

SHAPE DYNAMICS • COLOR DYNAMICS

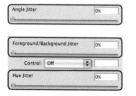

Angle Jitter	0%	20%	0%	20%
Foreground/Background Jitter	50%	50%	50%	50%
Hue Jitter	0%	50%	0%	50%

WATERCOLOR BRUSH 4

Default Brush

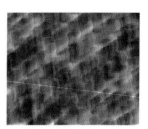

Hue Jitter 100%

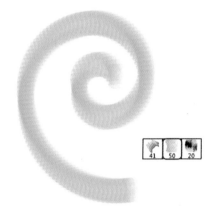

Scatter 50%

Opacity Jitter 100%

SCATTERING

Scatter	100%	100%	200%	200%
Count	1	9	1	9

BRUSH TIP SHAPE

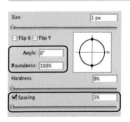

Angle	45°	45°	45°	45°
Roundness	100%	50%	30%	5%
Spacing	40%	40%	40%	40%

COLOR DYNAMICS • WET EDGES

Hue Jitter	50%	50%	50%	50%
Brightness Jitter	0%	0%	50%	50%
Wet Edges	Off	On	Off	On

SHAPE DYNAMICS • TRANSFER

Angle Jitter	0%	20%	0%	20%
Opacity Jitter	0%	0%	50%	50%
Flow Jitter	50%	50%	100%	100%

SHAPE DYNAMICS • DUAL BRUSH

Dual Brush:
Pastel Dark

Angle Jitter	0%	20%	0%	20%
Spacing	20%	20%	20%	20%
Count	1	1	3	3

SHAPE DYNAMICS • COLOR DYNAMICS

Size Jitter	50%	50%	50%	50%
Roundness Jitter	0%	0%	50%	50%
Brightness Jitter	0%	50%	0%	50%

WET BRUSH

Default Brush

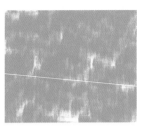

Scatter 150%

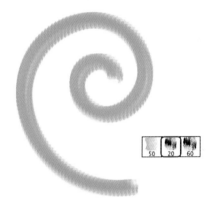

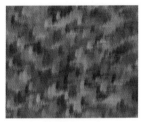

Foreground/Background Jitter 50%

Dual Brush: Chalk

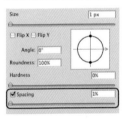

Spacing	25%	50%	50%	100%
Scatter	25%	25%	100%	100%

Size Jitter	50%	50%	100%	100%
Angle Jitter	0%	50%	0%	50%
Roundness Jitter	0%	0%	50%	50%

TRANSFER

Opacity Jitter	0%	50%	100%	100%
Flow Jitter	50%	50%	50%	100%

BRUSH TIP SHAPE

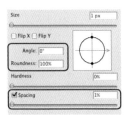

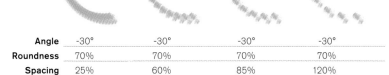

Angle	-30°	-30°	-30°	-30°
Roundness	70%	70%	70%	70%
Spacing	25%	60%	85%	120%

COLOR DYNAMICS • NOISE

Hue Jitter	50%	50%	100%	100%
Brightness Jitter	50%	50%	50%	50%
Noise	Off	On	Off	On

SCATTERING • WET EDGES

Scatter	50%	50%	200%	200%
Wet Edges	Off	On	Off	On

STIPPLE

Angle Jitter 50%
Roundness Jitter 50%

Angle 66°
Roundness 40%
Spacing 5%

Foreground/Background Jitter 100%
Brightness Jitter 50%

Spacing 20%
Scatter 80%
Count 1

SCATTERING

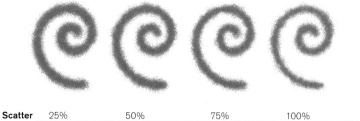

Scatter   25%   50%   75%   100%

BRUSH TIP SHAPE

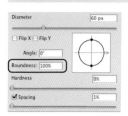

Roundness   25%   50%   75%   100%

COLOR DYNAMICS

Foreground/Background Jitter	100%	100%	100%	100%
Hue Jitter	25%	50%	75%	100%

SHAPE DYNAMICS

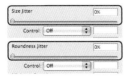 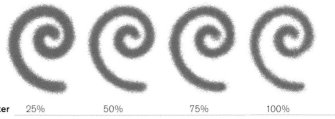

Size Jitter	25%	50%	75%	100%
Roundness Jitter	25%	50%	75%	100%

BRUSH TIP SHAPE

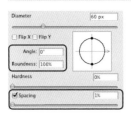 

Angle	0°	33°	66°	100°
Roundness	0%	33%	66%	100%
Spacing	1%	5%	10%	15%

SHAPE DYNAMICS • COLOR DYNAMICS

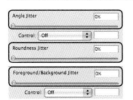 

Angle Jitter	25%	50%	75%	100%
Roundness Jitter	25%	50%	75%	100%
Foreground/Background Jitter	25%	50%	75%	100%

STIPPLE
DENSE

Size Jitter 50%
Foreground/Background Jitter 100%
Saturation Jitter 50%

Size Jitter 100%
Scatter 350%
Count 1

Foreground/Background Jitter 50%
Hue Jitter 50%
Saturation Jitter 50%

Spacing 15%
Size Jitter 50%
Wet Edges

SHAPE DYNAMICS

Size Jitter	25%	50%	75%	100%
Angle Jitter	25%	50%	75%	100%

SHAPE DYNAMICS

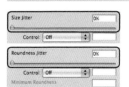

Size Jitter	25%	50%	75%	100%
Roundness Jitter	25%	50%	75%	100%

SCATTERING

Scatter	10%	50%	100%	150%
Count	1	2	3	4

COLOR DYNAMICS

Foreground/Background Jitter	25%	50%	75%	100%
Saturation Jitter	25%	50%	75%	100%

TRANSFER

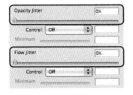 

Opacity Jitter	25%	50%	75%	100%
Flow Jitter	25%	50%	75%	100%

COLOR DYNAMICS

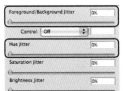 

Foreground/Background Jitter	25%	50%	75%	100%
Hue Jitter	25%	50%	75%	100%

CHARCOAL

Wet Edges

Angle 90°
Roundness 20%

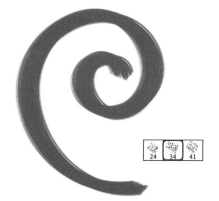

Scatter 200%
Count 3

Spacing 20%
Size Jitter 100%
Angle Jitter 100%

COLOR DYNAMICS

Hue Jitter	25%	50%	75%	100%
Purity	+25%	+50%	+75%	+100%

SCATTERING

Scatter	25%	50%	75%	100%
Count	2	2	2	2

SHAPE DYNAMICS

Size Jitter	25%	50%	75%	100%
Roundness Jitter	25%	50%	75%	100%

TRANSFER

Opacity Jitter	25%	50%	75%	100%
Flow Jitter	25%	50%	75%	100%

SHAPE DYNAMICS • WET EDGES

Size Jitter	25%	50%	75%	100%
Angle Jitter	25%	50%	75%	100%
Wet Edges	on	on	on	on

BRUSH TIP SHAPE

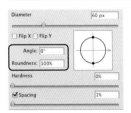

Angle	25%	50%	75%	100%
Roundness	25%	50%	75%	100%

SPRAY

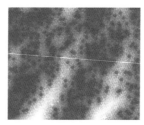

Scatter 100%
Count 2

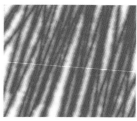

Roundness 100%
Size Jitter 100%
Angle Jitter 100%

Foreground/Background Jitter 100%
Saturation Jitter 100%
Purity +50%
Wet Edges

Roundness 20%
Spacing 15%

BRUSH TIP SHAPE

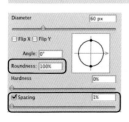

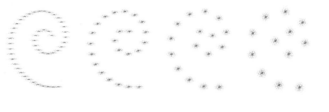

Roundness	25%	50%	75%	100%
Spacing	25%	50%	75%	100%

COLOR DYNAMICS

Foreground/Background Jitter	100%	100%	100%	100%
Hue Jitter	25%	50%	75%	100%

SCATTERING

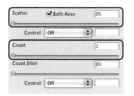

Scatter	25%	50%	75%	100%
Count	2	2	2	2

BRUSH TIP SHAPE • SHAPE DYNAMICS

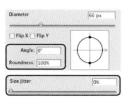

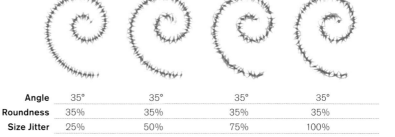

Angle	35°	35°	35°	35°
Roundness	35%	35%	35%	35%
Size Jitter	25%	50%	75%	100%

COLOR DYNAMICS • WET EDGES

Hue Jitter	25%	50%	75%	100%
Wet Edges	on	on	on	on

SHAPE DYNAMICS • NOISE

Size Jitter	25%	50%	75%	100%
Noise	on	on	on	on

AZALEA

Spacing 90%
Hue Jitter 25%

Spacing 90%
Angle Jitter 20%
Scatter 100%
Count 3
Count Jitter 60%
Foreground/Background Jitter 100%

Spacing 90%
Angle Jitter 20%
Count 5
Hue Jitter 100%

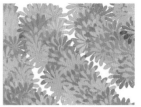

Spacing 7%
Angle Jitter 20%
Scatter 100%
Count 1
Hue Jitter 100%
Wet Edges

SETTINGS

Spacing 50%
Scatter 100%
Count 1
Hue Jitter 100%
Purity +100%

Spacing 50%
Scatter 100%
Count 2
Hue Jitter 100%
Purity +25%

Spacing 50%
Scatter 100%
Count 1
Hue Jitter 100%
Purity +100%

Spacing 50%
Size Jitter 100%
Foreground/Background
Jitter 100%
Brightness Jitter 50%
Purity +100%

Spacing 50%
Size Jitter 100%
Foreground/Background
Jitter 100%
Hue Jitter 40%
Brightness Jitter 50%
Purity +100%

Spacing 30%
Brightness Jitter 100%
Purity +100%

Spacing 30%
Foreground/Background
Jitter 25%
Hue Jitter 25%
Purity +50%

Spacing 30%
Foreground/Background
Jitter 25%
Hue Jitter 50%
Purity +50%

Spacing 50%
Angle Jitter 45%
Roundness Jitter 100%
Scatter 30%
Count 2
Hue Jitter 75%
Purity +75%

Spacing 50%
Angle Jitter 45%
Roundness Jitter 100%
Scatter 30%
Count 2
Hue Jitter 33%
Purity +75%
Wet Edges

SCATTERED ROSES

Spacing 75%
Scatter 100%
Count 1
Foreground/Background Jitter 100%
Brightness Jitter 100%

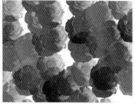

Spacing 75%; Scatter 150%
Count 3; Count Jitter 50%
Foreground/Background Jitter 50%
Hue Jitter 10%; Brightness Jitter 25%
Purity +100%; Wet Edges

Spacing 75%
Size Jitter 100%
Count 3
Count Jitter 50%
Hue Jitter 100%
Purity -50%
Noise

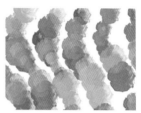

Spacing 75%
Size Jitter 100%
Count 3
Count Jitter 50%
Hue Jitter 100%
Purity +20%
Wet Edges

SETTINGS

Spacing 75%
Size Jitter 100%
Count 3
Hue Jitter 100%
Purity +20%

Spacing 50%
Size Jitter 50%
Count 1
Hue Jitter 50%
Purity -10%

Roundness 50%
Spacing 20%
Size Jitter 50%
Scatter 110%; Count 1
Foreground/Background
Jitter 100%
Hue Jitter 50%
Wet Edges

Angle 45°
Roundness 50%
Spacing 20%
Size Jitter 50%
Foreground/Background
Jitter 100%
Hue Jitter 50%

Angle 45°
Roundness 50%
Spacing 20%
Size Jitter 100%
Angle Jitter 25%
Foreground/Background
Jitter 100%
Hue Jitter 50%

Angle 45°; Rndnss 50%
Spacing 20%
Size Jitter 100%
Angle Jitter 25%
Foreground/Background
Jitter 100%
Hue Jitter 50%; Wet Edges
Purity +100%; Wet Edges

Roundness 50%
Spacing 20%
Size Jitter 100%
Angle Jitter 25%
Scatter 50%
Count 2; Hue Jitter 100%
Purity +100%

Spacing 75%
Scatter 100%
Count 5
Hue Jitter 100%

Spacing 75%
Scatter 100%
Count 16
Hue Jitter 100%
Wet Edges

Roundness 45%
Spacing 100%
Angle Jitter 20%
Foreground/Background
Jitter 100%
Hue Jitter 30%
Purity +100%

SCATTERED DAISIES

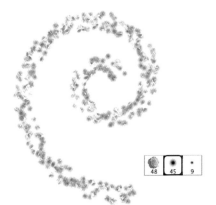

Scatter 200%
Count 2
Foreground/Background Jitter 100%
Hue Jitter 100%

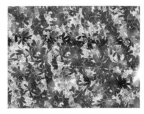

Count 6
Foreground/Background Jitter 100%
Hue Jitter 50%
Purity +100%
Wet Edges

Count 3
Hue Jitter 100%
Purity -40%

Foreground/Background Jitter 100%
Hue Jitter 100%
Purity +100%
Wet Edges

SETTINGS

Foreground/Background
Jitter 100%
Hue Jitter 100%
Purity +100%

Scatter 100%
Foreground/Background
Jitter 100%
Hue Jitter 100%
Purity +100%
Wet Edges

Scatter 33%
Count 9
Foreground/Background
Jitter 100%
Hue Jitter 100%

Hue Jitter 100%
Size Jitter 100%
Purity +100%

Spacing 1%
Size Jitter 100%
Hue Jitter 100%
Purity +100%

Size Jitter 100%
Foreground/Background
Jitter 100%
Hue Jitter 50%
Purity +100%

Angle 45°
Roundness 10%
Count 3
Hue Jitter 100%
Purity +100%

Angle 45°
Roundness 10%
Angle Jitter 20%
Count 3
Hue Jitter 100%
Purity +100%; Wet Edges

Spacing 100%
Count 6
Angle Jitter 20%
Foreground/Background
Jitter 100%
Purity +100%

Spacing 80%
Hue Jitter 100%
Purity +100%

DRIPPY WATERCOLOR

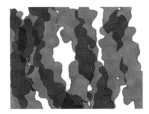

Foreground/Background Jitter 100%
Hue Jitter 10%
Purity +100%

Hue Jitter 100%
Purity -30%

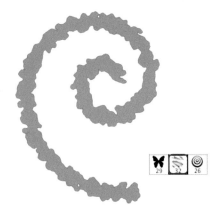

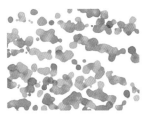

Spacing 100%
Hue Jitter 100%

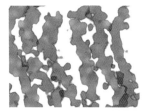

Count 3
Hue Jitter 40%
Purity +100%
Opacity Jitter 100%

SETTINGS

Spacing 100%
Foreground/Background
Jitter 100%
Purity +100%

Spacing 100%
Foreground/Background
Jitter 100%
Hue Jitter 100%
Purity +100%

Spacing 50%
Foreground/Background
Jitter 100%
Hue Jitter 100%
Brightness Jitter 100%

Spacing 120%
Foreground/Background
Jitter 100%
Hue Jitter 50%
Brightness Jitter 100%
Purity -30%

Spacing 120%
Count 8
Brightness Jitter 100%
Purity +100%

Spacing 120%
Scatter 400%
Count 8
Brightness Jitter 100%
Purity +100%

Spacing 120%
Scatter 400%
Count 8
Hue Jitter 100%
Brightness Jitter 100%
Purity +100%

Spacing 120%
Scatter 800%
Count 16
Foreground/Background
Jitter 100%
Purity +100%

Spacing 120%
Scatter 800%; Count 16
Foreground/Background
Jitter 100%
Hue Jitter 40%
Purity +50%

Spacing 400%
Scatter 650%; Count 16
Foreground/Background
Jitter 100%
Hue Jitter 40%
Purity +50%

SCATTERED FLOWERS MUMS

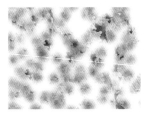

Foreground/Background Jitter 100%
Hue Jitter 40%
Purity +100%

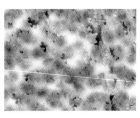

Spacing 10%
Foreground/Background Jitter 100%
Brightness Jitter 100%

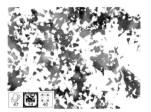

Dual Brush: Sampled Tip
Count 3
Hue Jitter 100%
Brightness Jitter 100%

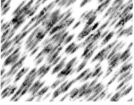

Angle 45°
Roundness 25%
Hue Jitter 100%
Brightness Jitter 100%
Purity +100%

SETTINGS

Angle 45°
Roundness 25%
Angle Jitter 45%
Hue Jitter 100%
Brightness Jitter 100%
Purity +100%

Angle 90°
Roundness 45%
Foreground/Background
Jitter 100%
Brightness Jitter 100%

Size Jitter 90%
Angle Jitter 45%
Foreground/Background
Jitter 40%
Hue Jitter 100%
Brightness Jitter 100%
Purity +100%; Wet Edges

Angle Jitter 45%
Hue Jitter 100%
Purity +100%

Angle Jitter 45%
Scatter 100%
Count 1
Hue Jitter 100%
Purity +100%
Wet Edges

Angle Jitter 45%
Scatter 100%
Count 2
Hue Jitter 100%
Purity +100%

Hardness 100%
Count 2
Hue Jitter 100%

Hardness 100%
Count 2
Hue Jitter 100%
Purity +100%

Hardness 100%
Count 2
Hue Jitter 100%
Purity +100%
Wet Edges

Spacing 15%
Scatter 450%
Count 1
Wet Edges

SCATTERED WILD FLOWERS

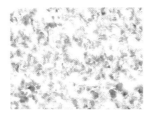

Angle 45°
Roundness 50%
Angle Jitter 45%
Count 2
Hue Jitter 100%

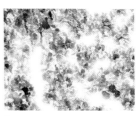

Scatter 150%
Count 1
Hue Jitter 25%
Brightness Jitter 100%
Purity +100%

Scatter 150%
Count 1
Hue Jitter 100%
Brightness Jitter 50%
Purity +100%
Wet Edges

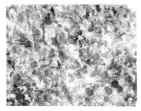

Count 6
Hue Jitter 100%
Brightness Jitter 100%
Purity -20%

SETTINGS

Count 6
Hue Jitter 100%
Brightness Jitter 100%
Purity -20%
Wet Edges

Count 6
Hue Jitter 100%
Brightness Jitter 100%
Purity +100%
Wet Edges

Wet Edges

Hue Jitter 100%
Purity +20%
Wet Edges

Spacing 10%
Size Jitter 50%
Angle Jitter 45%
Foreground/Background
Jitter 100%
Hue Jitter 100%
Purity +20%

Spacing 10%; Size
Jitter 50%; Angle
Jitter 45%; Scatter 105%
Count 1; Foreground/
Background Jitter 100%
Hue Jitter 100%
Purity +20%; Wet Edges

Spacing 10%; Size
Jitter 50%; Angle
Jitter 45%; Scatter 105%
Count 2; Foreground/
Background Jitter 100%
Hue Jitter 50%
Purity +20%; Wet Edges

Scatter 500%
Count 1
Foreground/Background
Jitter 100%
Brightness Jitter 100%
Purity +100%
Wet Edges

Scatter 0%
Count 4
Hue Jitter 100%
Brightness Jitter 25%

Hardness 100%
Spacing 25%
Hue Jitter 100%
Brightness Jitter 25%
Wet Edges

LARGE ROSES
WITH CHROMA

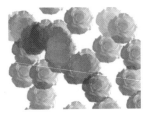

Wet Edges

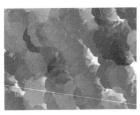

Scatter 200%
Count 2
Wet Edges

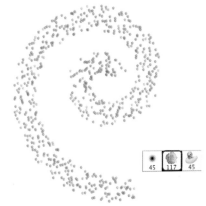

Scatter 300%
Count 2
Hue Jitter 100%
Purity +100%

Spacing 10%
Scatter 100%
Count 1
Foreground/Background Jitter 100%
Brightness Jitter 100%
Purity +100%

SETTINGS

Scatter 105%

Scatter 105%
Count 2
Wet Edges

Scatter 105%
Count 2
Hue Jitter 100%

Spacing 25%
Scatter 50%
Count 4
Foreground/Background
Jitter 100%

Spacing 100%
Scatter 15%
Count 2
Foreground/Background
Jitter 100%
Wet Edges

Size Jitter 60%
Scatter 400%
Count 1
Foreground/Background
Jitter 100%
Hue Jitter 100%
Purity -25%

Spacing 100%
Size Jitter 30%
Scatter 50%; Count 1
Foreground/Background
Jitter 100%
Hue Jitter 100%
Purity +100%

Spacing 100%
Size Jitter 30%
Scatter 50%; Count 1
Foreground/Background
Jitter 100%
Hue Jitter 100%
Purity +100%; Wet Edges

Spacing 75%
Size Jitter 30%
Scatter 50%; Count 1
Hue Jitter 100%
Brightness Jitter 60%
Purity +25%
Wet Edges

Spacing 75%
Size Jitter 30%
Scatter 50%
Count 3
Hue Jitter 100%
Brightness Jitter 60%

DUCKS NOT IN A ROW

Size Jitter 50%
Scatter 300%
Count 1
Count Jitter 14%
Foreground/Background Jitter 100%
Saturation Jitter 100%

Spacing 50%
Size Jitter 75%
Scatter 120%
Foreground/Background Jitter 100%
Hue Jitter 100%

Scatter 100%
Count 2
Foreground/Background Jitter 100%
Hue Jitter 100%
Purity -5%
Wet Edges

Scatter 100%
Count 1
Foreground/Background Jitter 100%
Hue Jitter 100%
Purity +100%
Wet Edges

SETTINGS

Scatter 100%
Count 1
Foreground/Background
Jitter 100%
Hue Jitter 100%
Purity +100%

Scatter 100%
Count 1
Foreground/Background
Jitter 100%
Hue Jitter 100%
Brightness Jitter 100%

Spacing 75%
Scatter 0%
Count 1

Spacing 75%
Scatter 100%
Count 2
Hue Jitter 100%
Brightness Jitter 100%

Spacing 75%; Size
Jitter 50%; Scatter 120%
Count 1; Foreground/
Background Jitter 100%
Hue Jitter 50%
Saturation Jitter 100%
Purity +50%

Size Jitter 100%
Angle Jitter 10%
Scatter 200%
Count 3
Hue Jitter 100%
Wet Edges

Size Jitter 100%
Angle Jitter 10%
Scatter 200%
Count 1
Hue Jitter 100%
Brightness Jitter 100%

Spacing 50%
Size Jitter 50%
Scatter 330%; Count 1
Foreground/Background
Jitter 100%
Hue Jitter 50%
Purity +100%

Scatter 0%
Count 1
Hue Jitter 50%
Purity +100%

Spacing 5%
Scatter 50%
Count 1
Foreground/Background
Jitter 50%
Hue Jitter 50%
Purity +100%

FALLING IVY LEAVES

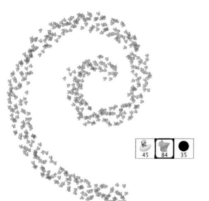

Size Jitter 75%
Angle Jitter 20%
Foreground/Background Jitter 100%
Purity +100%
Wet Edges

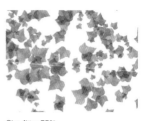

Size Jitter 75%
Angle Jitter 50%
Foreground/Background Jitter 100%
Hue Jitter 15%
Purity +100%

Angle 45°
Spacing 10%
Size Jitter 75%
Angle Jitter 75%
Foreground/Background Jitter 100%
Hue Jitter 50%

Angle 45°
Spacing 10%
Size Jitter 75%
Angle Jitter 75%
Foreground/Background Jitter 100%
Hue Jitter 50%
Brightness Jitter 100%

SETTINGS

Angle 45°; Spacing 10%
Size Jitter 75%; Angle
Jitter 75%; Foreground/
Background Jitter 100%
Hue Jitter 50%
Brightness Jitter 100%
Wet Edges

Scatter 110%
Count 1
Hue Jitter 95%
Wet Edges

Scatter 110%
Count 1
Hue Jitter 95%
Brightness Jitter 50%
Purity +40%

Spacing 100%
Scatter 60%; Count 2
Count Jitter 66%
Foreground/Background
Jitter 88%; Hue Jitter
10%; Brightness
Jitter 50%; Purity +100%
Wet Edges

Spacing 120%
Scatter 100%; Count 2
Count Jitter 45%
Foreground/Background
Jitter 100%
Brightness Jitter 100%
Wet Edges

Spacing 75%
Size Jitter 35%
Angle Jitter 50%
Scatter 10%
Count 1
Hue Jitter 55%
Wet Edges

Spacing 75%
Size Jitter 35%
Angle Jitter 50%
Scatter 300%
Count 1
Hue Jitter 55%

Size Jitter 35%
Angle Jitter 50%
Scatter 200%
Count 2
Hue Jitter 55%

Size Jitter 35%
Angle Jitter 50%
Scatter 200%
Count 2
Hue Jitter 55%
Purity +100%
Wet Edges

Size Jitter 35%
Angle Jitter 50%
Scatter 80%
Count 2
Hue Jitter 100%
Purity +75%

HYPNO LINES

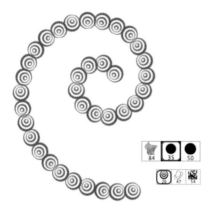

Spacing 100%
Foreground/Background Jitter 100%
Hue Jitter 100%
Purity +75%

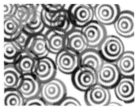

Size Jitter 86%
Foreground/Background Jitter 100%
Hue Jitter 100%

Angle 45°
Roundness 50%
Hardness 100%
Spacing 1%
Hue Jitter 50%
Purity +100%
Wet Edges

Angle 45°
Roundness 50%
Hardness 100%
Spacing 1%
Hue Jitter 10%
Purity -50%

SETTINGS

Foreground/Background
Jitter 100%
Hue Jitter 100%
Purity -50%

Foreground/Background
Jitter 100%
Hue Jitter 100%
Purity +20%
Wet Edges

Spacing 100%
Foreground/Background
Jitter 100%
Hue Jitter 100%
Purity +100%
Wet Edges

Spacing 100%
Hue Jitter 100%
Purity +100%

Spacing 100%
Scatter 500%
Count 16%
Hue Jitter 100%
Purity +100%

Spacing 100%
Roundness Jitter 100%
Scatter 1%
Count 1
Foreground/Background
Jitter 100%
Brightness Jitter 100%

Hardness 100%
Spacing 100%
Size Jitter 100%
Roundness Jitter 100%
Scatter 520%
Count 8

Spacing 50%
Size Jitter 100%
Roundness Jitter 100%
Scatter 0%
Count 1
Hue Jitter 100%
Wet Edges

Dual Brush:
Diameter 35px
Hue Jitter 66%

Dual Brush:
Diameter 30px
Foreground/Background
Jitter 50%
Hue Jitter 50%
Purity +100%
Wet Edges

TUMBLE PLANETS

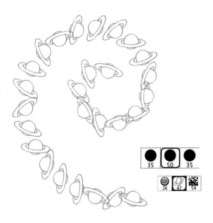

Foreground/Background Jitter 100%
Hue Jitter 100%
Purity -12%

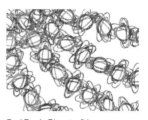

Dual Brush: Diameter 94 px
Spacing 12%; Count 4
Foreground/Background Jitter 100%
Hue Jitter 100%
Purity +100%
Wet Edges

Dual Brush: Diameter 40 px
Spacing 125%; Count 2
Foreground/Background Jitter 100%
Hue Jitter 100%
Brightness Jitter 100%
Purity -15%

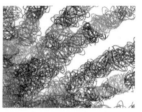

Dual Brush: Diameter 80 px
Spacing 33%; Scatter 33%; Count 2
Foreground/Background Jitter 100%
Hue Jitter 100%
Purity +100%

SETTINGS

Dual Brush:
Diameter 80 px
Spacing 33%
Scatter 33%; Count 2
Foreground/Background
Jitter 100%; Hue Jitter
100%; Purity +100%
Wet Edges

Dual Brush:
Diameter 30 px
Spacing 100%
Scatter 0%; Count 2
Foreground/Background
Jitter 100%
Hue Jitter 100%
Purity +100%

Dual Brush:
Diameter 30 px
Spacing 100%
Scatter 0%
Count 2
Hue Jitter 100%
Purity +100%

Dual Brush:
Diameter 30 px
Spacing 100%
Scatter 200%
Count 2
Hue Jitter 100%
Purity +100%

Dual Brush: Diameter
30 px; Spacing 30%
Scatter 200%; Count 6
Foreground/Background
Jitter 100%
Hue Jitter 100%
Brightness Jitter 100%
Purity +100%

Dual Brush: Diameter
30 px; Spacing 30%
Scatter 200%; Count 6
Foreground/Background
Jitter 100%
Hue Jitter 100%
Purity +100%; Wet Edges

Dual Brush:
Diameter 14 px
Spacing 10%
Scatter 200%; Count 2
Foreground/Background
Jitter 50%; Hue Jitter
100%; Purity +100%

Dual Brush:
Diameter 40 px
Spacing 150%
Scatter 0%; Count 3
Hue Jitter 100%
Brightness Jitter 100%
Purity +100%

Dual Brush:
Diameter 120 px
Spacing 150%
Scatter 0%; Count 3
Foreground/Background
Jitter 100%
Hue Jitter 100%

Dual Brush: Diameter
120 px; Spacing 150%
Scatter 0%; Count 10
Foreground/Background
Jitter 100%
Hue Jitter 100%
Wet Edges

GRANITE FLOW

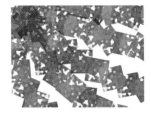

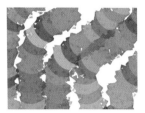

Dual Brush: Diameter 75 px
Spacing 80%; Count 1
Foreground/Background Jitter 100%
Wet Edges

Dual Brush: Diameter 75 px
Spacing 80%; Count 3
Foreground/Background Jitter 100%
Hue Jitter 100%
Wet Edges

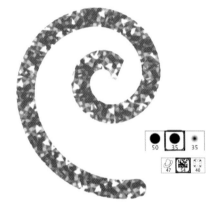

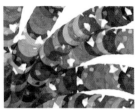

Dual Brush: Diameter 123 px
Spacing 80%; Count 1
Foreground/Background Jitter 100%
Hue Jitter 100%
Wet Edges

Dual Brush: Diameter 123 px
Spacing 80%; Count 1
Foreground/Background Jitter 100%
Hue Jitter 100%
Brightness Jitter 100%
Purity +100%
Wet Edges

SETTINGS

Dual Brush:
Diameter 123 px
Spacing 80%
Count 1
Foreground/Background
Jitter 100%
Hue Jitter 100%
Purity +100%

Dual Brush:
Diameter 31 px
Spacing 80%
Count 1
Foreground/Background
Jitter 100%
Hue Jitter 100%

Dual Brush:
Diameter 54 px
Spacing 80%
Count 1
Opacity Jitter 100%

Dual Brush:
Diameter 54 px
Spacing 80%
Count 1
Hue Jitter 20%
Saturation Jitter 100%

Dual Brush:
Diameter 54 px
Spacing 80%; Count 1
Foreground/Background
Jitter 100%
Hue Jitter 20%
Saturation Jitter 100%
Wet Edges

Scatter 260%
Count 1
Dual Brush:
Diameter 20 px
Spacing 80%
Count 1
Hue Jitter 60%

Size Jitter 100%
Dual Brush:
Diameter 54 px
Spacing 80%
Count 1
Hue Jitter 60%
Wet Edges

Dual Brush:
Diameter 54 px
Spacing 80%; Count 1
Foreground/Background
Jitter 100%; Hue
Jitter 30%; Purity -30%
Flow Jitter 100%

Dual Brush:
Diameter 54 px
Spacing 80%; Count 1
Foreground/Background
Jitter 100%; Hue
Jitter 100%; Purity -75%
Flow Jitter 100%

Scatter 160%
Count 2
Dual Brush:
Diameter 31 px
Spacing 80%
Count 1
Flow Jitter 100%

PETAL CRYSTALS

Dual Brush: Diameter 40 px
Spacing 25%; Scatter 0%; Count 1
Hue Jitter 100%
Purity +100%

Dual Brush: Diameter 22 px
Spacing 25%; Scatter 405%;
Count 1
Hue Jitter 100%
Wet Edges

Dual Brush: Diameter 56 px
Spacing 25%; Scatter 50%; Count 2
Hue Jitter 100%
Wet Edges

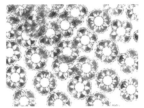

Dual Brush: Diameter 70 px
Spacing 115%; Scatter 10%; Count 3
Hue Jitter 33%
Purity +33%

SETTINGS

Dual Brush:
Diameter 70 px
Spacing 115%
Scatter 10%
Count 3
Hue Jitter 33%
Purity +33%
Wet Edges

Dual Brush:
Diameter 40 px
Spacing 25%
Scatter 0%; Count 1
Foreground/Background
Jitter 100%
Purity +100%
Wet Edges

Dual Brush:
Diameter 14 px
Spacing 25%
Scatter 150%; Count 1
Foreground/Background
Jitter 100%
Brightness Jitter 100%
Purity +100%; Wet Edges

Dual Brush:
Diameter 17 px
Spacing 25%
Scatter 100%; Count 1
Foreground/Background
Jitter 100%
Hue Jitter 100%
Purity +100%

Dual Brush:
Diameter 27 px
Spacing 85%
Scatter 0%; Count 2
Foreground/Background
Jitter 100%
Hue Jitter 100%
Purity +100%

Dual Brush:
Diameter 27 px
Spacing 85%; Scatter 0%
Count 2; Foreground/
Background Jitter 100%
Hue Jitter 50%
Purity +100%; Wet Edges

Dual Brush:
Diameter 20 px; Spacing
85%; Scatter 250%
Count 6; Foreground/
Background Jitter 100%
Hue Jitter 50%
Purity +100%; Wet Edges

Dual Brush:
Diameter 38 px
Spacing 125%
Scatter 0%; Count 4
Foreground/Background
Jitter 100%; Hue Jitter
50%; Purity -25%

Dual Brush: Diameter
38 px; Spacing 125%
Scatter 0%; Count 4
Foreground/Background
Jitter 30%; Hue
Jitter 30%; Brightness
Jitter 100%; Purity +100%

Dual Brush:
Diameter 38 px
Spacing 100%
Scatter 50%; Count 2
Hue Jitter 100%
Brightness Jitter 100%
Purity +100%

BUTTERFLY

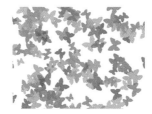

Wet Edges

Size Jitter 50%
Hue Jitter 10%

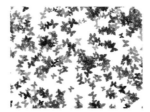

Scatter 1000%
Count 2
Count Jitter 80%
Brightness Jitter 25%
Purity +100%
Flow Jitter 60%

Hue Jitter 45%
Opacity Jitter 100%
Wet Edges

SETTINGS

Hue Jitter 45%
Opacity Jitter 100%
Wet Edges

Spacing 200%
Hue Jitter 100%

Spacing 200%
Hue Jitter 100%
Opacity Jitter 100%
Wet Edges

Scatter 300%
Count 2
Count Jitter 86%
Hue Jitter 100%
Purity +100%

Spacing 100%
Scatter 3%

Spacing 100%
Scatter 3%
Hue Jitter 50%
Wet Edges

Spacing 100%
Scatter 300%
Hue Jitter 50%

Scatter 115%
Count 2
Count Jitter 0%

Scatter 115%
Count 2
Count Jitter 0%
Brightness Jitter 100%

Spacing 75%
Scatter 200%
Count 2
Count Jitter 80%
Flow Jitter 100%
Wet Edges

FLAT BRISTLE

Default

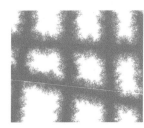

Size Jitter 100%
Angle Jitter 100%

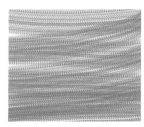

Spacing 25%

Saturation Jitter 100%
Purity +50%

BRUSH TIP SHAPE • WET EDGES

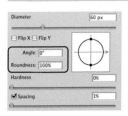

Angle	60°	40°	20°	0°
Roundness	50%	30%	10%	0%
Wet Edges	on	on	on	on

SHAPE DYNAMICS

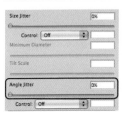

Angle Jitter	25%	50%	75%	100%

BRUSH TIP SHAPE

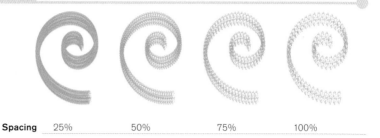

Spacing	25%	50%	75%	100%

BRUSH TIP SHAPE • COLOR DYNAMICS

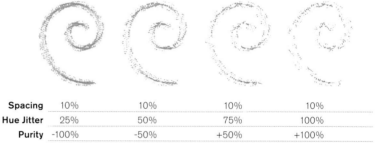

Spacing	10%	10%	10%	10%
Hue Jitter	25%	50%	75%	100%
Purity	-100%	-50%	+50%	+100%

SCATTERING

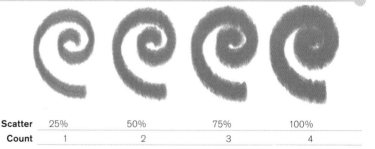

Scatter	25%	50%	75%	100%
Count	1	2	3	4

COLOR DYNAMICS

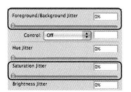

Foreground/Background Jitter	25%	50%	75%	100%
Saturation Jitter	25%	50%	75%	100%

ROUGH FLAT BRISTLE

Size Jitter 100%
Angle Jitter 100%

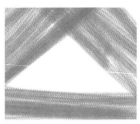

Angle 70°
Roundness 20%
Spacing 20%

Foreground/Background Jitter 50%
Hue Jitter 50%
Saturation Jitter 100%

Scatter 200%
Count 1

BRUSH TIP SHAPE

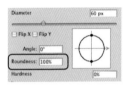

Roundness   25%   50%   75%   100%

SCATTERING

Scatter   25%   50%   75%   100%

SCATTERING

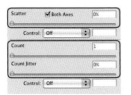

Scatter	200%	400%	600%	800%
Count	10	12	14	16
Count Jitter	100%	100%	100%	100%

COLOR DYNAMICS

Hue Jitter	25%	50%	75%	100%
Saturation Jitter	25%	50%	75%	100%

BRUSH TIP SHAPE

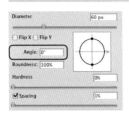

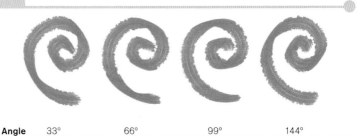

Angle	33°	66°	99°	144°

COLOR DYNAMICS

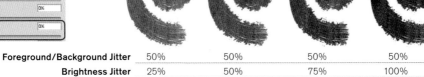

Foreground/Background Jitter	50%	50%	50%	50%
Brightness Jitter	25%	50%	75%	100%

ROUND BRISTLE

Angle 50°
Roundness 50%

Scatter 300%
Foreground/Background Jitter 50%
Hue Jitter 50%

Scatter 400%

Opacity Jitter 100%
Flow Jitter 100%
Wet Edges

COLOR DYNAMICS

Fgnd/Bgnd Jitter	25%	50%	75%	100%
Purity	+25%	+50%	+75%	+100%

BRUSH TIP SHAPE

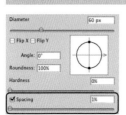

Spacing	25%	50%	75%	100%

BRUSH TIP SHAPE

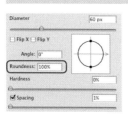

Roundness	25%	50%	75%	100%

SCATTERING

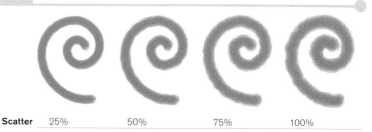

Scatter	25%	50%	75%	100%

SHAPE DYNAMICS • WET EDGES

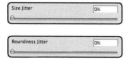

Size Jitter	25%	50%	75%	100%
Roundness Jitter	25%	50%	75%	100%
Wet Edges	on	on	on	on

COLOR DYNAMICS

Foreground/Background Jitter	100%	100%	100%	100%
Hue Jitter	25%	50%	75%	100%

SMOOTHER ROUND BRISTLE

Spacing 10%
Brightness Jitter 100%

Roundness 50%
Spacing 10%

Angle 33°
Roundness 20%

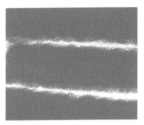

Scatter 300%

COLOR DYNAMICS

	25%	50%	75%	100%
Foreground/Background Jitter	25%	50%	75%	100%
Brightness Jitter	25%	50%	75%	100%

SHAPE DYNAMICS

	25%	50%	75%	100%
Size Jitter	25%	50%	75%	100%

BRUSH TIP SHAPE

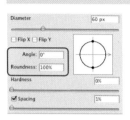

Angle	25°	50°	75°	100°
Roundness	25%	50%	75%	100%

COLOR DYNAMICS

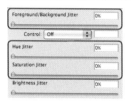

Foreground/Background Jitter	50%	50%	50%	50%
Hue Jitter	25%	50%	75%	100%
Saturation Jitter	25%	50%	75%	100%

SCATTERING • WET EDGES

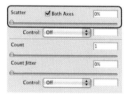

Scatter	25%	50%	75%	100%
Wet Edges	on	on	on	on

TRANSFER

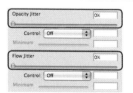

Opacity Jitter	25%	50%	75%	100%
Flow Jitter	25%	50%	75%	100%

ROUGH ROUND BRISTLE

Scatter 50%

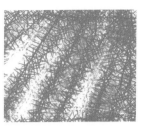

Dual Brush: Spacing 100%

Hue Jitter 100%
Dual Brush: Spacing 20%
Dual Brush: Scatter 200%

Scatter 50%
Angle Jitter 50°
Roundness Jitter 50%

BRUSH TIP SHAPE

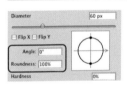

	Angle	0°	33°	66°	100°
	Roundness	25%	50%	75%	100%

BRUSH TIP SHAPE

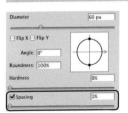

Spacing	25%	50%	75%	100%

BRUSH TIP SHAPE • WET EDGES

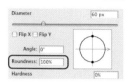

Roundness	25%	50%	75%	100%
Wet Edges	on	on	on	on

DUAL BRUSH

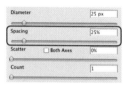

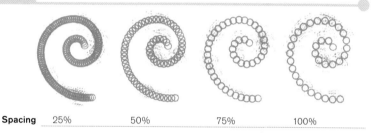

Spacing	25%	50%	75%	100%

SCATTERING • NOISE

Scatter	100%	150%	200%	400%
Noise	on	on	on	on

TRANSFER • NOISE

Opacity Jitter	25%	50%	75%	100%
Flow Jitter	25%	50%	75%	100%
Noise	on	on	on	on

ROUGH ROUND BRISTLE

Default Brush

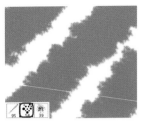

Dual Brush: Rough Dry Brush

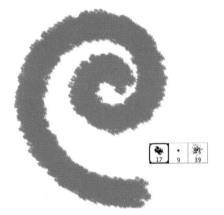

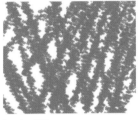

Spacing 32%
Size Jitter 100%

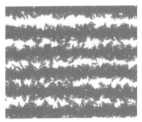

Size Jitter 100%
Angle Jitter 100%
Roundness Jitter 100%

BRUSH TIP SHAPE

Angle	33°	66°	99°	122°
Roundness	25%	50%	75%	100%

TRANSFER

Opacity Jitter	100%	75%	50%	25%
Flow Jitter	25%	50%	75%	100%

SHAPE DYNAMICS • WET EDGES

Size Jitter	25%	50%	75%	100%
Wet Edges	on	on	on	on

SCATTERING

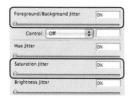

Scatter	25%	50%	75%	100%

COLOR DYNAMICS

Foreground/Background Jitter	25%	50%	75%	100%
Saturation Jitter	25%	50%	75%	100%

BRUSH TIP SHAPE

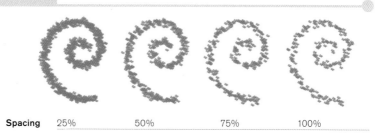

Spacing	25%	50%	75%	100%

DRIPPY WATER

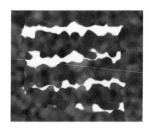

Foreground/Background Jitter 100%

Spacing 10%
Scatter 1000%

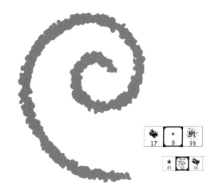

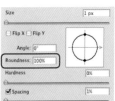

Saturation Jitter 50%
Wet Edges

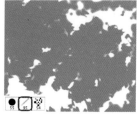

Dual Brush: Paint Brush Tool
Texture Comb
Spacing 33%

BRUSH TIP SHAPE

Roundness   25%   50%   75%   100%

SCATTERING

Scatter   25%   50%   75%   100%

SHAPE DYNAMICS

Size Jitter	25%	50%	75%	100%
Angle Jitter	25%	50%	75%	100%

COLOR DYNAMICS

Hue Jitter	25%	50%	75%	100%

BRUSH TIP SHAPE

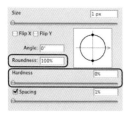

Roundness	25%	50%	75%	100%
Hardness	25%	50%	75%	100%

DUAL BRUSH

Dual Brush:
Assorted
Brushes
Library,
Circle 3

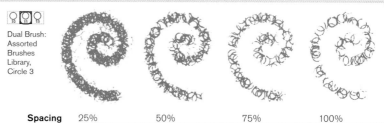

Spacing	25%	50%	75%	100%

DRY BRUSH
ON TOWEL

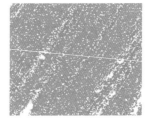

Wet Edges

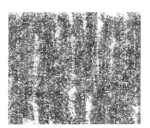

Hue Jitter 100%
Purity +100%

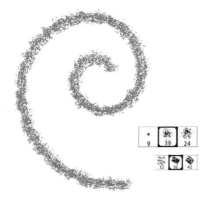

Opacity Jitter 100%
Flow Jitter 100%

Dual Brush: Hard Elliptical
Spacing 150%

COLOR DYNAMICS

	Hue Jitter			
Hue Jitter	25%	50%	75%	100%
Saturation Jitter	25%	50%	75%	100%

SCATTERING

Scatter	100%	200%	300%	600%
Count	1	10	15	16
Count Jitter	10%	20%	40%	50%

BRUSH TIP SHAPE

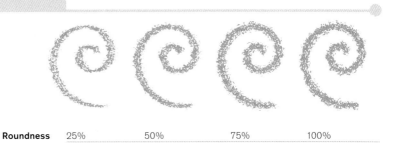

| Roundness | 25% | 50% | 75% | 100% |

BRUSH TIP SHAPE

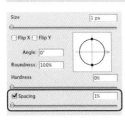
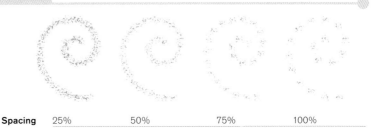

| Spacing | 25% | 50% | 75% | 100% |

SHAPE DYNAMICS

Size Jitter	25%	50%	75%	100%
Minimum Diameter	0%	0%	0%	0%
Roundness Jitter	25%	50%	75%	100%

TRANSFER

| Opacity Jitter | 25% | 50% | 75% | 100% |
| Flow Jitter | 25% | 50% | 75% | 100% |

HEAVY SCATTER FLOW

Default Brush

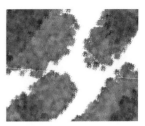

Foreground/Background Jitter 100%
Hue Jitter 10%

Angle 33°
Roundness 33%

Size Jitter 25%

SHAPE DYNAMICS

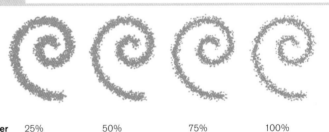

| Size Jitter | 25% | 50% | 75% | 100% |

BRUSH TIP SHAPE

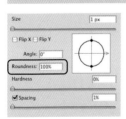

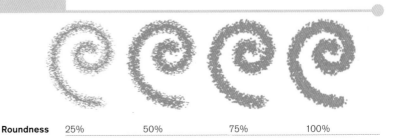

| Roundness | 25% | 50% | 75% | 100% |

DUAL BRUSH

Dual Brush:
Special
Effects
Library,
Azalea

Spacing	25%	50%	75%	100%

COLOR DYNAMICS

Foreground/Background Jitter	25%	50%	75%	100%
Purity	-50%	-25%	+25%	+50%

COLOR DYNAMICS

Brightness Jitter	25%	50%	75%	100%

BRUSH TIP SHAPE

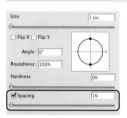 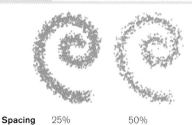 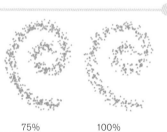

Spacing	25%	50%	75%	100%

HEAVY STIPPLE FLOW

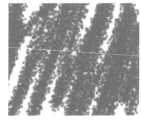

Default Brush

Angle 33°
Roundness 5%

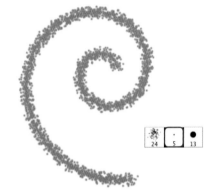

Scatter 150%

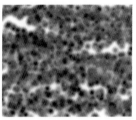

Foreground/Background Jitter 100%
Hue Jitter 100%

DUAL BRUSH

Dual Brush:
Rough
Round
Brush

Spacing	20%	40%	60%	80%

COLOR DYNAMICS

Foreground Background Jitter	25%	50%	75%	100%

BRUSH TIP SHAPE

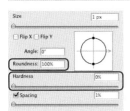

Roundness	25%	50%	75%	100%
Hardness	25%	50%	75%	100%

SHAPE DYNAMICS

Size Jitter	25%	50%	75%	100%

BRUSH TIP SHAPE

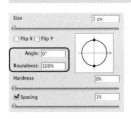

Angle	1°	33°	66°	100°
Roundness	25%	50%	75%	100%

SCATTERING

Scatter	25%	50%	75%	100%

BRUSH ON LIGHT WEAVE

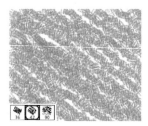

Dual Brush: Spacing 50%

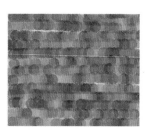

Spacing 33%
Saturation Jitter 100%
Wet Edges

Hardness 0%
Spacing 40%

Default Brush

SHAPE DYNAMICS

Size Jitter 25%   50%   75%   100%

BRUSH TIP SHAPE

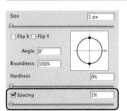

Spacing 25%   50%   75%   100%

COLOR DYNAMICS

Foreground/Background Jitter	25%	50%	75%	100%
Saturation Jitter	25%	50%	75%	100%

BRUSH TIP SHAPE

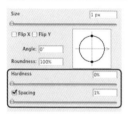

Hardness	25%	50%	75%	100%
Spacing	100%	50%	75%	25%

SCATTERING

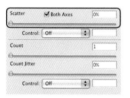

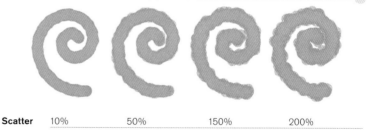

Scatter	10%	50%	150%	200%

BRUSH TIP SHAPE

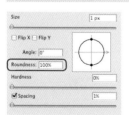

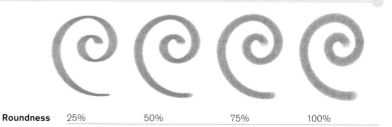

Roundness	25%	50%	75%	100%

LIGHT OIL FLAT TIP

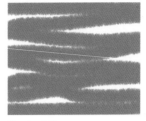

Size Jitter 50%

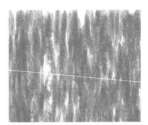

Scatter 500%

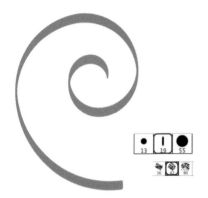

Saturation Jitter 50%
Purity +50%

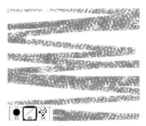

Dual Brush: Paintbrush Tool
Texture Comb
Spacing 15%

BRUSH TIP SHAPE

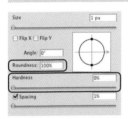

Roundness	25%	50%	75%	100%
Hardness	25%	50%	75%	100%

SHAPE DYNAMICS

Size Jitter	25%	50%	75%	100%

SCATTERING

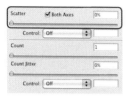

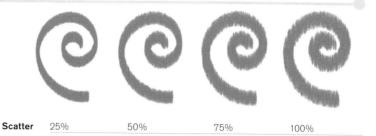

| **Scatter** | 25% | 50% | 75% | 100% |

DUAL BRUSH

Dual Brush:
Chalk

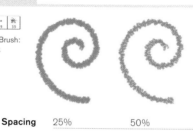

| **Spacing** | 25% | 50% | 75% | 100% |

COLOR DYNAMICS

| **Hue Jitter** | 25% | 50% | 75% | 100% |
| **Saturation Jitter** | 25% | 50% | 75% | 100% |

SHAPE DYNAMICS

| **Angle Jitter** | 25° | 50° | 75° | 100° |
| **Roundness Jitter** | 25% | 50% | 75% | 100% |

PAINT ON ROUGH TEXTURE

Opacity Jitter 50%
Wet Edges

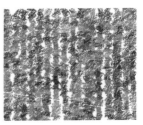

Foreground/Background Jitter 100%
Purity -50%

Scatter 50%
Count 16

Saturation Jitter 50%

BRUSH TIP SHAPE

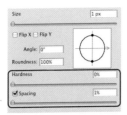

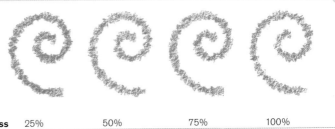

Hardness	25%	50%	75%	100%
Spacing	25%	50%	75%	100%

FLOW

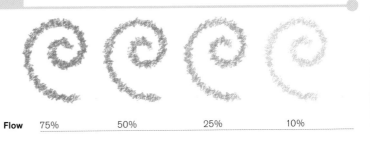

Flow	75%	50%	25%	10%

BRUSH TIP SHAPE

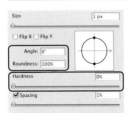

Angle	33°	66°	99°	122°
Roundness	50%	50%	50%	50%
Hardness	25%	50%	75%	100%

COLOR DYNAMICS

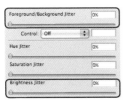

Foreground/Background Jitter	25%	50%	75%	100%
Brightness Jitter	25%	50%	75%	100%

TRANSFER

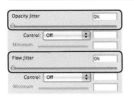

Opacity Jitter	25%	50%	75%	100%
Flow Jitter	25%	50%	75%	100%

DUAL BRUSH

Dual Brush:
Assorted
Brushes
Library,
Ornament 1

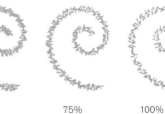

Spacing	25%	50%	75%	100%

PAINT BRUSH TOOL TEXTURE COMB

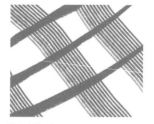

Default Brush

Wet Edges

Hue Jitter 100%

Dual Brush: Size 100 px
Foreground/Background Jitter 50%
Saturation Jitter 100%

SHAPE DYNAMICS

Size Jitter	25%	50%	75%	100%
Angle Jitter	25%	50%	75%	100%

BRUSH TIP SHAPE

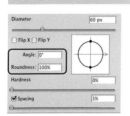

Angle	33°	66°	99°	122°
Roundness	25%	50%	75%	100%

SCATTERING

Count	2	4	6	8
Count Jitter	20%	15%	10%	5%

COLOR DYNAMICS

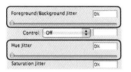

Foreground/Background Jitter	25%	50%	75%	100%
Hue Jitter	25%	50%	75%	100%

SHAPE DYNAMICS

Roundness Jitter	25%	50%	75%	100%
Minimum Roundness	1%	1%	1%	1%

TRANSFER

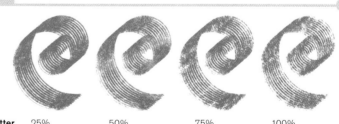

Opacity Jitter	25%	50%	75%	100%
Flow Jitter	25%	50%	75%	100%

ROUGH DRY

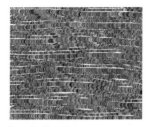

Saturation Jitter 50%
Brightness Jitter 50%

Size Jitter 100%
Noise

Default Brush

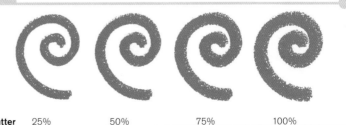

Size Jitter 50%
Foreground/Background Jitter 100%
Opacity Jitter 100%

BRUSH TIP SHAPE

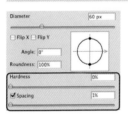

Diameter	60 px
Flip X ☐ Flip Y	
Angle:	0°
Roundness:	100%
Hardness	0%
☑ Spacing	1%

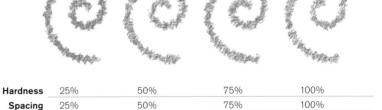

Hardness	25%	50%	75%	100%
Spacing	25%	50%	75%	100%

SCATTERING

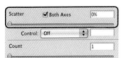

Scatter	☑ Both Axes	0%
Control:	Off	
Count		1

Scatter	25%	50%	75%	100%

SHAPE DYNAMICS

Angle Jitter	25%	50%	75%	100%
Roundness Jitter	100%	75%	50%	25%

COLOR DYNAMICS

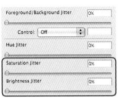

Saturation Jitter	25%	50%	75%	100%
Brightness Jitter	25%	50%	75%	100%

BRUSH TIP SHAPE

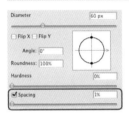

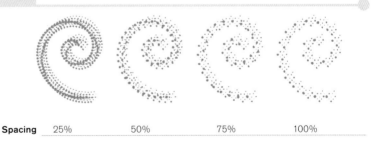

Spacing	25%	50%	75%	100%

SHAPE DYNAMICS

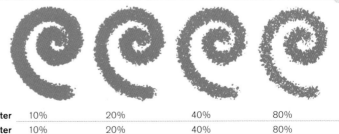

Size Jitter	10%	20%	40%	80%
Angle Jitter	10%	20%	40%	80%
Roundness Jitter	10%	20%	40%	80%

ROUGH INK

Default Brush

Size Jitter 100%
Angle Jitter 100%
Wet Edges

Scatter 350%

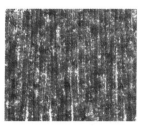

Foreground/Background Jitter 100%
Opacity Jitter 100%

COLOR DYNAMICS

Foreground/Background Jitter	25%	50%	75%	100%

DUAL BRUSH

Dual Brush:
Rough Dry
Brush

Spacing	10%	20%	40%	80%

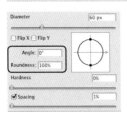

BRUSH TIP SHAPE

Angle	33°	33°	33°	33°
Roundness	25%	50%	75%	100%

SCATTERING

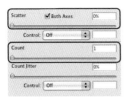

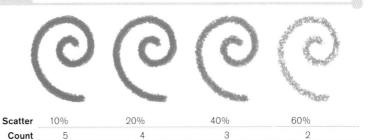

Scatter	10%	20%	40%	60%
Count	5	4	3	2

TRANSFER

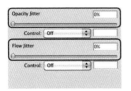

Opacity Jitter	25%	50%	75%	100%
Flow Jitter	25%	50%	75%	100%

SHAPE DYNAMICS • COLOR DYNAMICS

Size Jitter	25%	50%	75%	100%
Hue Jitter	25%	50%	75%	100%

SCATTERED DRY

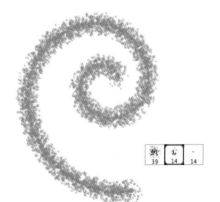

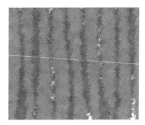

Scatter 150%
Foreground/Background Jitter 50%
Wet Edges

Angle 40°
Roundness 50%
Spacing 1%

Size Jitter 50%
Noise
Wet Edges

Flow 25%
Scatter 200%
Count 6
Count Jitter 100%

SCATTERING

Scatter	200%	150%	75%	1%
Count	4	3	2	1

DUAL BRUSH

Dual Brush:
Sampled
Tip

Spacing	81%	60%	40%	20%

SCATTERING

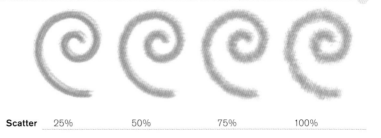

	Scatter	25%	50%	75%	100%

COLOR DYNAMICS

	Hue Jitter	100%	75%	50%	25%
	Saturation Jitter	25%	50%	75%	100%

DUAL BRUSH

Dual Brush:
Soft Round

	Spacing	25%	50%	75%	100%

BRUSH TIP SHAPE

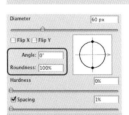

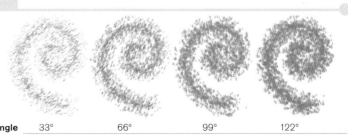

	Angle	33°	66°	99°	122°
	Roundness	25%	50%	75%	100%

LARGE TEXTURED STROKE

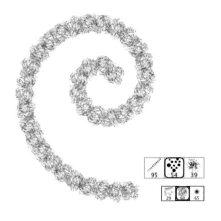

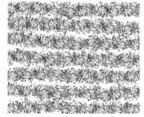

Size Jitter 100%
Roundness Jitter 100%
Saturation Jitter 100%
Purity +100%

Foreground/Background Jitter 100%
Hue Jitter 100%

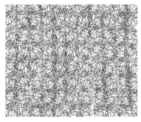

Angle 30°
Roundness 50%
Scatter 10%

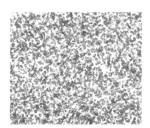

Spacing 25%
Noise
Wet Edges

DUAL BRUSH

Dual Brush:
Spatter

Diameter	1 px
Spacing	1%
Scatter ☐ Both Axes	0%
Count	1

Scatter   25%   50%   75%   100%

BRUSH TIP SHAPE

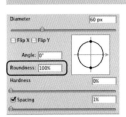

Diameter	60 px
☐ Flip X ☐ Flip Y	
Angle:	0°
Roundness:	100%
Hardness	0%
☑ Spacing	1%

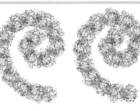

Roundness   25%   50%   75%   100%

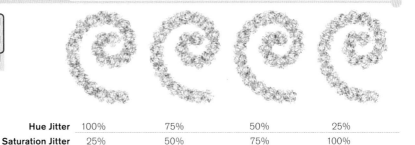

COLOR DYNAMICS

Hue Jitter	100%	75%	50%	25%
Saturation Jitter	25%	50%	75%	100%

TRANSFER

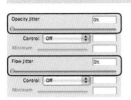

Opacity Jitter	100%	75%	50%	25%
Flow Jitter	25%	50%	75%	100%

BRUSH TIP SHAPE

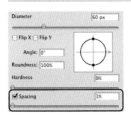
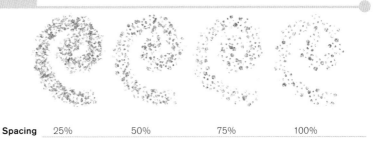

Spacing	25%	50%	75%	100%

DUAL BRUSH • COLOR DYNAMICS

Dual Brush: Sampled Tip

Spacing	25%	50%	75%	100%
Hue Jitter	80%	80%	80%	80%

BRUSH WITH THICK FLOW MEDIUM TIP

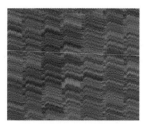

Foreground/Background Jitter 100%

Angle 42°
Wet Edges

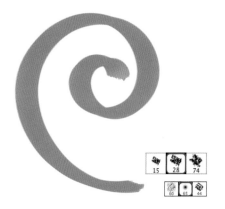

Scatter 220%
Count 3
Count Jitter 50%

Flow 25%

BRUSH TIP SHAPE

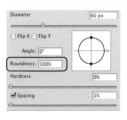

Roundness	25%	50%	75%	100%

BRUSH TIP SHAPE

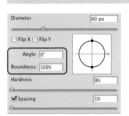

Angle	25°	50°	75°	100°
Roundness	25%	50%	75%	100%

DUAL BRUSH

Dual Brush:
Hard
Elliptical

Spacing	25%	50%	75%	100%

COLOR DYNAMICS

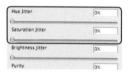

Hue Jitter	25%	50%	75%	100%
Saturation Jitter	25%	50%	75%	100%

SCATTERING

Scatter	25%	50%	75%	100%

SHAPE DYNAMICS

Size Jitter	25%	50%	75%	100%
Angle Jitter	25%	50%	75%	100%
Roundness Jitter	25%	50%	75%	100%

OIL MEDIUM BRUSH WET EDGES

Default Brush

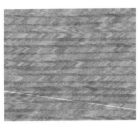

Saturation Jitter 50%
Opacity Jitter 50%

Roundness 80%
Spacing 50%

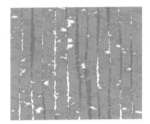

Scatter 500%
Count 3

COLOR DYNAMICS

Saturation Jitter   25%   50%   75%   100%

BRUSH TIP SHAPE

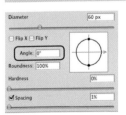

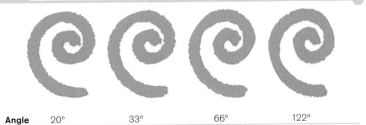

Angle   20°   33°   66°   122°

BRUSH TIP SHAPE

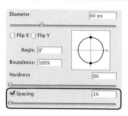

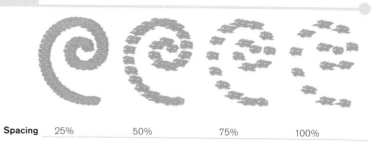

Spacing	25%	50%	75%	100%

BRUSH TIP SHAPE

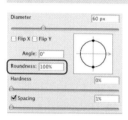

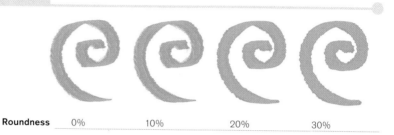

Roundness	0%	10%	20%	30%

TRANSFER

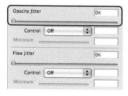

Opacity Jitter	25%	50%	75%	100%

COLOR DYNAMICS

Foreground/Background Jitter	100%	75%	50%	25%
Hue Jitter	25%	50%	75%	100%

BRUSH LIGHT TEXTURE

Scatter 200%
Count 4
Count Jitter

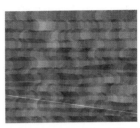

Foreground/Background Jitter 100%
Saturation Jitter 50%
Wet Edges

Spacing 50%

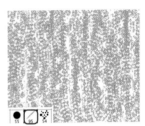

Dual Brush: Paint Brush Tool
Texture Comb
Spacing 10%

COLOR DYNAMICS

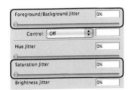

Foreground/Background Jitter	100%	75%	50%	25%
Saturation Jitter	25%	50%	75%	100%

BRUSH TIP SHAPE

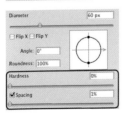

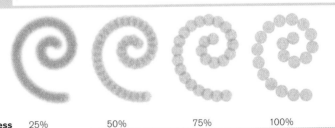

Hardness	25%	50%	75%	100%
Spacing	25%	50%	75%	100%

DUAL BRUSH

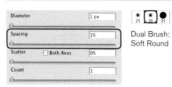

Dual Brush:
Soft Round

Spacing	25%	50%	75%	100%

SCATTERING

Scatter	25%	50%	75%	100%

BRUSH TIP SHAPE

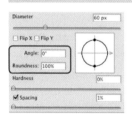

Angle	25°	50°	75°	100°
Roundness	25%	50%	75%	100%

COLOR DYNAMICS

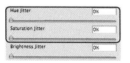

Hue Jitter	100%	75%	50%	25%
Saturation Jitter	25%	50%	75%	100%

WATERCOLOR HEAVY LOADED

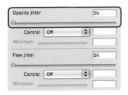

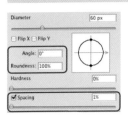

Wet Edges

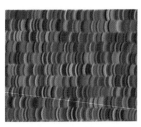

Foreground/Background Jitter 100%
Saturation Jitter 100%

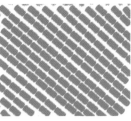

Spacing 100%

Flow 25%
Foreground/Background Jitter 25%

TRANSFER

	Opacity Jitter	25%	50%	75%	100%

BRUSH TIP SHAPE

	55°	55°	55°	55°
Angle	55°	55°	55°	55°
Roundness	36%	36%	36%	36%
Spacing	25%	50%	75%	100%

COLOR DYNAMICS

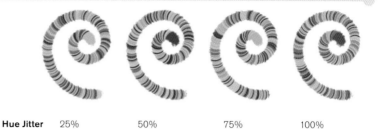

Hue Jitter	25%	50%	75%	100%
Saturation Jitter	100%	75%	50%	25%

BRUSH TIP SHAPE

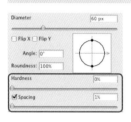
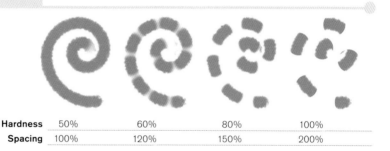

Hardness	50%	60%	80%	100%
Spacing	100%	120%	150%	200%

BRUSH TIP SHAPE • WET EDGES

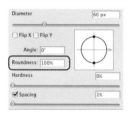

Roundness	25%	50%	75%	100%
Wet Edges	on	on	on	on

COLOR DYNAMICS

Foreground/Background Jitter	20%	40%	80%	100%

WATERCOLOR HEAVY PIGMENT

Default Brush

Size Jitter 100%
Hue Jitter 50%

Scatter 200%

Opacity Jitter 50%
Noise

BRUSH TIP SHAPE

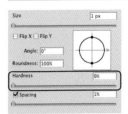

Size	1 px
Flip X Flip Y	
Angle:	0°
Roundness:	100%
Hardness	0%
Spacing	1%

Hardness   25%   50%   75%   100%

DUAL BRUSH

Diameter	1 px
Spacing	1%
Scatter Both Axes	0%
Count	1

Dual Brush:
Paint Brush
Tool Texture
Comb

Spacing   1%   10%   20%   30%

COLOR DYNAMICS

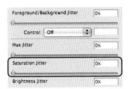

Saturation Jitter	25%	50%	75%	100%

SHAPE DYNAMICS • NOISE

Size Jitter	25%	50%	75%	100%
Angle Jitter	100%	75%	50%	25%
Noise	on	on	on	on

BRUSH TIP SHAPE

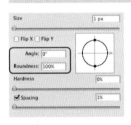

Angle	25°	50°	75°	100°
Roundness	33%	33%	33%	33%

SHAPE DYNAMICS

Size Jitter	25%	50%	75%	100%
Angle Jitter	25%	50%	75%	100%

WATERCOLOR HEAVY MEDIUM TIP

Hue Jitter 50%
Saturation Jitter 50%

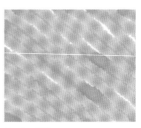

Spacing 68%

Scatter 250%
Count 8

Foreground/Background Jitter 100%
Saturation Jitter 50%
Purity +100%

BRUSH TIP SHAPE

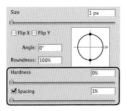

Hardness	100%	100%	100%	100%
Spacing	25%	50%	75%	100%

BRUSH TIP SHAPE

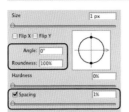

Angle	9°	9°	9°	9°
Roundness	25%	50%	75%	100%
Spacing	100%	100%	100%	100%

COLOR DYNAMICS

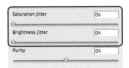

Saturation Jitter	25%	50%	75%	100%
Brightness Jitter	100%	75%	50%	25%

SHAPE DYNAMICS

Size Jitter	25%	50%	75%	100%
Roundness Jitter	25%	50%	75%	100%

BRUSH TIP SHAPE

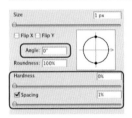

Angle	25°	50°	75°	100°
Hardness	25%	50%	75%	100%
Spacing	100%	100%	100%	100%

TRANSFER

Opacity Jitter	25%	50%	75%	100%

WATERCOLOR FAT TIP

Hardness 50%
Spacing 50%

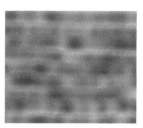

Foreground/Background Jitter 100%
Hue Jitter 100%
Purity +100%

Size Jitter 100%
Angle Jitter 50%
Saturation Jitter 50%

Scatter 300%
Count 3

BRUSH TIP SHAPE

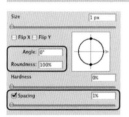

Angle	30°	30°	30°	30°
Roundness	30%	30%	30%	30%
Spacing	25%	50%	75%	100%

BRUSH TIP SHAPE

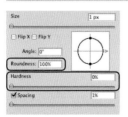

Roundness	25%	50%	75%	100%
Hardness	25%	50%	75%	100%

SHAPE DYNAMICS

Size Jitter	80%	40%	20%	10%

BRUSH TIP SHAPE

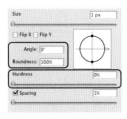

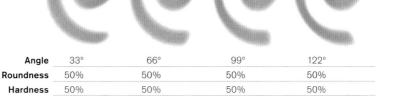

Angle	33°	66°	99°	122°
Roundness	50%	50%	50%	50%
Hardness	50%	50%	50%	50%

COLOR DYNAMICS

Saturation Jitter	25%	50%	75%	100%

SCATTERING

Scatter	25%	50%	75%	100%
Count	4	4	4	4
Count Jitter	100%	100%	100%	100%

WATERCOLOR TEXTURED SURFACE

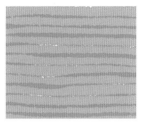

Default Brush

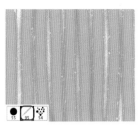

Dual Brush: Paintbrush Tool
Texture Comb

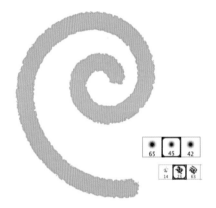

Foreground/Background Jitter 50%
Brightness Jitter 50%

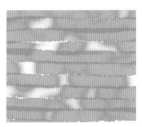

Scatter 700%
Count 5
Count Jitter 100%

BRUSH TIP SHAPE • NOISE

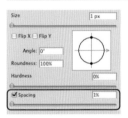

Spacing	1%	33%	66%	100%
Noise	on	on	on	on

COLOR DYNAMICS

Brightness Jitter	25%	50%	75%	100%

BRUSH TIP SHAPE

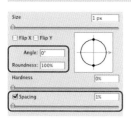

Angle	30°	30°	30°	30°
Roundness	25%	50%	75%	100%
Spacing	25%	50%	75%	100%

COLOR DYNAMICS

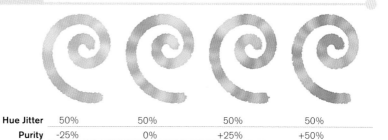

Hue Jitter	50%	50%	50%	50%
Purity	-25%	0%	+25%	+50%

BRUSH TIP SHAPE

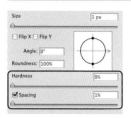

Hardness	25%	50%	75%	100%
Spacing	25%	50%	75%	100%

TRANSFER

Flow Jitter	25%	50%	75%	100%

WATERCOLOR LIGHT OPACITY

Foreground/Background Jitter 100%
Purity +100%

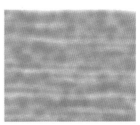

Opacity Jitter 50%

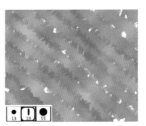

Dual Brush: Hard Elliptical
Size 66 px
Hue Jitter 25%

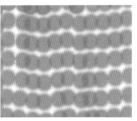

Hardness 50%
Spacing 100%

SHAPE DYNAMICS

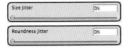

Size Jitter	100%	75%	50%	25%
Roundness Jitter	25%	50%	75%	100%

COLOR DYNAMICS

Brightness Jitter	25%	50%	75%	100%

BRUSH TIP SHAPE

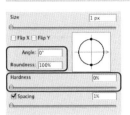

Angle	45°	45°	45°	45°
Roundness	20%	20%	20%	20%
Hardness	25%	50%	75%	100%

BRUSH TIP SHAPE

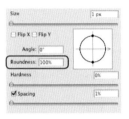
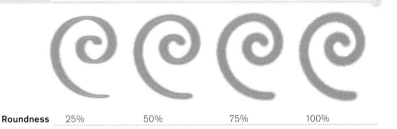

Roundness	25%	50%	75%	100%

SCATTERING

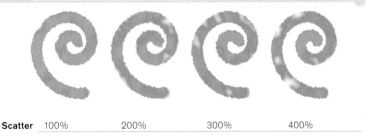

Scatter	100%	200%	300%	400%

BRUSH TIP SHAPE

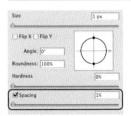
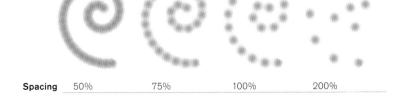

Spacing	50%	75%	100%	200%

Textures

Within the Brushes panel you'll find the Texture Settings (see page 32 for more information about the settings themselves). There are many textures available to apply to the brushes and they are organized in nine pattern libraries that come with Photoshop. You can add your own pattern libraries, either that you have created yourself or that you've downloaded (see page 345).

Texture Swatches

This section of the Brush Directory shows a sample swatch of each texture that has been painted at 100% with the default settings using the Multiply or Subtract Blend mode. For clarity, some have been "inverted," as indicated by (I) after the texture name (1, above right) and others have had the brush applied several times, as indicated by the number in brackets, e.g. (x5), after the texture name. Give this a try if your texture is a little weak.

Texture Swatches colors

Some of the textures have their own colors that have been used (the textures in the Color Paper Library, for instance). In other cases, the Foreground Color is applied and you'll find the libraries have been "color-coded" so you can see where one library ends and another begins.

To load other Photoshop pattern libraries:

You can load the pattern libraries that come with Photoshop by going to the Texture Settings in the Brushes panel.

1 Click the Texture drop-down menu and go to the menu on the side where you can select the library you want to load.
2 To load one of the libraries listed in the bottom section of the menu, simply select it.
3 A dialog box appears asking whether you want to replace the existing textures/patterns or if you want to append (add) the new library to the existing one.

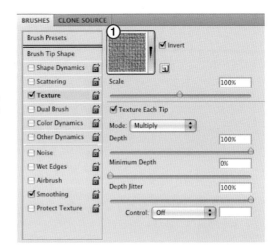

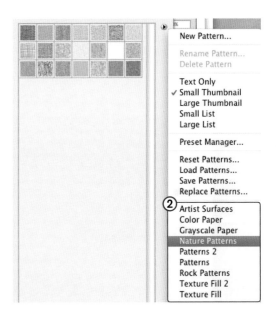

ARTIST SURFACES

Dark Coarse Weave

Stone

Burlap

Berber

ARTIST SURFACES

Extra Heavy Canvas

Coarse Weave

Granite

Gauze

ARTIST SURFACES

Heavy Weave

Parchment

Canvas

Washed Watercolor Paper

ARTIST SURFACES

Watercolor

Oil Pastel Light

Hard Charcoal Light

Wax Crayon on
Charcoal Paper

ARTIST SURFACES

Wax Crayon on Sketch Pad

Brush Pen on Canvas

Wax Crayon on Vellum

Gouache Light on Watercolor

ARTIST SURFACES   COLOR PAPER

Oil Pastel on Canvas

Aqua

Beige with White Flecks

Blue Crepe (I) (x6)

COLOR PAPER

Blue Dust (I)

Blue Specks (I) (x6)

Blue Textured

Blue Vellum

COLOR PAPER

Buff Textured

Gold Metallic (I)

Gold Parchment (I)

Gold Vellum

COLOR PAPER

Graph Paper (I) (x6)

Gray Vellum

Green and Black

Green with Fibers

COLOR PAPER

Kraft Paper

Kraft Waffle

Leaf

Linen Weave (I) (x6)

COLOR PAPER

Marbled (I) (x6)

Metallic Black (I)

Metallic Flecks (I) (x6)

Notebook (I) (x6)

COLOR PAPER

Peach Pebbled

Pink Textured (I)

Pink with Flecks

Red Textured (I)

COLOR PAPER

Red Vellum

Sketch Paper (I) (x6)

White Columns (I) (x6)

White Diagonal (I) (x6)

COLOR PAPER

White Stationery (I) (x6)

White Textured (I) (x6)

White with Wood (I) (x6)

Yellow Lined

GRAYSCALE PAPER

Black Weave

Charcoal Flecks

Crepe

Dark Gray Flecks

GRAYSCALE PAPER

Fibers

Fibers 2

Gray Granite (x8)

Homemade Paper (x8)

GRAYSCALE PAPER

Kraft Paper

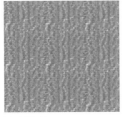

Kraft Waffle

Lined

Linen

GRAYSCALE PAPER

Marbled

Metallic Flecks (x8)

Pebbled (x8)

Stationery (x10)

GRAYSCALE PAPER   NATURE PATTERNS

Textured (x8)

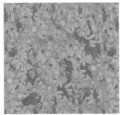

Blue Daisies (I)

Leaves (I)

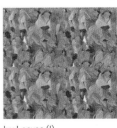

Ivy Leaves (I)

NATURE PATTERNS

Yellow Mums

Purple Daisies (I)

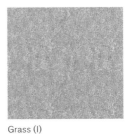

Grass (I)

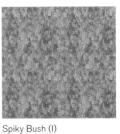

Spiky Bush (I)

PATTERNS 2

Carpet

Coarse Weave

Crystals

Denim

PATTERNS 2

Purple

Rough

Slate

Stone

PATTERNS 2

Streaks

Stucco

Water

PATTERNS

Bubbles

PATTERNS

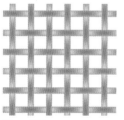

Woven Flat

Woven Wide

Zebra

Wrinkles

PATTERNS

Woven

Wood

Waffle

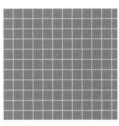
Tiles Smooth

PATTERNS

Tie Dye

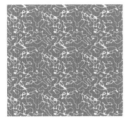
Strings

Satin

Rusted Metal

PATTERNS

Optical Squares

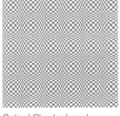
Optical Checkerboard

Nebula

Molecular

PATTERNS

Metallic Snakeskin

Metal Landscape

Herringbone

Fractures

PATTERNS / ROCK PATTERNS

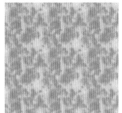

Clouds

Cells

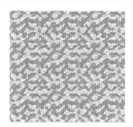

Ant Farm

Black Marble

ROCK PATTERNS

Stones

Gravel

Granite

Red Rocks

ROCK PATTERNS

Rock Wall

Light Marble

Textured Tile

Dirt

TEXTURE FILL 2

Shingles

Shredded Plastic

Sparse Basic Noise

Strands

TEXTURE FILL 2

Stucco 1

Stucco 2

Stucco 3

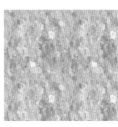

Stucco 4

TEXTURE FILL 2

Styrofoam

Thick Hair

Towel

Weave 1

TEXTURE FILL 2

Weave 2

Weave 3

Weave 4

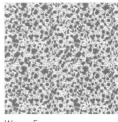

Weave 5

TEXTURE FILL 2   TEXTURE FILL

Web

Clouds

Amoeba

Bark

TEXTURE FILL

Blistered Paint

Burlap

Canvas

Concrete

TEXTURE FILL

Confetti

Denim

Driven Snow

Footprints

TEXTURE FILL

Frosted Glass

Frozen Rain

Leather

Lichen

TEXTURE FILL

Loose Threads

Mountains

Noise

Rust Flakes

TEXTURE FILL

Screen Door

Shag Rug

LOADING OTHER PATTERN LIBRARIES

Having seen this selection of patterns that you can use as textures with your brushes, you may be ready to expand and try others. You'll find many free libraries available on the Internet.

To load pattern libraries you've downloaded:
1 Once you have downloaded the library, open the Texture Settings in the Brushes panel in Photoshop.
2 Click the menu where you select the textures and select Load Patterns.
3 Navigate to the pattern library you want to load, click it, and click Load to add it to the libraries.
4 Then load the library you have just downloaded. The library name will appear at the bottom of the menu, but not until you next launch Photoshop.

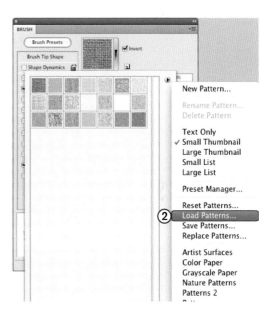

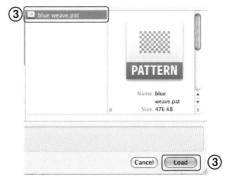

Photoshop CS5 Bristle Brushes

Photoshop CS5 introduced Bristle Brushes, which allow for the creation of more realistic, natural-looking strokes through the addition of a richer set of controls than were available with Photoshop's earlier brushes. In addition to the regular brush controls found in the Brushes panel, when you have a bristle brush selected a further set of controls—Bristle Qualities—is added to the Brushes panel.

1 Bristle brushes can be identified in the Brushes Presets panel or Brush Tip thumbnails in the Brushes panel by their distinctive Brush Tip icons.

2 The Bristle Qualities panel lets you control the number of settings that can be applied to the brushes.

3 The first setting you can adjust is the basic shape of the bristle brush.

4 Bristles lets you control the number of bristles.

5 Length changes the length of the bristles.

6 Thickness controls the width of the brush's individual bristles.

7 Stiffness controls how rigid the brush's bristles are. Using a lower value means the brush shape will be squashed more easily.

8 If you are painting with a mouse, the Angle setting lets you set the angle at which the brush stroke is applied. This has no effect if you're using a graphics tablet.

9 If your computer is fitted with an Open GL-based video card, you can choose to see the Bristle Brush Preview, which displays a preview of the bristle brush, adjusting the cursor to indicate the level of pressure you are applying and any tilt (assuming you are using a graphics tablet). You can turn the Bristle Brush Preview on or off using the Bristle Brush Preview icon at the bottom of the Brushes panel or on the Brush Presets panel.

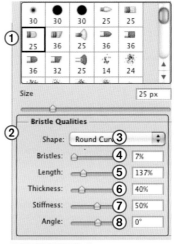

Bristle Brushes and Bristle Qualities in the Brushes panel

Bristle Brush Preview

Bristle Brush Preview icon

PHOTOSHOP CS5 BRISTLE BRUSH PREVIEWS

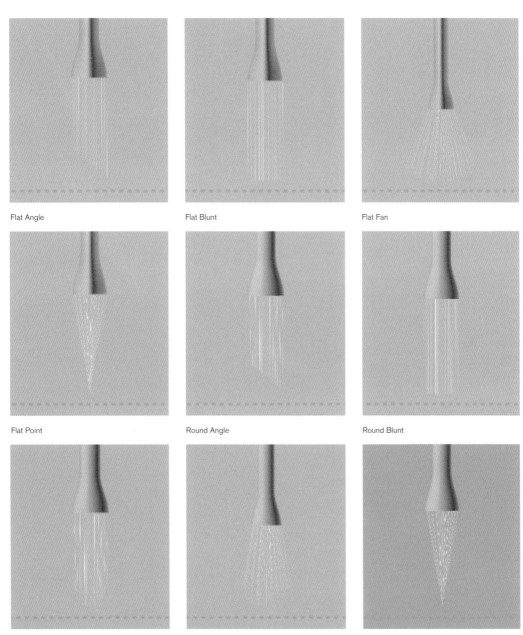

Flat Angle

Flat Blunt

Flat Fan

Flat Point

Round Angle

Round Blunt

Round Curve

Round Fan

Round Point

ROUND POINT STIFF

Default Brush

Stiffness 50%
Opacity Jitter 50%

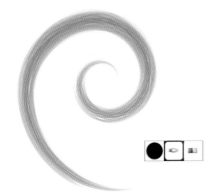

Thickness 1%
Stiffness 1%

Angle Jitter 50%
Wet Edges

SETTINGS

Scatter 30%

Stiffness 1%
Angle Jitter 0%

Thickness 100%
Angle Jitter 45%
Wet Edges

Spacing 25%

Saturation Jitter 100%

Length 500%
Thickness 200%
Angle Jitter 50%

Bristles 50%
Length 50%
Stiffness 50%

Hue Jitter 50%
Angle Jitter 100%

Spacing 25%
Flow Jitter 100%

Scatter 100%
Count 10
Count Jitter 20%

ROUND BLUNT
MEDIUM STIFF

Wet Edges

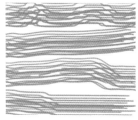

Length 25%
Thickness 18%

Bristles 50%
Stiffness 5%

Brightness Jitter 50%
Wet Edges

SETTINGS

Angle Jitter 100%
Control: Initial Direction

Opacity Jitter 50%
Flow Jitter 50%

Length 400%
Spacing 50%

Hue Jitter 20%
Wet Edges

Stiffness 1%

Thickness 40%

Length 20%
Spacing 20%
Scatter 200%
Count 10
Wet Edges

Thickness 50%
Spacing 50%

Angle Jitter 50%
Brightness Jitter 50%
Noise

Length 25%
Thickness 10%

ROUND CURVE LOW BRISTLE PERCENT

Hue Jitter 10%

Wet Edges

Angle Jitter 20%

Default Brush

SETTINGS

Length 50%
Stiffness 50%
Wet Edges

Spacing 50%
Brightness Jitter 50%

Length 50%
Stiffness 50%
Wet Edges

Bristles 20%
Spacing 50%
Hue Jitter 10%

Angle Jitter 55%

Bristles 30%
Length 30%
Stiffness 30%

Stiffness 10%
Hue Jitter 20%
Wet Edges

Scatter 100%

Angle Jitter 20%
Hue Jitter 20%
Saturation Jitter 20%

Thickness 25%
Stiffness 100%

ROUND ANGLE LOW STIFFNESS

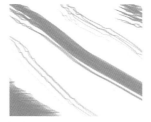

Bristles 10%

Spacing 60%

Stiffness 80%
Angle Jitter 20%
Wet Edges

Spacing 20%
Saturation Jitter 50%

SETTINGS

Length 25%
Spacing 25%

Opacity Jitter 25%
Flow Jitter 25%
Wet Edges

Bristles 7%

Scatter 50%
Hue Jitter 10%
Wet Edges

Length 25%

Stiffness 75%
Spacing 30%

Spacing 10%
Angle Jitter 30%
Scatter 10%

Saturation Jitter 20%

Bristles 100%
Stiffness 1%

Angle Jitter 50%
Flow Jitter 100%

ROUND FAN STIFF THIN BRISTLES

Wet Edges

Default Brush

Angle Jitter 50%
Brightness Jitter 30%
Control: Pen Pressure

Scatter 150%
Count 5
Count Jitter 40%
Wet Edges
Control: Pen Pressure

SETTINGS

Saturation Jitter 50%

Thickness 25%
Stiffness 25%

Spacing 10%
Wet Edges

Stiffness 25%
Opacity Jitter 25%

Scatter 50%
Count 2

Spacing 10%
Hue Jitter 100%
Wet Edges

Spacing 12%
Angle Jitter 100%
Opacity Jitter 100%

Bristles 15%
Length 25%
Stiffness 25%

Bristles 30%
Hue Jitter 30%

Scatter 1%
Count 4

FLAT POINT
MEDIUM STIFF

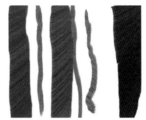

Foreground/Background Jitter 50%
Control: Pen Tilt

Bristles 4%

Scatter 50%
Control: Pen Pressure

Spacing 60%
Brightness Jitter 50%

SETTINGS

Thickness 50%
Spacing 15%
Angle Jitter 50%

Length 200%
Spacing 5%

Scatter 10%
Wet Edges

Length 40%
Stiffness 20%

Length 50%
Thickness 50%
Stiffness 100%

Angle Jitter 50%
Flow Jitter 50%
Control: Initial Direction
Wet Edges

Stiffness 1%
Spacing 20%

Scatter 20%
Count 5
Count Jitter 100%

Dual Brush: Dune Grass

Bristles 10%
Length 60%

FLAT BLUNT SHORT STIFF

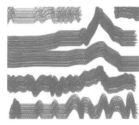

Default Brush

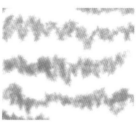

Bristles 50%
Angle Jitter 50%
Control: Pen Tilt

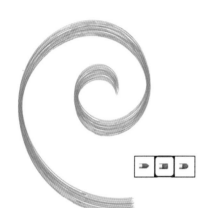

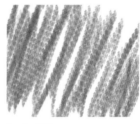

Spacing 50%
Foreground/Background Jitter 20%

Length 20%
Stiffness 10%

SETTINGS

Thickness 20%
Stiffness 50%

Hue Jitter 10%
Saturation Jitter 20%
Control: Pen Pressure

Spacing 10%
Angle Jitter 50%
Control: Pen Pressure

Length 40%
Saturation Jitter 50%
Opacity Jitter 50%

Bristles 13%
Stiffness 100%
Foreground/Background
Jitter 40%

Bristles 20%
Length 200%
Thickness 50%

Scatter 10%
Count 10
Count Jitter 100%

Stiffness 50%

Thickness 50%
Length 25%

Flow Jitter 100%
Control: Pen Pressure

FLAT CURVE THIN STIFF BRISTLES

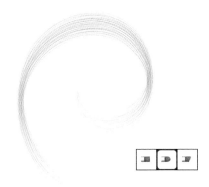

Default Brush

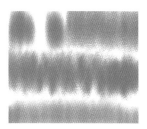

Scatter 100%
Count 10
Count Jitter 10%
Control: Pen Pressure

Wet Edges

Stiffness 10%

SETTINGS

Spacing 25%

Length 80%
Foreground/Background
Jitter 20%

Bristles 80%
Stiffness 50%
Opacity Jitter 20%

Scatter 70%

Saturation Jitter 50%
Brightness Jitter 50%

Stiffness 100%

Bristles 80%
Length 300%

Angle Jitter 50%
Wet Edges

Stiffness 30%
Flow Jitter 50%

Spacing 20%

FLAT ANGLE LOW BRISTLE COUNT

Wet Edges

Foreground/Background Jitter 100%
Control: Pen Pressure

Stiffness 25%
Spacing 10%

Scatter 200%
Count 4

SETTINGS

Scatter 90%

Length 50%
Thickness 50%

Scatter 10%
Flow Jitter 50%

Stiffness 50%
Hue Jitter 50%

Stiffness 20%
Foreground/Background
Jitter 80%
Hue Jitter 20%

Thickness 10%
Spacing 50%

Length 200%
Thickness 200%

Angle Jitter 50%

Scatter 20%
Opacity Jitter 20%
Noise
Wet Edges

Bristles 60%
Stiffness 70%

FLAT FAN HIGH BRISTLE COUNT

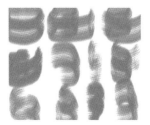

Default Brush

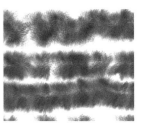

Angle Jitter 20%
Control: Rotation
Foreground/Background Jitter 100%
Control: Pen Pressure

Wet Edges

Bristles 100%
Length 25%
Thickness 20%
Stiffness 60%

SETTINGS

Wet Edges

Foreground/Background
Jitter 100%
Control: Pen Pressure
Noise

Spacing 10%
Scatter 10%
Count 3

Angle Jitter 30%
Control: Initial Direction
Opacity Jitter 50%
Control: Pen Pressure

Length 150%
Stiffness 100%

Bristles 20%
Scatter 150%

Stiffness 20%
Wet Edges

Angle Jitter 100%
Control: Direction
Foreground/Background
Jitter 100%
Control: Pen Pressure

Bristles 100%
Length 25%
Stiffness 40%
Wet Edges

Scatter 1%
Count 4
Saturation Jitter 50%

FLAT BLUNT STIFF

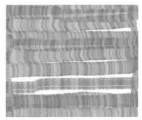

Spacing 12%
Scatter 5%
Foreground/Background Jitter 50%
Control: Pen Pressure

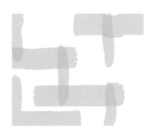

Wet Edges

Stiffness 35%

Bristles 50%
Thickness 25%
Stiffness 50%

SETTINGS

Stiffness 30%
Opacity Jitter 50%
Control: Pen Pressure

Scatter 75%
Count 2

Bristles 100%
Length 150%

Foreground/Background
Jitter 50%
Control: Pen Pressure

Scatter 70%
Opacity Jitter 50%
Control: Pen Pressure
Noise

Scatter 10%
Hue Jitter 20%
Opacity Jitter 10%
Wet Edges

Thickness 20%
Stiffness 10%
Spacing 20%

Foreground/Background
Jitter 10%
Saturation Jitter 50%
Opacity Jitter 50%

Angle Jitter 50%
Scatter 10%
Count 2

Length 25%
Spacing 10%

FLAT ANGLE SHORT MEDIUM STIFF

Angle Jitter 20%
Foreground/Background Jitter 50%
Control: Pen Pressure

Scatter 100%
Foreground/Background Jitter 20%

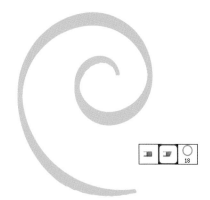

Angle Jitter 50%
Control: Pen Pressure

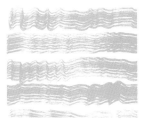

Bristles 20%
Thickness 20%
Stiffness 40%

SETTINGS

Spacing 25%

Length 25%
Stiffness 20%
Foreground/Background
Jitter 50%
Control: Pen Pressure

Bristles 20%
Hue Jitter 20%

Length 200%
Wet Edges

Spacing 10%
Foreground/Background
Jitter 25%

Scatter 50%
Count 2
Wet Edges

Angle Jitter 25%
Opacity Jitter 20%
Control: Pen Pressure

Bristles 40%
Stiffness 10%
Saturation Jitter 20%
Wet Edges

Bristles 80%
Length 50%
Thickness 50%

Scatter 200%
Count 3
Count Jitter 100%
Control: Pen Pressure
Hue Jitter 20%

FLAT BLUNT
WITH TEXTURE

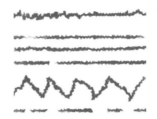

Angle Jitter 30%
Control: Pen Pressure

Default Brush

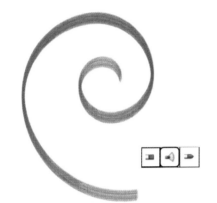

Scatter 0%
Foreground/Background Jitter 20%
Control: Pen Pressure
Wet Edges

Spacing 25%
Scatter 50%
Foreground/Background Jitter 100%

SETTINGS

Scatter 10%
Count 16

Spacing 10%
Angle Jitter 30%
Control: Pen Pressure

Angle Jitter 10%
Scatter 200%
Count 3
Wet Edges

Stiffness 35%

Flow Jitter 50%
Control: Pen Pressure

Bristles 50%
Length 40%
Saturation Jitter 50%

Stiffness 50%
Spacing 10%
Scatter 20%
Wet Edges

Bristles 20%
Foreground/Background
Jitter 100%

Angle Jitter 50%
Control: Pen Pressure

Spacing 1%
Scatter 20%
Saturation Jitter 30%

ROUND FAN
WITH TEXTURE

Wet Edges

Thickness 50%
Foreground/Background Jitter 100%
Control: Pen Pressure

Scatter 150%
Count 4

Bristles 70%
Spacing 60%
Wet Edges

SETTINGS

Bristles 10%
Length 25%
Thickness 25%
Stiffness 50%

Hue Jitter 50%
Brightness Jitter 50%

Spacing 50%

Thickness 50%
Angle Jitter 30%
Scatter 100%
Control: Pen Pressure

Length 50%
Flow Jitter 50%
Wet Edges

Stiffness 20%
Scatter 200%
Hue Jitter 10%

Bristles 100%
Length 300%
Thickness 50%

Stiffness 25%
Hue Jitter 50%
Brightness Jitter 50%

Spacing 1%
Angle Jitter 50%
Scatter 50%
Foreground/Background
Jitter 20%
Control: Pen Pressure

Spacing 80%
Scatter 5%
Opacity Jitter 50%
Control: Pen Pressure
Wet Edges

FLAT POINT SCATTER NO SPACING

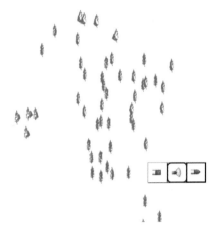

Default Brush

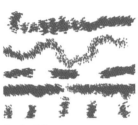

Spacing 10%
Scatter 200%

Hue Jitter 80%
Wet Edges

Bristles 100%
Stiffness 20%
Spacing 25%

SETTINGS

Thickness 60%
Scatter 50%
Hue Jitter 40%
Control: Pen Pressure

Stiffness 20%
Spacing 20%
Saturation Jitter 50%

Spacing 50%
Angle Jitter 50%
Wet Edges

Bristles 80%
Thickness 25%
Spacing 5%

Stiffness 20%
Spacing 11%
Foreground/Background
Jitter 100%
Control: Pen Pressure

Length 100%
Spacing 20%

Bristles 20%
Spacing 30%
Scatter 50%
Count 5
Count Jitter 100%
Control: Pen Pressure

Spacing 10%
Brightness Jitter 80%
Flow Jitter 50%

Thickness 50%
Stiffness 100%
Spacing 1%

Spacing 11%
Wet Edges

ROUND POINT
THIN BRISTLE

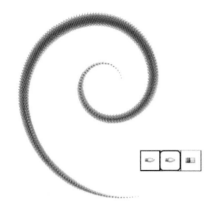

Stiffness 50%
Foreground/Background Jitter 100%
Control: Pen Pressure

Spacing 20%
Scatter 50%
Control: Pen Pressure
Wet Edges

Bristles 100%
Spacing 2%

Angle Jitter 50%
Control: Pen Pressure

SETTINGS

Scatter 200%

Length 250%
Foreground/Background
Jitter 50%
Control: Pen Pressure

Opacity Jitter 100%
Control: Pen Pressure
Wet Edges

Spacing 25%
Angle Jitter 20%
Hue Jitter 20%

Scatter 50%
Count 2
Count Jitter 100%
Control: Pen Pressure

Stiffness 30%
Spacing 1%
Saturation Jitter: 20%
Wet Edges

Length 50%
Thickness 20%

Spacing 50%
Scatter 10%
Foreground/Background
Jitter 50%

Spacing 5%
Hue Jitter 20%
Saturation Jitter 20%
Wet Edges

Bristles 10%
Thickness 30%
Stiffness 50%

ROUND POINT LOW BRISTLE COUNT

Default Brush

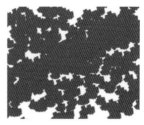

Scatter 100%
Count 3
Count Jitter 50%
Control: Pen Pressure

Hue Jitter 50%

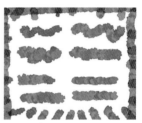

Angle Jitter 50%
Control: Initial Direction
Foreground/Background Jitter 100%
Control: Pen Pressure
Wet Edges

SETTINGS

Bristles 30%
Hue Jitter 50%

Angle Jitter 50%
Control: Direction

Length 100%
Scatter 20%
Brightness Jitter 20%
Control: Pen Pressure
Wet Edges

Stiffness 30%
Brightness Jitter 30%
Hue Jitter 20%

Length 200%
Thickness 10%
Foreground/Background
Jitter 20%
Control: Pen Pressure

Stiffness 30%
Spacing 25%

Scatter 150%
Count 5

Angle Jitter 100%
Saturation Jitter 20%
Control: Initial Direction
Wet Edges

Stiffness 40%
Spacing 5%
Scatter 10%

Scatter 200%
Foreground/Background
Jitter 100%
Noise
Wet Edges

ROUND BLUNT STREAKS

Length 200%
Stiffness 50%

Bristles 60%
Stiffness 80%
Spacing 10%
Wet Edges

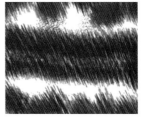

Scatter 50%
Foreground/Background Jitter 100%
Control: Pen Pressure

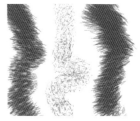

Angle Jitter 50%
Control: Initial Direction

SETTINGS

Scatter 90%

Thickness 50%
Stiffness 80%

Bristles 50%
Spacing 20%
Flow Jitter 100%
Control: Pen Pressure

Stiffness 20%
Scatter 5%
Opacity Jitter 50%
Wet Edges

Length 150%

Length 10%
Stiffness 100%
Thickness 50%
Spacing 50%

Length 50%
Thickness 100%
Scatter 60%
Count 5

Stiffness 20%
Scatter 10%
Hue Jitter 20%

Foreground/Background
Jitter 100%
Control: Pen Pressure
Flow Jitter 100%
Control: Pen Pressure
Wet Edges

Stiffness 50%
Scatter 200%

FLAT BLUNT STREAKS

Bristles 50%

Thickness 50%

Scatter 150%
Control: Pen Pressure

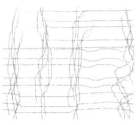

Scatter 150%
Hue Jitter 50%

SETTINGS

Bristles 20%
Thickness 20%
Spacing 20%
Flow Jitter 50%
Control: Pen Pressure

Bristles 50%
Length 150%
Stiffness 80%

Length 150%
Foreground/Background
Jitter 100%
Control: Pen Pressure

Length 200%
Thickness 20%
Angle Jitter 50%
Control: Initial Direction

Thickness 60%
Stiffness 30%
Hue Jitter 20%

Bristles 100%
Spacing 25%
Saturation Jitter 20%
Wet Edges

Length 50%
Thickness 20%
Stiffness 20%
Brightness Jitter 50%
Wet Edges

Bristles 70%
Length 50%
Thickness 20%
Hue Jitter 50%

Bristles 50%
Wet Edges

Thickness 50%
Length 50%
Spacing 1%
Scatter 90%

FLAT FAN THICK STIFF WET EDGE

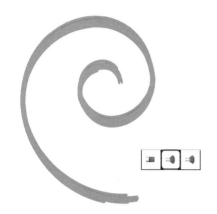

Angle Jitter 50%
Control: Pen Pressure

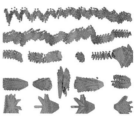

Stiffness 40%
Spacing 10%
Foreground/Background Jitter 100%
Control: Pen Pressure

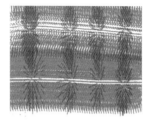

Bristles 40%
Length 200%
Thickness 20%
Stiffness 60%

Hue Jitter 50%

SETTINGS

Bristles 50%

Length 500%

Scatter 50%
Control: Pen Pressure

Stiffness 50%
Spacing 33%
Scatter 10%
Foreground/Background
Jitter 50%

Bristles 35%
Length 90%
Thickness 30%
Stiffness 80%

Angle Jitter 30%
Flow Jitter 50%

Scatter 90%

Stiffness 20%
Brightness
Jitter 80%

Scatter 0%

Brightness Jitter 50%

FLAT FAN SINGLE BRISTLE DUAL BRUSH

Default Brush

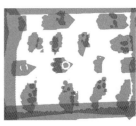

Stiffness 20%
Spacing 5%
Wet Edges

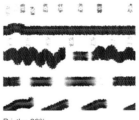

Bristles 89%
Foreground/Background Jitter 100%
Control: Pen Pressure

Length 200%
Thickness 30%
Opacity Jitter 50%

SETTINGS

Scatter 60%
Count 6
Count Jitter 60%
Control: Pen Pressure

Foreground/Background
Jitter 100%
Opacity Jitter 50%
Control: Pen Pressure

Bristles 30%
Length 200%

Stiffness 50%
Flow Jitter 20%

Thickness 50%
Scatter 5%
Saturation Jitter 50%

Spacing 50%

Bristles 50%
Thickness 20%
Stiffness 80%

Angle Jitter 50%
Scatter 150%

Stiffness 10%
Spacing 10%
Hue Jitter 50%

Length 200%
Stiffness 50%
Saturation Jitter 30%

FLAT SINGLE BRISTLE WET EDGE

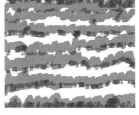

Default Brush

Stiffness 1%

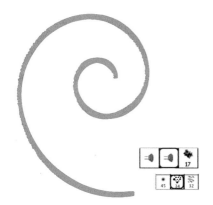

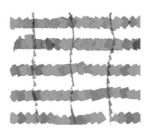

Length 30%
Spacing 25%
Brightness Jitter 20%

Bristles 20%
Spacing 12%
Opacity Jitter 50%

SETTINGS

Bristles 100%

Scatter 10%
Control: Pen Pressure

Angle Jitter 30%
Control: Direction

Bristles 10%
Length 25%
Thickness 25%
Stiffness 50%

Scatter 70%
Control: Pen Pressure

Spacing 50%

Stiffness 30%
Foreground/Background
Jitter 50%

Scatter 70%
Count 4
Opacity Jitter 20%
Control: Pen Pressure

Bristles 25%
Thickness 10%
Hue Jitter 10%

Stiffness 100%
Spacing 50%
Scatter 70%
Brightness Jitter 30%

BASICS OF PAINTING

Before you start applying brushes to your digital art, you
should have sound knowledge of the relevant elements that
make such creativity possible. Document settings, layers,
and color and blend modes are just some of the tools that
will help you to master digital painting techniques.

Setting Up and Working With Your Document

Before you start a new document you need to think about how you intend to use your image. Documents that are going to be printed need to be set up differently than those that are only going to be viewed on screen (on a Web page, for instance).

The document resolution determines the level of detail it contains. Resolution is measured in Pixels Per Inch (ppi) though often you'll hear it (incorrectly) referred to as Dots Per Inch (dpi). The higher a document's ppi, the greater the level of detail when you zoom in on an image.

When you're creating an image that will only be viewed on screen, resolution isn't an issue. You simply create the document with the pixel dimensions you require.

If you're going to print your image, you should be safe if you set it up with a resolution of 300ppi (2).

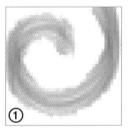 

When you print a file that doesn't have a high enough resolution, the printed results can be disappointing. In the example above, the swirl on the left has been created at 72ppi, the swirl on the right, 300ppi. The left-hand example is pixelated and lacking in detail.

CREATING YOUR CANVAS

When you start a new document, you need to specify what size you want your image to be. Here, size refers both to the physical dimensions of your artwork and the level of detail that the artwork contains.

The physical dimensions are referred to as the canvas size (width and height) and the level of detail is determined by the resolution of the document.

To create a new document:
1 Go to File > New.
2 Fill in the details for your new image. As explained above, if you are preparing an image to display only on screen, change the measurement units to pixels and select the dimensions you need.
3 Click OK.

The New dialog box

ALTERING CANVAS SIZE

To alter the dimensions of your image, go to Image > Canvas Size. But be careful! If you decrease the size of the canvas, Photoshop will crop some of your image away.

1 You can change the units to pixels, centimeters, or inches—whatever works best for you.
2 The Relative check box lets you specify the amount to be added to the canvas rather than the default option, which sets the total width and height of the altered canvas.
3 The Anchor area lets you position your existing artwork in relation to your new canvas size by clicking on one of the nine squares.
4 If you are extending your canvas, then the Canvas extension color lets you choose what color you want the extended canvas to be.

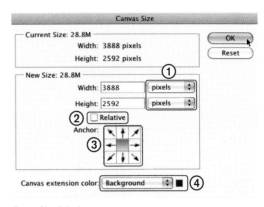

Canvas Size dialog box

Keyboard shortcut
To access Canvas Size:
Ctrl/Cmd+Alt+C

RESIZING AN IMAGE

To change the dimensions and/or resolution of an image, use Image > Image Size. Increasing the size of an image in Photoshop can easily lead to a disappointing loss of quality, although Photoshop is now fairly adept at increasing the resolution (up to about 130%). Try to anticipate whether you will need a large document before you start your work.
1 Constrain Proportions maintains the art's aspect ratio, which means that Photoshop won't squeeze or squash your image into its new dimensions.
2 Resample Image lets Photoshop create pixels in or drop pixels from your artwork.
3 Tell Photoshop how to resample the image from the drop-down menu. It's not ideal to increase image size, but the Bicubic smoother can help.

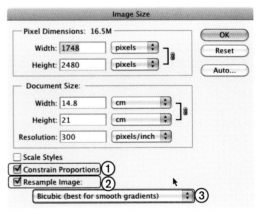

Image Size dialog box

SHOWING AND HIDING PANELS

There are many panels down the right-hand side of the screen. All the panels can be accessed from the Window menu. Each panel offers specific settings and they have a menu in the top right-hand corner offering additional options.

1 From the Window menu, choose a panel name to open that panel.

2 You'll see a tick next to panels that are already open. If you select a panel name that is already open, it will close.

> **Keyboard shortcut**
> To hide or show all open panels:
> Tab

Window menu

UNDO AND HISTORY

Undo
Photoshop's approach to undoing your work is not like other programs. The Edit > Undo command (Ctrl/Cmd+Z) toggles between Undoing and Redoing your last action and so doesn't allow you to undo beyond your last step.

The History panel
To go back further than your last step, the History panel (Window > History) shows a list of commands and actions you've performed in the order you carried them out.

1 This small blue arrow points to the image state you're currently looking at. Dragging the arrow up or down the list of states lets you Undo and Redo over multiple states. As you undo actions, you'll see them fade out. Until you carry out a new command, you can still redo the actions you have undone by dragging the arrow down the list again.

2 You can click the area at the top of the History panel to revert the file to its original state.

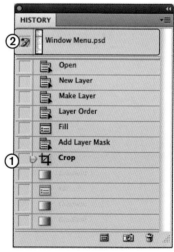

History panel

> **Keyboard shortcuts**
> Undo and Redo: Ctrl/Cmd+Z
>
> Up through History: Ctrl/Cmd+Alt+Z
>
> Down: Ctrl/Cmd+Shift+Z

SAVING YOUR WORK

Although Photoshop doesn't often crash, it is sensible to save your work regularly. Save by going to File > Save.

The File > Save As… command creates a new image file based on the document you're currently working with.

Using Save As is useful when you're experimenting with your image and are uncertain whether you want to commit yourself to changing the original file. Use it to save a copy.

ABOUT FILE FORMATS

When you save your work, Photoshop needs to know what type of image file you want to save. Photoshop can create a lot of different file formats and the file format you choose can make a significant difference as to how you can use your image later. Before you save a file, you should think about what you might want to use the image for. The most popular file formats are listed below:

1 Photoshop: this is the format you should use to save your work-in-progress. The Photoshop format saves all the Photoshop elements, such as layers, paths etc., with the file so that you can carry on making changes when you re-open it. It saves the file with a .psd suffix.

2 JPEG is an ideal format for archiving completed work and is also useful for images intended for use on the Web. JPEG is not suitable for saving work-in-progress because it removes Photoshop elements such as layers from the file. You should save all files at "maximum" quality to avoid any deterioration in the image unless you are saving them for the Web. JPEGs are saved with a .jpg suffix.

3 TIFF files are an alternative to the Photoshop file format. They are widely used in print publishing and retain most of the editability of a Photoshop file, saving the layers. TIFFs are saved with a .tif suffix.

① ✓ Photoshop
   BMP
   CompuServe GIF
   Dicom
   Photoshop EPS
   FXG
   IFF Format
② JPEG
   Large Document Format
   PCX
   Photoshop PDF
   Photoshop 2.0
   Photoshop Raw
   PICT File
   PICT Resource
   Pixar
   PNG
   Portable Bit Map
   Scitex CT
   Targa
③ TIFF
   Photoshop DCS 1.0
   Photoshop DCS 2.0

File format list from the Save or Save As dialog box

Color Modes—RGB and CMYK

Images for screen viewing need to describe color differently from images that are going to be printed on a professional press. The different ways Photoshop uses to describe color are called Color Modes.

RGB mode uses levels of red, green, and blue light to describe colors. It works in the same way as a computer screen or digital camera. Use RGB for images you want to view on screen or if you're not sure where you finally want to use your image.

CMYK imitates the mixing of cyan, magenta, yellow, and black (K) inks used in professional printing. If you intend to have your work printed professionally, use CMYK. You tell Photoshop which color mode to use when creating a new image.

Although most home printers use cyan, magenta, yellow, and black inks, generally the printer's own software deals with converting your image from RGB to CMYK as you print. Unless you are getting bad results from printing in RGB, you won't usually have to convert an image to CMYK in order to print it at home.

You can also change the color mode of an existing image, but you may notice some colors change and lose intensity, especially when you go from RGB to CMYK.

This is because RGB and CMYK, while they contain many of the same colors, don't share exactly the same range of colors. The range of colors a color mode contains is known as its "gamut."

It is best to create your image in RGB since it contains a greater gamut than CMYK. You will need to bear in mind that if you do need to switch to CMYK, some of the colors may seem a little faded. You can avoid this by picking in gamut colors when you are painting (see opposite).

If you are working in RGB and need to check how your image will look in CMYK, go to View > Proof Setting, making sure the CMYK option is selected, and then go to View > Proof Colors.

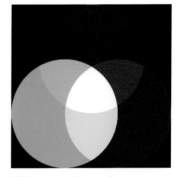

RGB mode: mixing light together

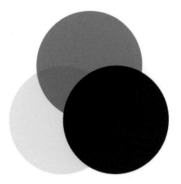

CMYK mode: mixing inks together

Keyboard shortcut
To switch Proof Colors on and off:
Ctrl/Cmd+Y

COLOR MODES AND CHOOSING COLORS

1 To find out how to select colors, see page 26. Using either the Color Picker or Color panel, you can select both RGB and CMYK colors.

2 The Out of Gamut Warning (the ! sign in the triangle) appears when you've chosen colors that are in the RGB range but not in the CMYK range. It will be adjusted if you subsequently change your image from RGB to CMYK.

3 To change an RGB color to its closest CMYK color, click the color square next to the Gamut Warning.

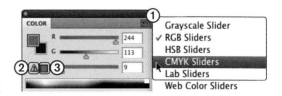

Color panel—selecting a new Foreground Color swatch

CREATING AND SAVING SWATCHES

Use the Swatches Palette (Window > Swatches) to access and keep frequently used colors, or use it to access color libraries that are pre-installed as well as libraries you've created yourself.

1 Clicking on a specific color swatch selects it as the Foreground Color, and you can double-click the swatch to rename it.

2 From the menu on the side, you can change the way your swatches display in the Swatches panel.

3 Click the New Swatch icon to add the present Foreground Color to the Swatches panel.

4 To delete a color from the Swatches panel, drag the swatch to the Trash icon at the bottom right of the Swatches panel.

5 You can load other swatch libraries by selecting Load Swatches in the Swatches panel menu.

6 If you want to create your own swatch libraries, go to Save Swatches in the Swatches panel menu. Photoshop will ask you to save the collection as an .aco file, which you can load into Photoshop using the Load Colors… command from the Swatches panel menu.

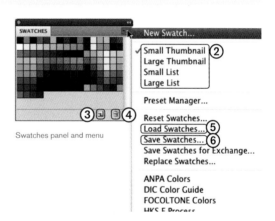

Swatches panel and menu

Swatches panel in small list view

How Layers Work

Layers are crucial for painting because they let you separate an image into individual elements that can be edited and moved without affecting the rest of the image. Without them you'll find that painting is a tricky matter.

Layers are stacked one on top of the other; where you paint there will be pixels, while the rest of the layer is transparent, allowing the pixels on lower layers to show through.

It is generally best practice to begin a new layer for each new object you are painting. It will mean it is much easier to make changes (moving, deleting sections, etc.) without being destructive to the rest of your painting.

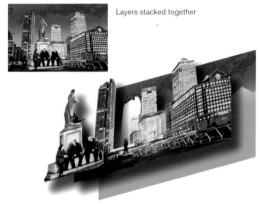

Layers stacked together

Layers "exploded" for you to see

USING AND CREATING LAYERS

The Layers panel (Window > Layers) lets you create and manage layers.

1 When you're using layers, the selected layer is displayed with a blue background in the Layers panel. Layers have to be selected before you can move or paint on them. To select a layer, click on it once.

2 You can create new layers with the Create New Layer icon at the bottom of the panel.

3 If you want to delete a layer, drag it to the Trash icon.

4 You can re-order the layers (they appear one on top of the other according to their stacking order in the panel) by clicking and dragging a layer up or down the stacking order. You'll see a black line appear while you are dragging indicating the new position for the layer.

5 It's often useful to be able to hide layers so you can see the whole image or painting underneath. Just click the eye to the left of the layer name to hide the layer.

6 It's very useful to know that every time you Paste (Edit > Paste or Ctrl/Cmd+V) into your painting a new layer is created.

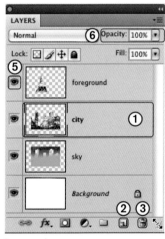

Layers panel

Keyboard shortcuts

To bring up the Layers panel: F9

To hide all layers except the one you have selected:
Alt+click the eye beside the selected layer

To show all layers again:
Repeat the process

RENAMING LAYERS

Although Photoshop automatically gives your layer a name, it's not very descriptive, so it's useful to get in the habit of renaming as something more meaningful. To name a layer, double-click its name in the Layers panel.

Renaming a layer

TRANSPARENT AREAS IN LAYERS AND THE BACKGROUND LAYER

Transparent areas in layers
Photoshop indicates the transparent areas of your layers in a gray checkerboard pattern.

Background layers
When you create a new painting, or open most images for the first time, you'll find that in Photoshop the base is called "Background." It isn't really a layer because it can't be moved and it can't contain any transparent areas.

To convert the background into a normal layer, double-click it in the Layers panel. Photoshop will suggest that you rename it and when you click OK it will become a normal layer.

Transparency areas are displayed with a checkerboard pattern

Double-click the Background to turn it into a layer

MOVING AND LOCKING LAYERS

Moving what you've painted on a layer

If you want to move the pixels you have painted on a layer, select it and use the Move Tool (pictured left) to drag the layer around the canvas.

Locking and unlocking layers
Clicking the lock icons at the top of the Layer menu locks and unlocks changes being made to: transparency (1), pixels (i.e. existing content) (2), and position (3) of selected layers. The final icon (4) locks and unlocks all of these properties.

About Selections

Once you have done some painting in Photoshop you may want to change a section of it—perhaps to apply an effect, delete it, or move it. A selection is the way you indicate to Photoshop the part of your painting you want to alter. Whichever tool you use to make the selection (there are several), Photoshop indicates the selected area with a dotted border that appears to shimmer and move (known as "marching ants"!).

Only the pixels inside the selection border will be affected by any changes, while those outside won't be touched.

For instance, if you select an area and then paint on your canvas, only the area that is selected will change color. You can also cut or copy the selected area and paste it into another document.

The dotted line shows the selected area. The solid circle is a brush. The brush only paints into the selected area.

Making a Selection

RECTANGULAR AND ELLIPTICAL MARQUEE TOOLS

There is a range of different tools for selecting areas. Use the Marquee tools to make simple rectangular or elliptical selections.

Clicking and dragging with either of the tools creates a selected area.

Hold down the Shift key while dragging to constrain the selection to either a square or circle. Hold down the Alt key while dragging to create a selection from its center.

Marquee tools

Keyboard shortcut
To select the Marquee tools:
Shift+M

LASSO TOOL

You can use the Lasso Tool to create irregular, freehand-shaped selections.

Click and drag with the Lasso to draw around the area you want to select. You don't have to try to make the whole selection all in one go. See opposite to learn how you can add to and subtract from the selection in order to build the selected area bit by bit.

Lasso Tool

Keyboard shortcut
To select the Lasso tools:
Shift+L

POLYGONAL LASSO TOOL

Use the Polygonal Lasso Tool to create straight-edged selections.

Click to anchor a selection edge. Click again elsewhere to create a line between the two clicks. Continue clicking to define the edges of the selection.

Double-click to close the selection.

Hold down the Alt key to be able to draw freehand lines.

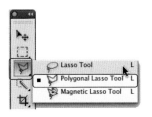

Polygonal Lasso Tool

Keyboard shortcut
Hold down the Alt key while using the Polygonal Lasso to draw freehand borders.

QUICK SELECTION TOOL

The Quick Selection Tool lets you create a selection by "painting" onto the canvas. Photoshop tries to anticipate where the edges are in what you're selecting and expands your "painted" stroke out toward defined edges in an image.

Quick Selection Tool in the toolbar

To use the Quick Selection Tool:

1 Select the Quick Selection Tool from the toolbar.
2 Use the Options bar to select a brush size appropriate to the area that you want to select.

Quick Selection options on the Options bar

3 Click and drag over some of the area you want to select to start the selection. When you release the mouse, Photoshop will create a new selection border.
4 To add more to the selection, click the Add to Selection icon and drag over the area that you want to add to the selection.
5 To subtract from the selection, click the Subtract from Selection icon and drag over the area that you want to remove from the selection.

Keyboard shortcut
Hold down Shift and then drag to Add to a Quick Selection; Alt to take away.

MAGIC WAND TOOL

Use the Magic Wand Tool to select areas of similar color in an image without having to trace around edges, as you would have to using the Lasso Tool.

How large an area the tool selects when you click depends on how similar the colors are to the pixel you clicked on. The range of colored pixels you select is determined by the tolerance setting in the Options bar. With tolerance at 0, only pixels the same color will be selected. With tolerance of 255, all pixels will be selected.

Magic Wand Tool in the toolbar

Magic Wand options on the Options bar

1 The Contiguous check box limits your selection to similar colors immediately adjacent to where you click with the Magic Wand Tool; unchecked it selects similar colors over the whole canvas.
2 If you select fewer or more pixels than you intended, adjust the Tolerance setting and try again.

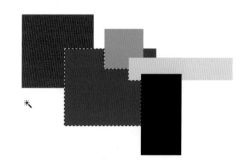

Modifying Selections

Deselecting
You can get rid of a selection by clicking away from it with a selection tool or by going to Select > Deselect.

Keyboard shortcuts
To deselect: Ctrl/Cmd+D

To reselect: Ctrl/Cmd+Shift+D

To invert a selection: Ctrl/Cmd+I

Reselecting
Should you need to load your last selection again, go to Select > Reselect.

Inverting a selection
It's often easier to select the part of the image you don't want to have selected and then inverse the selection. Go to Select > Inverse Selection.

The New, the Add to, Subtract from, and Intersect with Selection icons from the Options bar

Combining selections
When you have a selection tool active, the Options bar always displays four buttons. Once you've made an initial selection, click one of these buttons and the next selection you make will:
1 Make a new selection;
2 Add to the existing selection;
3 Subtract from the existing selection;
4 Find the area where the existing selection and new selection intersect.

Keyboard shortcuts
Add to a selection by holding down the Shift key as you drag.

Subtract from a selection by holding down the Alt key as you drag.

Find the Intersection between your current selection and where you are dragging by holding down Alt+Shift as you drag.

RESIZING, MOVING, AND ROTATING SELECTION

Often you'll want to alter a selection by resizing, moving, or rotating it. When you transform a selection, you just change the shape or position of the selection; you don't affect any actual pixels.

To transform your selection (you must have created one already):

1 Choose Select > Transform Selection.

2 A transform rectangle appears around your selection.

3 To move the selection, click and drag inside the rectangle to reposition the selection.

4 Click and drag on the resize handles at the edges and in the middle to resize the selection.

5 Rotate your selection by moving your cursor just outside the transform rectangle and dragging in the direction you want your selection to rotate.

6 When you have finished modifying your selection border, either click the Commit Transform icon if you are happy with the results or the Cancel Transform icon to cancel it.

Magic Wand options on the Options bar

> **Keyboard shortcuts**
>
> Clicking on a resize handle around the Transform Selection rectangle and then holding down a modifier key on the keyboard changes the way the resize handles work:
>
> Ctrl/Cmd allows you to move handles independently.
>
> Ctrl/Cmd+Shift gives a perspective-like transformation.

SAVING AND RELOADING SELECTIONS

Selections are fairly transitory. When you close a document, Photoshop forgets any selections you created in it unless you deliberately choose to save those selections and then save the document.

To save a selection for later use:

1 With a selection created, go to Selection > Save Selection.

2 Name your selection and click OK.

To reload a saved selection:

1 Go to Selection > Load Selection.

2 Choose your saved selection from the Load Selection dialog box's Channels drop-down menu.

3 Click OK.

Save Selection dialog box

Load Selection dialog box

Filters and the Filter Gallery

Photoshop's Filter menu provides a wide range of commands that can be used to apply special effects and enhancements to paintings.

Filters alter the pixels you apply them to so it's a good idea to duplicate a layer before you apply a filter to it. This way you can easily return to your unfiltered image. You can also use a feature called Smart Filters to avoid making permanent changes. Of special interest to artists is the collection known as the Filter Gallery filters—choose Filter > Filter Gallery... to find them. The filters from the Filter Gallery won't work if you aren't in the RGB color mode (see page 376).

Above: The left half of the image has not been filtered. The right half has had the Glass filter applied to it. Glass can be found at Filter > Distort > Glass.

USING THE FILTER GALLERY

1 Select the area you want to filter (unless you want to apply the filter to your whole painting).
2 Go to Filter > Filter Gallery... to bring up the Filter Gallery dialog box.
3 On the left of the dialog box is a preview of your image along with icons to let you zoom in and out.
4 To the right of the preview are groups of different effects to apply. Click on the arrow next to a group's folder icon to see all the different effects in that group. Choose an effect by clicking it. Photoshop will update the image preview.
5 Sliders that control the settings for the effects are located under the OK and Cancel buttons on the far right.
6 More than one effect can be used at a time. Click the New Effect button to add another effect. Delete effects using the Trash icon.
7 If you have more than one effect applied, you can adjust its setting by clicking its name in the list of effects.
8 Hide and show effects by clicking the eye icons. Click OK to apply the filter effects.

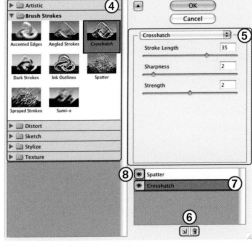

Filter Gallery dialog box controls

FADING FILTERS

If you want to modify the effects of a filter, you can use Edit > Fade Filter… (Photoshop changes the name of this command according to the last filter used, so if the last filter you used was the Glass filter, the command would say Edit > Fade Glass…). You can only fade a filter right after you've applied it.

Fading allows you to refine the effects of your last filter by:
1 Blending it back into your unfiltered original using an Opacity slider.
2 Applying Blend Modes (see page 390).

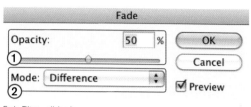

Fade Filter… dialog box

Keyboard shortcut
To access Fade Filter…:
Ctrl/Cmd+Shift+F

USING SMART FILTERS

Filters can permanently alter your work, which can restrict your chances of experimentation. In more recent versions of Photoshop (CS3 onward) you can apply a Smart Filter, which will allow you to tweak or even abandon filters you have applied.

To use a Smart Filter:
1 After you select the layer you want to filter, go to Filter > Convert to Smart Filter. This changes the layer into a "Smart Object" and the Smart Object icon appears in the Layer Preview in the Layers panel.
2 Apply a filter to the layer.
3 Once you have applied a filter, it appears in a list below the filter, as shown.
4 Hide and show the Smart Filter effect by clicking the eye icon.
5 You can change the settings for the Smart Filter effect by double-clicking the name of the filter you want to change.

Layer 0 has a Smart Object icon in its bottom right-hand corner.

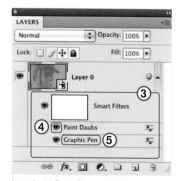

Layer 0 with Smart Filters attached

Using Layer Masks

Layer masks allow you to use Photoshop's paint tools to hide and show or blend portions of layers.

Working with layer masks

1 Select the layer that you want to add a mask to.

2 Click the Add Layer Mask icon.

3 Photoshop adds a Layer Mask thumbnail to the right of the Layer thumbnail on the Layers panel. You'll notice a thin black highlight around the Layer Mask thumbnail, which means the layer mask is active. Clicking the Layer thumbnail activates the layer; clicking the Layer Mask thumbnail activates the layer mask.

4 Paint on the layer mask to hide or reveal the layer's content. While the layer mask is active you can only paint in black, white, or different shades of gray. Painting in black hides the part of the layer you paint over (like a mask) and painting in white reveals it. Shades of gray create a semitransparent effect with lighter shades being more transparent and darker shades less transparent. Painting with a soft-edged brush creates soft transitions in the mask. Hard-edged brushes create hard transitions.

5 Delete layer masks by dragging the Layer Mask thumbnail to the Trash icon. When you do this, Photoshop will ask if you want to apply the mask before deleting or whether you simply want to delete the mask. The Apply option will delete all masked content from the layer. The Delete option will simply remove the mask and return your layer to its unmasked state.

The Layers panel: On the Falcon layer, the Layer Mask thumbnail sits to the right of the Layer thumbnail. Note the thin outline, which lets you know that the layer mask is active.

CREATING A LAYER MASK FROM A SELECTION

If you've created a selection and want to use it as the basis for a layer mask then, with your selection active, create a layer as above. Photoshop will generate a mask based on your selection.

VIEWING LAYER MASKS

The Layer Mask thumbnail in the Layers panel offers a small preview of your layer mask, but sometimes it's useful to be able to see the mask in more detail, or to be able to hide it completely.

Changing layer mask views

1 To view a layer mask without the layer, hold down the Alt key and click the layer mask's thumbnail. Alt-clicking the thumbnail again will return you to a normal view of your image.
2 To temporarily hide a layer mask, Shift-click the Layer Mask thumbnail.
3 To view the layer mask as a semi-opaque overlay over your image, hold down Shift+Alt and click the layer mask. You can continue to edit your mask in this mode.
4 To change the color of the layer mask overlay, double-click the layer mask in the Channels panel and click the color swatch to choose the tint that you'd prefer to see the overlay in.

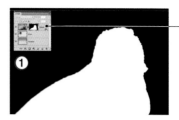

Alt-click the Layer Mask thumbnail to hide the image with only the layer mask showing.

Shift-click the Layer Mask thumbnail to hide the mask with only the image showing without the mask applied.

Layer mask displayed as semi-opaque overlay.

Layer Mask Display Options dialog box

GRADIENTS AND GRAYS IN LAYER MASKS

In a layer mask, painting in gray provides different levels of transparency depending on the tint you are using, so you can use grays to create a variety of effects.

1 For instance, if you drag a gradient over a layer mask, you can blend gradually between one image and another.
2 Painting with gray lets you create a semi-opaque effect where you can see part of your painting below.

A gradient on a layer mask blends one layer into another.

Layer Effects and Styles

You can apply layer effects to your layers to add special touches such as glows and shadows. Photoshop thinks of more than one effect applied to a layer as a layer style.

Layer effects and styles are based on the content of your layer. If you apply a drop shadow to a layer, and then amend the layer content, the shadow will update automatically.

1 Select the layer you want to apply the effect to, double-click the Add a Layer Style icon, and Photoshop will display the Layer Style dialog box.

2 Click on the name of an effect from the left-hand column of the Layer Style dialog box to see all available settings for that style. This is where you can change the effect's settings. When you've finished defining your settings, click the OK button.

3 Once layer effects are added to a layer, they are displayed in the Layers panel.

4 You can control the visibility of the layer effects using the eye icon.

5 Delete layer effects by dragging them to the Trash icon.

6 Return to the Layer Style dialog box by double-clicking the name of the effect you wish to edit in the Layers panel.

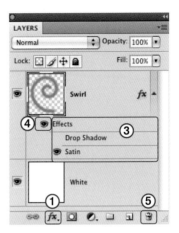

The Layers panel. The Swirl layer has two effects attached to it: Drop Shadow, which has its visibility turned off, and Satin, which is visible.

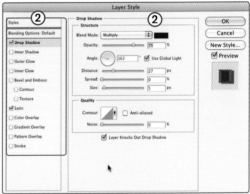

Layer Style dialog box

REUSING LAYER EFFECTS AND STYLES

If you want to be able to reuse your layer effects on other layers, you can save them as a style. First select the layer with effects you wish to reuse, then go to Window > Styles to bring up the Styles panel.

1 In the Styles panel, click the New Styles icon to add a style to the panel.

2 To apply a style, select a layer, then click the style you want to apply in the Styles panel.

LAYER EFFECTS EXAMPLES

Drop Shadow

Gradient Overlay

Bevel/Emboss

Pattern Overlay

Satin

Inner Shadow

The Blend Modes

When you paint or add layers to your painting, you can choose how the pixels "blend" together by selecting a blend mode. Blend modes work by reading the color of a pixel on the lower layer, and then looking at the color of the pixels on top, and blending them together according to different calculations, creating different colored effects. You can also use blend modes in layer effects and the Fade Filter… command.

In blending terminology, you have "base," "blend," and "result" pixels. If you painted in red over a flat blue background, blue would be the base color, red the blend color, and, depending on the blending mode, the colors would blend to generate different colors.

Blend modes menu from the Options bar

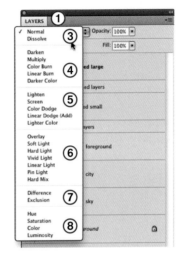

Blend modes menu from the Layers panel

To use blend modes:

1 Define a blend mode for a layer in the Layers panel. Layer blend modes can be changed at any time.

2 Blend modes for brushes are set on the Options bar when you have a brush tool selected.

3 The blend modes are organized into groups in the blend mode menu, with the first section containing Normal, which is the default setting, and Dissolve.

4 The results of the Darken section are always darker than the original.

5 The results in the Lighten section are always lighter than the original.

6 The Overlay section darkens dark colors and lightens light colors, increasing contrast.

7 The Difference modes invert the original colors.

8 The final section blends either the color values (Hue), color intensity (Saturation), or Brightness values (Luminosity).

BLEND MODE EXAMPLES

Dissolve: Works on semitransparent or softened edges, creating a dissolved effect.

Darken: Any colors that are darker will be preserved while lighter colors are replaced.

Multiply: Similar to Darken, but usually retaining more detail.

Color Burn: Produces color similar to but darker than the blend color—increases contrast in base pixels. Leaves whites untouched.

Linear Burn: Similar to Color Burn, but decreases brightness in the base pixels. Leaves whites untouched.

Darker Color: Always chooses the darker colored pixel.

Lighten: Lighter colors are preserved; darker colors are replaced.

Screen: Similar to Lighten, but usually preserves more detail.

Color Dodge: Produces a color that's similar to but lighter than the blend color—decreases contrast. Leaves blacks untouched.

BLEND MODE EXAMPLES

Linear Dodge: Produces a color that's lighter than the blend color–increases brightness in the base pixels. Leaves blacks untouched.

Lighter Color: Always chooses the lighter colored pixel.

Overlay: Colors are lightened or darkened according to whether they are shadows or highlights.

Soft Light: Similar to Overlay mode but the pixels from the base layer are given more emphasis.

Hard Light: Similar to Overlay mode but the pixels from the blend layer are given more emphasis.

Vivid Light: Another variety of Overlay. Pixels are lightened and darkened by increasing their contrast.

Linear Light: Another Overlay variation. Pixels are lightened and darkened by increasing their brightness.

Pin Light: Another Overlay variant. Pin light favors blend pixels.

Hard Mix: All pixels change to primary colors: red, green, blue, cyan, yellow, magenta, white, or black.

BLEND MODE EXAMPLES

Difference: Changes pixels to their negative color and black doesn't change anything at all.

Exclusion: Very similar to Difference, except there is far less contrast.

Hue: Uses the color of the blend pixel to mix with the saturation and brightness of the base pixel.

Saturation: Uses the saturation of the blend pixel to mix with the color and brightness of the base pixel.

Color: Lets you add color without changing brightness values. Very useful for re-coloring artwork.

Luminosity: Uses the brightness of the blend pixel to mix with the color and saturation of the base pixel.

Using Adjustment Layers

Adjustment layers alter the color balance, brightness, etc., of the layers below them.

1 To create an adjustment layer, click the Add Adjustment Layer icon on the Layers menu and choose the adjustment you want to use.

2 Photoshop will open the Adjustments panel. The controls available will reflect the adjustment you choose. (Here you can see the Hue/Saturation adjustment controls.)

3 Adjustment layers affect all the layers below them in the Layers panel. If you only want to affect the layer immediately below your adjustment layer, click the This Adjustment Affects All Layers Below icon.

4 Make your adjustments using the appropriate controls. To compare your picture before applying the adjustment layer to how it will look with the layer, click the Eye icon.

5 Some adjustment controls are easier to use if you expand the Adjustments panel with the Switch Panel to Expanded View icon.

6 To reset all adjustment settings, click the Reset to Adjustment Default icon.

7 Delete adjustments by clicking the Trash icon.

8 When you create an adjustment layer, Photoshop automatically creates a layer mask, letting you paint out areas in your artwork so they are masked and therefore not affected by the adjustment layers.

Adjustment layers are very useful in that they don't commit you to making lasting changes to the colors and tones in your image. However, if you change color modes, for instance from RGB to CMYK, you may find that the effects of adjustment layers alter, leaving you with a very different look. To avoid this, when you change color mode, first flatten your adjustment layers by selecting the layer in the Layers panel, then go to Layer Menu > Merge Down.

Layers panel with Adjustment Layers menu

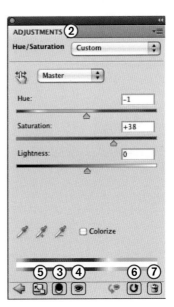

Adjustments panel in Hue/Saturation mode

LEVELS ADJUSTMENT LAYERS

Levels Adjustment Layers are used to adjust contrast and color balance across an image. The Levels controls in the Adjustments panel are organized around a graph, called a histogram, which shows the distribution of brightness levels in an image. Beneath the histogram are three input sliders that allow you to alter how bright or dark your image is.

1 Drag the Shadows slider to the right to make dark pixels darker.

2 The Midtones slider will lighten or darken pixels that have a medium brightness.

3 Drag the Highlights slider to the left to lighten light pixels.

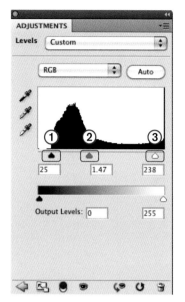

Adjustments panel in Levels mode

CURVES ADJUSTMENT LAYERS

Curves Adjustment Layers are similar to Levels and even feature a histogram, input sliders, and eyedropper tools that can be used in the same way as the controls in Levels Adjustment Layers (see above).

Curves Adjustment Layers, however, offer a much finer degree of control than Levels Adjustment Layers. Rather than simply giving you control over shadows, highlights, and midtones, Curves Adjustment Layers let you place points along a line that represents the gradual transition between dark and light pixels. Once a point is added, by clicking on the line, dragging the point downward darkens pixels and dragging upward lightens them (this behavior is reversed if you are in the CMYK color mode).

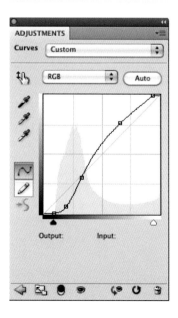

Adjustments panel in Curves mode

HUE/SATURATION ADJUSTMENT LAYER

The Hue/Saturation Adjustment Layer lets you control three separate components of your image: its hue (color), saturation (richness of color), and lightness (brightness).

1 Moving the Hue slider changes the colors in your image by moving them through the spectrum.

2 The Saturation slider alters the intensity of colors. Low saturation values create grayer images; high saturation values create vibrant, rich colors.

3 The Lightness slider simply darkens or lightens images.

4 The Hue/Saturation Adjustment Layer alters all colors in an image unless you use the menu above the sliders to restrict the effects to a specific color range.

5 You can also use the eyedropper tools to select specific colors you want to alter in your painting. Click the first eyedropper and then click a pixel in your painting that matches the colors you want to change.

6 Add or subtract colors using the Add To Sample and Subtract From Sample buttons.

7 There is also a Color Range slider at the bottom of the Hue/Saturation Adjustment Layers panel. You can drag the Color Range slider to redefine the color range you have selected. The small triangles outside of the Color Range slider control how altered colors transition into unmodified colors.

8 Use the Colorize check box to create a two-tone effect.

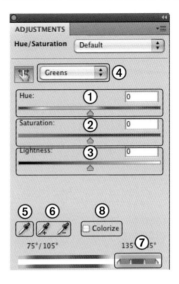

Adjustments panel in Hue/Saturation mode

COLOR BALANCE ADJUSTMENT LAYER

The Color Balance Adjustment Layer changes
the overall color cast of an image and lets you
manipulate the casts in the shadows, midtones,
or highlights of your artwork.
1 First decide on the tonal range in your image
  that you want to affect: Shadows, Midtones,
  or Highlights.
2 Three sliders let you adjust colors by moving
  them toward their opposite in the spectrum, for
  instance Cyan opposes Red. Moving the Cyan
  slider to the right toward the Red would alter
  Cyan pixels, adding Red to their tint.
3 The Preserve Luminosity check box makes
  sure that the full tonal range of your image is
  retained. This means the overall contrast of your
  picture will be maintained.

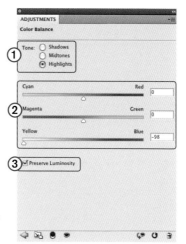

Adjustments panel in
Color Balance mode

BLACK & WHITE ADJUSTMENT LAYER

Use the Black & White Adjustment Layer
to transform layers below it into Grayscale
(black and white).
1 The various color sliders let you control how
  colors are translated into black and white. For
  instance, if you wanted the pixels that were
  yellow in the colored artwork to be transformed
  into a light gray, you would drag the Yellows
  slider to the left. If you wanted the yellows to
  transform into a darker gray, you would drag the
  Yellows slider to the right.
2 The Tint check box lets you apply a tint to your
  transformed image.

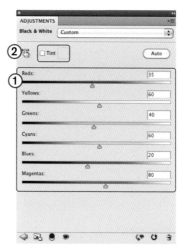

Adjustments panel in
Black & White mode

About the Pen Tools

Photoshop's pen tools create "paths" that can be filled with color, have borders added, or can be used as the basis for creating a selection.

1 To create a path, click with the Pen Tool to create anchor points. Anchor points are the square nodes—usually where the line changes direction.

2 The lines between the anchor points are called segments.

3 Anchor points can have direction handles coming from them that are used to shape the slope of curves.

4 There are three kinds of points: Points with no direction handles; smooth curve points, where the handles are related to each other, see-sawing as you move them; and corner points where the direction handles can be moved independently of each other.

Pen tools

Path with anchor points, segments, and direction handles

PATHS PANEL

Outlines created with the Pen Tool are saved and managed from the Paths panel (Window > Paths). Click a path's name in the Path panel to activate the path.

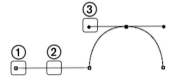

Paths panel

Delete a path
1 Drag the path name to the Trash icon.

Rename a path
2 Double-click a path name to rename a path.

Create a path from an existing selection
3 First make a selection using one of the standard selection tools. Click the Make Work Path From Selection icon.

Load a path as a selection
4 To use a path as the basis for a selection, select the path in the Paths panel, then click the Load Path as Selection icon.

Fill a path with color
5 To fill a path with color, first change the Foreground Color to the color you want to fill the path with. Select the path, then click the Fill Path With Foreground Color icon.

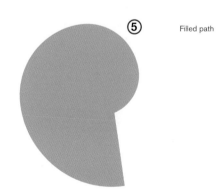

Filled path

USING THE PATHS PANEL (CONT.)

To put a brush stroke on a path:
6 Select the Brush Tool and set its options
to the style you wish to use for the border
of your path.
7 Select your path and click on the Stroke Path
With Brush icon (see 7 on the previous page).

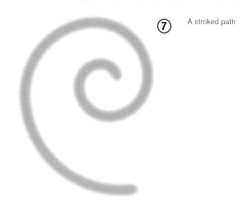

⑦   A stroked path

USING THE PEN TOOL

Creating paths
The Pen Tool creates, deletes, and adds anchor
points to a path.
1 Once you have selected the Pen Tool, go to the
Options bar and click the Paths button to create
paths rather than shape layers.
2 Then click your painting to add anchor points
that are corner points.
3 Clicking and dragging pulls out direction
handles to create a smooth curve.
4 Clicking the first anchor point once again
"closes" a path and completes a shape.

Continuing a path you have started
Click and drag the last point on the path (the
endpoint) to continue drawing a path with a curve
(you'll be pulling out a direction handle). Continue
clicking and dragging or just clicking.

Adding and deleting anchor points
Delete anchor points by moving the Pen Tool over
an existing anchor point. The cursor changes to a
pen with a minus and you can click and release to
delete the point.
   Add anchor points to a path by moving the Pen
Tool over a path segment and click to add new
anchor points.

BASICS OF PAINTING

DIRECT SELECTION TOOL

The Direct Selection Tool lets you select and move anchor points, curve segments, and direction handles. It is the tool you use to edit a path you have created with the Pen Tool.

Before you start editing, make sure you have deselected the path. Then to select a point, click it with the Direct Selection Tool and the small square will appear to fill in. Once you have selected it, you can move the point by dragging.

Direct Selection Tool

Keyboard shortcut
To select the Direct Selection Tool: Shift + A
To select the Path Selection Tool: A

PATH SELECTION TOOL

An entire path can be moved without altering its shape by using the Path Selection Tool.

To select a path, click it using the Path Selection Tool. Photoshop selects the whole path, ready for you to move it.

Path Selection Tool

CONVERT POINT TOOL

Use the Convert Point Tool to change an anchor point into one of these three types:
1 Corner anchor points with no handles.
2 Corner anchor points with independent handles.
3 Smooth anchor points where the direction lines are related to each other, see-sawing as you move them.
Click an anchor point with handles to remove the handles. Drag out from an anchor point without handles to add smooth curve handles.

Click hold and drag curve handles to convert a smooth anchor point into a corner anchor point (see-sawing to non-see-sawing where you can move each point independently).

Convert Point Tool

USING THE PEN TOOL TIPS

Although it takes a bit of practice to get used to using keyboard shortcuts, once you've mastered them you'll find they make creating and editing paths much easier and quicker.

Keyboard shortcuts and tips
Use the Pen Tool to create a path.

Click, hold, and drag to pull out smooth direction handles as you place anchor points.

Delete anchor points by clicking them.

Add anchor points by clicking the active path where you want to add points.

Move anchor points by holding down Ctrl/Cmd.

Alter direction lines by holding down Alt and dragging direction handles or dragging from a point to add direction handles.

CREATING SHAPE LAYERS WITH THE PEN TOOL

1 To create Shape Layers with the Pen Tool, first select the Pen Tool, and then, before you start drawing, click the Shape Layers button on the Options bar.
2 Photoshop creates a new layer in the Layers panel. The layer is filled with the Foreground Color.
3 To change the fill color of your shape layer, double-click the shape layer's Layer thumbnail, select a color, from the Color Picker, and then click OK.

Shape Layers button on Options bar

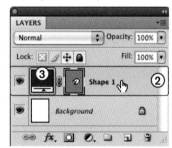

Shape layer in Layers panel

CREATING SELECTIONS WITH THE PEN TOOL

1 To create selections from a path, select the Pen Tool and click the Paths button on the Options bar.
2 Photoshop creates a path in the Paths panel.
3 When you've finished drawing your path, click the Load Path As Selection icon.

Paths button on the Options bar

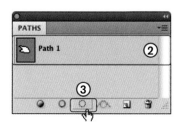

Paths panel

Painting with Other Programs

Corel Painter and Adobe Illustrator are other widely used programs for producing painterly effects on the computer. Corel Painter focuses on painting and has fewer photographic controls than Photoshop; Illustrator is more of a drawing and illustrative program.

Corel Painter

Corel Painter is a dedicated painting application that uses pixels as Photoshop does.

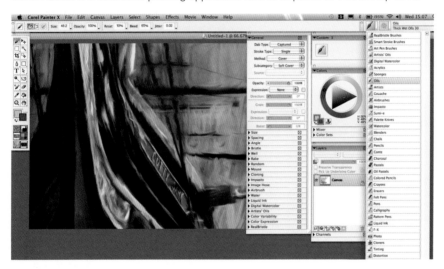

WHY USE PAINTER?

Painter lets you experiment with color, composition, and brush strokes, without the toxins, mess, and expense associated with traditional art.

Painter's natural-media painting and drawing tools let you choose your tools as you would in real life.

If you were to paint traditionally using watercolor paints, for instance, you would choose your brush and paints, mix up your color, and start painting on your paper. A number of things would influence the look of your painting. For example, the temperature may affect how long it takes for the paint to dry and in turn how much the paint runs. The wind may blow the wet paint in a certain direction.

All these factors can be used and controlled in Painter to create images that mimic real life. Unlike real life however, you can undo mistakes.

HOW TO USE PAINTER

Use Painter as though you were preparing to paint in real life:

1 Create your canvas and choose the Brush Tool from the toolbar.
2 Choose the type of brush you wish to paint with—there is a wide range of brushes to choose from, such as oils, acrylics, or chalk.
3 Choose the style of brush. The style describes the brush tip and how the brush will apply the paint to the surface.
4 Change the brush preset settings to customize your brush.
5 Choose a color from the color wheel, the color sets, or mix up your own from various colors using the color mixer.

Now you're ready to begin painting.

CHOOSE YOUR BRUSH TOOL AND CATEGORY

To choose your type of brush (category):

1 Choose the Brush Tool from the toolbar.
2 Choose the type of brush you need from the brush category drop-down menu on the upper right of your screen.

Be aware that watercolor brushes require a watercolor layer, which will be generated automatically when you start painting. If you subsequently want to use a different type of brush, you'll need to switch to a normal layer before you start painting.

The drawing brush categories include various pencils, chalks, and pens. The painting categories include watercolor, oils, acrylics, impasto, and palette knives. There are a number of brushes for blending your paint and some for erasing pixels. Painter also has a few tools that will paint in the style of an artist, for example the Van Gogh brush. For copying areas there are Cloning brushes, and for effects you can use Effect brushes.

Keyboard shortcut
To choose the Brush Tool from the toolbar: press b

THE VARIANTS

To choose the brush "variant" once you have chosen your brush category:

1 Go to the Variant drop-down menu at the top right-hand side of the screen.
2 Click the arrow and scroll down to the variant you want to use.
3 Change the Brush Size, Opacity, Reset, Feature, Grain, Bleed, and Jitter settings to create the brush you want.

Some of the brush variants don't have all these options.

CHOOSE A COLOR

To choose a color using the Color Palette:

1 Display the Colors panel by going to Window > Color Palettes > Show Colors.
2 Drag the outer slider on the circle to choose the hue.
3 Drag the slider in the triangle to choose the saturation and brightness you require.

To create colors using the Color Mixer:

4 Display the Colors panel by going to Window > Color Palettes > Show Mixer.
5 Paint in the color area with multiple colors.
6 Mix the colors using the palette knife.
7 Sample the color you require from the mixing area.

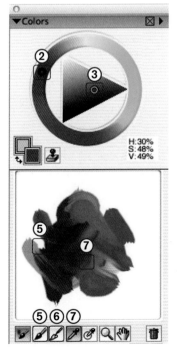

Keyboard shortcuts

To show and hide the Colors Palette: Ctrl/Cmd+1

To show and hide the Color Mixer Palette: Ctrl/Cmd+2

CONTROL PALETTE

To change the brush variant settings:

1 Display the Control palette by going to Window > Brush Controls > Show General.
2 Click on the name of the setting you want to change in the list and the settings appear.
3 You can adjust the settings and then test your brush by making some trial strokes.

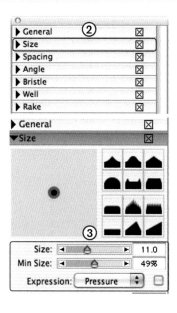

USE THE BRUSH CREATOR

To create your own colors with the Brush Creator:

1 Display the Brush Creator panel by going to Window > Show Brush Creator.
2 Click one of the three options at the top: Randomizer, Transposer, or Stroke Designer.
3 Each option displays settings that you can change.
4 Once you have adjusted the settings, test the brush in the white area to the right.
5 If the white test area becomes too full of test paint strokes, click Clear to start again.

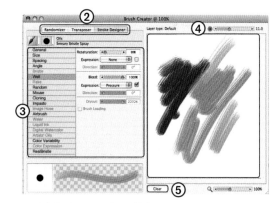

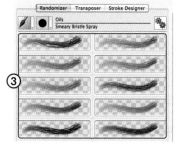

Keyboard shortcut
To bring up the Brush Creator:
Ctrl/Cmd+B

Adobe Illustrator

Adobe Illustrator is a vector drawing program used more for illustrative work than painting.

WHY USE ILLUSTRATOR?

Illustrator is a vector drawing program, while Photoshop and Painter are both raster image programs.

"Vector" refers to an image that is created mathematically using lines and points, while a raster image is created using pixels or dots. Being defined mathematically means that a vector image is easy to enlarge without losing any quality, whereas with raster images the pixels/dots get larger as you enlarge the image, so you lose detail.

1 and 2 The edge of a vector-defined circle is completely smooth.

3 and 4 In contrast, the edge of a rasterized circle, which is created using pixels/dots, has a step effect along the edge.

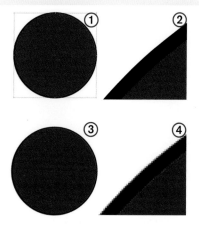

ILLUSTRATOR BRUSHES

To apply a brush stroke to an Illustrator path:
1 Select the path you want to apply the stroke to and click the Stroke icon at the bottom of the toolbar to bring it to the front.
2 Go to Window > Brushes.
3 Choose a brush stroke to apply it to the path you have selected.

More brushes are available from Window > Brush Libraries > Choose Brush Set.

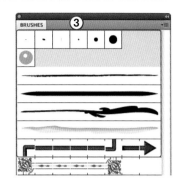

ILLUSTRATOR'S FOUR TYPES OF BRUSHES

1 Calligraphic Brush: Emulates a calligraphic pen by varying the width of the stroke depending on the angle.
2 Scatter Brush: Scatters a vector object along the stroke. The options allow you to vary its size, uniformity, rotation, etc.
3 Art Brush: Takes a vector shape and stretches it along the stroke, allowing you to create strokes that look hand drawn.
4 Pattern Brush: Similar to the Scatter Brush, but the shapes that are scattered along the stroke are distorted to keep the stroke line smooth.

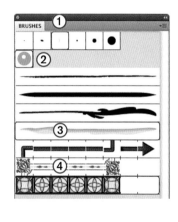

EXPORTING TO PHOTOSHOP

Vector files can be exported to Photoshop by copying the Illustrator artwork and pasting it into Photoshop. You will still be able to edit the paths if you use Edit > Paste as Smart Object (see Creating Your Own Brushes, pages 44–47).

INDEX

CREDITS

This book would not exist without Moira Clinch, who lives with a creative mind that bubbles up with ideas like a spring. This Photoshop Brushes Directory was her concept.

Nor would it exist without the hard work of first the Contributors: Richard Bird, Andrew Moreton, and Tim Wilson; and then of course Senior Editor at Quarto, Katie Crous.

I would also like to thank my good friend Kayode Olafimihan, who always helps me when I can't see the wood for the trees and has supported me throughout the production of this book.

Images p371, 378, and 386 © Andrew Moreton

Quarto would like to thank the following artists for kindly supplying images for inclusion in this book:

p2–3, 20–21 David Carron www.avadav.com

p12 Gina Walton www.starwalt.com

p13 Ricardo Medina www.fabiopanichi.com

p14–15 Mike Nash www.mike–nash.com

p16 Michael Lai www.mikeylikeydesign.com

p17, 18 Jonathan Wong www.artofwong.com

p19 Rob Shields www.robshields.net

All other images are the copyright of Quarto Publishing plc. While every effort has been made to credit contributors, Quarto would like to apologize should there have been any omissions or errors, and would be pleased to make the appropriate correction for future editions of the book.